Ethics: The Key Thinkers

KEY THINKERS

The *Key Thinkers* series is aimed at undergraduate students and offers clear, concise and accessible edited guides to the key thinkers in each of the central topics in philosophy. Each book offers a comprehensive overview of the major thinkers who have contributed to the historical development of a key area of philosophy, providing a survey of their major works and the evolution of the central ideas in that area.

Key Thinkers in Philosophy available now from Bloomsbury:

Aesthetics, Edited by Alessandro Giovannelli
Epistemology, Edited by Stephen Hetherington
Philosophy of Language, Edited by Barry Lee
Philosophy of Religion, Edited by Jeffrey J. Jordan
Philosophy of Science, Edited by James Robert Brown

Ethics: The Key Thinkers

EDITED BY
TOM ANGIER

BLOOMSBURY
LONDON · NEW DELHI · NEW YORK · SYDNEY

Bloomsbury Academic

An imprint of Bloomsbury Publishing Plc

50 Bedford Square
London
WC1B 3DP
UK

175 Fifth Avenue
New York
NY 10010
USA

www.bloomsbury.com

British Library Cataloguing-in-Publication Data
A catalogue record for this book is available from the British Library.

ISBN: HB: 978-1-4411-6453-7
PB: 978-1-4411-4939-8

Library of Congress Cataloging-in-Publication Data
Ethics: the key thinkers/edited by Tom Angier.
p. cm. – (Key thinkers)
Includes bibliographical references and index.
ISBN 978-1-4411-6453-7 – ISBN 978-1-4411-4939-8 (pbk.) –
ISBN 978-1-4411-5102-5 (epub) – ISBN 978-1-4411-1382-5 (ebook (pdf))
1. Ethics. 2. Ethicists. I. Angier, Tom P. S.
BJ1031.E77 2012
170.92'2–dc23
2012006889

Typeset by Deanta Global Publishing Services, Chennai, India
Printed and bound in India

Contents

Notes on contributors

Tom Angier is Lecturer in Philosophy at the University of Kent, Canterbury. While his thematic interests lie in ethical and political theory, his historical interests centre on two periods: nineteenth century (post-Kantian) and ancient Greek philosophy. He has two monographs: *Either Kierkegaard/Or Nietzsche: Moral Philosophy in a New Key* (Ashgate 2006), and *Technē in Aristotle's Ethics: Crafting the Moral Life* (Continuum 2010). His current research is on well-being and second nature in the context of Aristotelian virtue theory.

Vivian Boland O. P. studied philosophy and theology in Dublin, Edinburgh and Rome. He has taught at the Dominican House of Studies in Dublin, at St Mary's University College in London and at Blackfriars in Oxford. His publications include *Ideas in God According to St Thomas Aquinas* (Brill, 1996) and *St Thomas Aquinas* (Continuum Library of Educational Thought, 2007). His research has been centred on various aspects of Aquinas' work, particularly his moral and educational thought, his anthropology and his understanding of philosophy and theology.

Krister Bykvist is Fellow and Tutor in Philosophy at Jesus College, Oxford. He is the author of *Utilitarianism: A Guide for the Perplexed* (Continuum, 2009), and his recent articles include 'No good fit – Why the fitting attitude analysis of value fails' (*Mind* 18, 2009, pp. 763–92) and 'Can unstable preferences provide a stable standard of well-being?' (*Economics and Philosophy* 26:1, 2010, pp. 1–26). His current research is on well-being, value theory and moral uncertainty.

Timothy Chappell is Professor of Philosophy and Director of the Ethics Centre at the Open University, and Visiting Research Fellow in Philosophy at the University of St Andrews, Scotland. He works on ethics, ancient philosophy, epistemology and philosophy of religion. His recent books include: *Human Values: New Essays on Ethics and Natural Law* (edited with D. Oderberg, 2004), *The Inescapable Self* (2005), *Reading Plato's Theaetetus* (2005), *Values and Virtues: Aristotelianism in Contemporary Ethics* (editor, 2006), *The Problem of Moral Demandingness* (2009) and *Ethics and Experience* (2009).

Ken Gemes came to Birkbeck College, University of London, in 2000, having taught for 10 years at Yale University, Connecticut, USA. His research interests include philosophy of science, philosophy of logic and Nietzsche. His latest publications are 'Freud and Nietzsche on Sublimation' in the *Journal Of Nietzsche Studies* 38:38–59 (2009), and 'We Remain of Necessity Strangers to Ourselves: The Key Message of Nietzsche's *Genealogy*', 191–208 in C.D. Acampora (ed.), *Nietzsche's 'On the Genealogy of Morals': Critical Essays* (2006).

Jacob Klein gained his PhD on 'Nature and Reason in Stoic Ethics' from Cornell University, New York, USA, in 2010 and now teaches at Colgate University, New York, USA. His current research focuses on the Stoic theory of practical reason. His paper 'Stoic Eudaimonism and the Natural Law Tradition' is appearing in November 2012 in *Reason, Religion and Natural Law: From Plato to Spinoza*, ed. Jonathan Jacobs (Oxford University Press).

Peter Millican is Gilbert Ryle Fellow and Professor of Philosophy at Hertford College, Oxford University, Visiting Professor at the University of York, and Illumni David Hume Fellow at Edinburgh University. From 2005 until 2010 he was co-editor of *Hume Studies*, and his publications include detailed studies of Hume's views on induction, causation, free will and miracles, several editions of Hume's works (printed or electronic) and the collection *Reading Hume on Human Understanding* (Oxford, 2002). His other major interests include ethics, logic and language, philosophy of religion and the connections between computer science and philosophy, in which he recently instituted a new joint degree programme at Oxford University.

Sean Sayers is Professor of Philosophy at the University of Kent, Canterbury. He has written extensively on topics in Hegelian and Marxist philosophy. His books include: *Marx and Alienation: Essays* on *Hegelian Themes* (2011), *Plato's Republic: An Introduction* (1999), *Marxism and Human Nature* (1998, paperback 2007), *Reality and Reason: Dialectic and the Theory of Knowledge* (1985) and *Hegel, Marx and Dialectic: A Debate* (1980). He was one of the founders of *Radical Philosophy* (1972) and of 'The Marx and Philosophy Society' (2003). He is the founder and Editor in Chief of the online *Marx and Philosophy Review of Books* (2010).

Christoph Schuringa is a doctoral candidate in the Department of Philosophy at Birkbeck, University of London, writing a dissertation on Nietzsche supervised by Ken Gemes. He is currently a DAAD scholar at the T.U. Berlin, working with Günter Abel, and has published several papers on Nietzsche.

David Solomon is the H.B. and W.P. White Director of the Centre for Ethics and Culture at the University of Notre Dame, where he has been a member of the Department of Philosophy since 1968. His most recent books are *Medical Ethics at Notre Dame* (2009) and *The Common Good: Aristotelian and Confucian Perspectives* (forthcoming in 2012). His main research interests are in contemporary ethical theory, the history of moral philosophy and bioethics. He is currently completing a history that will focus on the manner in which Anglophone academic ethics in the twentieth century engaged (or failed to engage) the broader culture.

Ralph Walker studied philosophy at McGill University in Montréal and at Oxford University. He was a Tutor at Magdalen College, Oxford from 1972 to 2011 and has also taught in Uganda, Brazil, Czechoslovakia and the Czech and Slovak Republics. His main interests centre on the nature of truth and on the work of Kant, subjects he takes to be closely related. He has published three books: *Kant* (1978), *The Coherence Theory of Truth* (1989) and *Kant and the Moral Law* (1998).

Kenneth R. Westphal is Professorial Fellow in the School of Philosophy at the University of East Anglia (Norwich). His primary research interest is rational justification in the non-formal domains of theoretical and practical philosophy. He is author of *Kant's Transcendental Proof of Realism* (Cambridge 2004) and editor of

The Blackwell Guide to Hegel's Phenomenology of Spirit (2009). His recent articles include 'Urteilskraft, gegenseitige Anerkennung und rationale Rechtfertigung' (in H.-D. Klein, ed., *Ethik als prima philosophia?*, 2011) and 'Norm Acquisition, Rational Judgement and Moral Particularism' (*Theory and Research in Education* 10.1, 2012). He is completing a monograph with the tentative title of 'Hume, Kant and the Proper Construction of Justice'.

Acknowledgements

I would like to thank all the contributors to this volume for maintaining a very high standard of scholarly and philosophical excellence. They have made this collection a model of how philosophy and the history of philosophy can inform each other, to the clear (and I would say indispensable) benefit of both.

I would also like to thank all those at Bloomsbury Academic who have helped in the preparation of the text. In particular, I'm grateful to David Avital, who invited me to edit *Ethics: The Key Thinkers*. Thanks are also due to Timothy Chappell and Rachel Barney, who sent me very helpful comments on my chapter on Plato.

Introduction

The view that 'doing the history of philosophy' can substantially be divorced from 'doing philosophy' is now not uncommon. Indeed, despite the example of philosophy's finest recent practitioners – Charles Taylor, for instance, Bernard Williams, Terence Irwin or Alasdair MacIntyre – it is perhaps an increasingly common view (at least in the leading Anglo-American universities). Drawing on my own experience, I can recall a faculty member whose door bore the legend 'No History of Philosophy Beyond This Point', along with attempts to remove set texts from the curriculum and replace them with assorted extracts. It is unsurprising that these attitudes and initiatives came from philosophers working at the more technical, science-influenced end of the discipline, since here the bonds between philosophy and its history are arguably at their weakest. But in ethics, at least, the attempt to sunder philosophy from its historical development is almost always impoverishing, not to say positively destructive. Why so?

To begin with, it makes likely the recapitulation of episodes in the history of philosophy of which one is unaware. One thinks here of 'moral particularism', for example, which has been elaborated and debated largely without engaging the 1960s literature on situation ethics.[1] Similarly, John McDowell's vital notion of 'second nature' has been developed without reference to the natural law tradition, in which the Thomistic idea of realizing one's moral nature through *habitus* and 'connatural knowledge' has long been a topic of interest.[2] Clearly, the risks here are not simply of repeating ideas and arguments from the past but rather of missing problems and distinctions that have already been illuminated and rehearsed. A case in point might be the recent rich literature on the emotions, which tends to treat 'emotion' as a homogeneous category, thereby papering over distinctions that were earlier captured by terms such as 'passion', 'affection' and 'sentiment'.[3] It is cases like this that make the history of moral philosophy of direct and continuing relevance, offering conceptual nuance and issuing theoretical challenges, where otherwise current assumptions and prejudices would hold unreasonable sway.

Narrating the history of Western ethics, which is the task of this volume, will, I hope, go some way to avoiding these kinds of intellectual pitfall. While this narrative – from Plato to MacIntyre – is inevitably full of lacunae, its further and fundamental aim is to show how an understanding of any part of the history of moral philosophy is inextricably informed by the parts preceding it. No great moral philosopher works in a vacuum, and an assessment of his achievement cannot prescind, therefore, from what Nietzsche calls the 'genealogy' of his ideas and arguments. Not that this collection constitutes (as does Nietzsche's *On the Genealogy of Morality*) a *parti pris* narrative, designed to vindicate one ethical theory or approach over others.[4] The latter genre of writing is very valuable, but is far better suited to a single-authored text: one could cite, for example, Jacques Maritain's *Moral Philosophy*, Alasdair MacIntyre's *After Virtue* or John Rist's *Real Ethics*.[5] Rather, this collection is meant to demonstrate the conceptual and argumentative threads that bind the history of Western moral philosophy together, and which make it a genuine unity in the first place. Which voices within that history are persuasive, and to what degree, is up to the reader to decide.

I begin the story of Western ethics with Plato, its first comprehensive and systematic exponent. I argue that central to Plato's philosophy is a concern with goodness and specifically with the virtues: qualities like courage, temperance and justice. Like later Greek and mediaeval thinkers, Plato assumes that virtue is necessary for happiness, an assumption that remains unchallenged until the modern period. But this leaves open what, exactly, the virtues consist in. Plato's initial view here is that they consist in forms of knowledge or expertise, which he models on craft-knowledge. On a traditional interpretation, this is an unfortunate 'intellectualist' stance, which is remedied only in the *Republic*, where it is admitted that the soul contains independently motivating desires. I then challenge this developmentalist account with one that sees far more continuity between the early and middle dialogues. But this still leaves open a crucial issue, namely, what virtue-knowledge is knowledge *of*. Here I canvas two main possibilities: the *Protagoras*' notion that virtue is knowledge of how to maximize pleasure and the *Republic*'s idea that it is a kind of mathematical knowledge whose ultimate source lies in the 'Form of the Good'. For different reasons, I argue that neither of these answers is satisfactory, either *per se* or by Plato's own admission. The search for an analysis of goodness and virtue remains fundamentally unresolved.

Timothy Chappell continues this narrative with a survey of Aristotle's ethics. Like Plato, Aristotle's central moral heuristic is virtue, but unlike Plato, his non-dialogical, succinct style has afforded him substantial influence on recent philosophy. Accepting what I called the 'traditional interpretation' of Plato's development, Chappell argues that Aristotle affirms the *Republic*'s view that moral virtue requires lengthy pre-cognitive, affective training or habituation, which is strikingly similar to the *mimēsis* or imitation of character analysed in Aristotle's *Poetics*. Such character-formation does not, Chappell insists, follow any precise formulae, and Aristotle certainly never offers general blueprints for right action of the kind sought by modern moral philosophers. True, Aristotle does believe that humans have a 'function', which enjoins them to specifically rational action and emotion, and he holds that moral virtues constitute 'means' between two correlative vices. But neither of these claims generates, says Chappell, an ethical decision-procedure; on the contrary, humans are best off if they transcend the human function altogether, and Aristotle's mean is not only given different schemata in different places, but also raises too many internal problems to constitute a 'doctrine'. Ultimately, Chappell concludes, the character-virtues are theoretically basic and irreducible for Aristotle, amounting to 'ways of seeing' the world which express the moral vision of the good person.

Although the Stoics succeed Aristotle in the history of ethics, Jacob Klein shows how, in key ways, their legacy amounts to a rigorous reworking of the early ('Socratic') Plato. Where the latter arguably leaves room for components other than virtue in the happy life, the Stoics maintain that virtue is the sole component. And where Socrates leaves the object of virtue-knowledge vague, the Stoics claim that virtue (*qua* the 'craft of life') is knowledge of how to conform to 'nature'. Whether 'nature' here is human or cosmic, virtue on the Stoic view is clearly purely cognitive and very hard to attain: the 'sage', indeed, is the only person, according to Stoic theory, who can achieve happiness. But why, Klein asks, assume that virtue is the only good? Because, the Stoics answer, supposed 'goods' like wealth and health are not invariably beneficial and moreover are not always attainable (hence a providential order could not require them as part of the essential human good). This raises the further and pressing question of how the Stoic agent should *act*, given that no external aim is acknowledged by him as a genuine 'good'. To this the Stoics reply that, while external goals are admittedly strictly 'indifferent', some indifferents are properly preferred, whereas others are properly dispreferred. Virtue, then, consists in having true, reliable beliefs, which guide one to preferred indifferents – not to independently valuable ends. Such, Klein holds, is the austere moral vision of the Stoics.

With Thomas Aquinas, we jump to the mediaeval period, but remain, as Vivian Boland makes clear, fundamentally in the same moral thought-world as the Greeks – specifically, that of Aristotle. Aquinas follows Aristotle's privileging of the contemplative over the practical life, even if his Christian conception of *contemplatio* differs from Aristotle's *theôria*. He also follows Aristotle in understanding the cognitive and desiderative aspects of human rationality as inextricably intertwined. Against the Stoics, therefore, Aquinas insists that passions can be rational, and that rational passions inform fully engaged human action. Indeed, although reason should exercise a 'constitutional' rule over the passions, its rule should never, on his view, be despotic, since our nature is 'graced' by our emotive capacities. What, then, of the role of virtue, which is just as vital for Aquinas as it is for Aristotle? According to Aquinas, virtue is a disposition (*habitus*), which is developed by the habituation of our passions in line with the requirements of reason. These requirements are, he stresses, never fundamentally in tension with our nature, but actually fulfil it – because they are what he calls 'connatural' with it. And this conception of the virtues as fulfilling our nature underlies Aquinas' celebrated 'natural law' theory: human nature, he holds, is inclined to virtuous ends, and human reason is capable of discerning these ends without any direct divine assistance.

Hume marks a significant break with both ancient and mediaeval moral thought, as Peter Millican shows. Although Hume, like previous moral philosophers, places virtue at the centre of ethics, the rationale of virtue now becomes utility, where this is constructed out of the extant passions of wholly 'naturalized' moral agents. Hence there is now no room, unlike in Aquinas, for the 'monkish virtues' – celibate chastity, humility, self-mortification, etc. – which Hume condemns as useless for both individual and society. Rather, any supposed virtue must prove itself at the bar of this-worldly values, the kind of values lauded by the ascendant class of property-owners in eighteenth-century England. *Contra* many readings of Hume, then, he is not a thorough-going sceptic or wholesale debunker of moral norms. Indeed, Hume thinks that natural 'fellow-feeling' and the 'artificial' virtue of justice are highly beneficial. It is just that such norms now find their grounding not in any transcendent realm but in the contingencies of human convention and sentiment. While this makes Hume very attractive to subsequent thinkers influenced by evolutionary and game theory, it might also make him vulnerable to later, radical challengers of the moral *status quo* like Nietzsche. For when challenged to show that his virtues of sympathy, mercy, sociability etc. are more than expressions of a depleted, unambitious sub-Christian morality, it is not clear that Hume has a convincing response.

Kant's ethics contrasts with Hume's in several respects, as Ralph Walker emphasizes. While Hume may take beliefs to be motivating, the essential motivating factor here is passion or sentiment, whereas for Kant it is the moral law, which specifies one's duties through what he calls the 'categorical imperative'. On a common reading of Kant, any other form of motivation – not least the desire for happiness – is non-moral, a function of mere passion or 'inclination'. But Walker argues that Kant allows other forms of motivation, so long as reason is a determining part of the mix (in this way, Walker brings Kant closer to Aristotle than to the Stoics). Kant also parts company with Hume in his attitude to universality. Whereas for Hume, moral action is grounded in contingent passions, for Kant this is simply to denature morality, which is necessarily universal in its prescriptions. But Walker criticizes Kant at this point: for even if universalizability is a necessary mark of the moral, it is not (he argues) a sufficient one, and Kant fails to see the importance of how moral maxims are specified in the first place. Perhaps the other formulae of the categorical imperative can help Kant out at this juncture, especially the attractive formula of treating rational agents as 'ends in themselves'. But even if so,

Walker is in little doubt that Kant's moral rationalism stands in need of revision. The chapter ends with an excursus on Kant's influential conceptions of freedom and autonomy.

Although Hegel appears to accuse Kant's ethics of empty formalism, Kenneth Westphal holds that Hegel's account of morality is 'fundamentally Kantian'. This is because Hegel adopts Kant's notion of the autonomy of the will and follows his call for a 'practical anthropology' in which to embody the principles of pure practical reason. In this way, Hegel ends up producing (in the *Philosophy of Right*) a work which conjoins the moral and the political – following the Greek subsumption of both under the term 'justice'. What, then, is at the core of Hegel's theory of justice? At its core, argues Westphal, is the view that personal freedom not only can be, but also is necessarily realized in a set of institutions (family, civil society and government). *Pace* the notion that freedom is a matter simply of escaping constraint, Hegel maintains that true freedom involves limits on individuals' idiosyncratic ends. This yields a higher, 'social freedom', which allows citizens to express their practical identity through social membership. At the same time, this does not destroy autonomy, since individuals can endorse that membership. Thus Hegel steers a course between liberal individualism, which fails to recognize irreducibly social goods, and communitarianism, which fails to protect individuals with a sufficiently robust conception of universal reason. If States follow these prescriptions, they will realize their 'rational core', thereby optimizing the well-being of their citizens.

As Westphal acknowledges, this ambitious and optimistic vision, with its echoes of the Aristotelian-Thomistic ethical synthesis, was soon confronted with a social world shattered by both Napoleon's invasion of Germany and the advent of industrial capitalism. Into this world stepped Karl Marx, who, although critical of Hegel's 'bourgeois' idealism, always remained committed (according to Sean Sayers) to Hegel's methodology. Key to this methodology is the idea that history develops through progressive stages, a progression Marx (unlike Hegel) sees as driven by working-class consciousness. Also key here is the idea that history's progress is marked by the incremental realization of humanity's 'species-being', that is, the mode in which humans flourish as a species. Unlike Hegel, however, Marx locates the principal obstacle to such realization in capitalism, which, he thinks, not only traps people in relentless toil, but also creates new needs it cannot satisfy. What is needed, then, according to Marx, is a form of economy designed to afford holistic satisfaction, satisfaction for human beings 'rich in needs', as opposed to the narrow, hedonistic satisfactions conceived of by Benthamite utilitarianism. While Marx goes some way to outlining this form of economy – he speaks of communal property and distribution according to need – his Hegelian historicism ultimately precludes, Sayers argues, any concrete, universalistic prescriptions that would hold for all time.

John Stuart Mill's utilitarianism appears in tension not only with Marx's anti-hedonism, but also with Kant's duty-based ethics – though according to Krister Bykvist, the tensions here are less than might be supposed. For a start, Marx's notion of holistic satisfaction may not be that far from Mill's own notion of 'higher pleasures', which he thought in principle available to all, and which Bykvist thinks can be squared with his general hedonism. After a similarly charitable reading of Mill's (in)famous 'proof' of the principle of utility, Bykvist goes on to tackle the form of utilitarianism endorsed by Mill, which some have construed as 'rule-utilitarianism'. Rule-utilitarianism holds that acts should be done if and only if they fall under rules that maximize happiness when universally followed. But, argues Bykvist, Mill in fact holds that rules should be consulted only insofar as they are needed to calculate the consequences of individual acts, thereby making his position a version of act-utilitarianism. Where Mill does come close to Kant, perhaps, is in his support (*contra* Bentham) for moral rights. Whereas Bentham had proclaimed the latter 'nonsense upon stilts', Mill is sympathetic to moral rights, and speaks in *On Liberty* as if they were wholly compatible with 'utility as the ultimate appeal on all ethical questions'. As Bykvist admits, squaring moral rights with act-utilitarianism is a tall order, but he suggests that Mill is to be commended for trying.

Juxtaposing Mill with Nietzsche would have offended both thinkers, and it is difficult to say who would have taken more offence. Then again, as Ken Gemes and Christoph Schuringa imply, given Nietzsche's avowed 'immoralism', he may not have been entitled to take offence in the first place. Certainly, if Nietzsche wants to abolish all moralities, then moral offence would seem an illegitimate attitude to adopt. But not only is this possibility hard to make sense of, there is also little evidence for it in his texts. Rather, Nietzsche's real target is Judaeo-Christian morality, which he takes to have had baleful consequences, in particular for European culture. How so? At this point, Gemes and Schuringa unpack Nietzsche's *Genealogy*, in which he traces the 'sickness' of Christian ethics back to its supposed origin in the Jewish revolt against all that is noble, 'strong', self-respecting and guilt-free. This is intended to reveal a contingent, embarrassing origin for Christian values, thereby initiating (though not accomplishing) a critique of Christian humility, selflessness, guilt, etc. And this paves the way, in turn, for a second, positive 'revaluation', in which Nietzsche adjures his readers to overcome nihilism and 'create' their own, individual values. As Gemes and Schuringa note, it is difficult to see how these new values are to be grounded, but they conclude that artists inspired by Nietzsche – like Rilke, Yeats, Mann, Lawrence and Shaw – may provide the best answers to this.

Finally, David Solomon turns to Alasdair MacIntyre, one of the greatest, and historically one of the best informed moral philosophers of the twentieth century. Solomon begins by outlining how, from the start of his career, MacIntyre reacted against the dominance of Kantianism and utilitarianism in normative theory, following instead various Oxford philosophers in their call for a resurrection of Aristotelian naturalism. The consummation of this research project is MacIntyre's *After Virtue* (1981), which Solomon explicates at length. Key to *After Virtue* is the claim that contemporary culture is basically emotivist in its approach to ethical questions. It is so because, in short, its paradigm representatives are the manager, therapist and aesthete, who cannot affirm universal, objective ends, but construe all proposed ends as mere expressions of personal, emotive preference. In place of this ethical dystopia, MacIntyre argues for a return to Aristotelianism, which makes conceptual and metaphysical room for a genuine moral teleology. Although *After Virtue* replaces Aristotle's 'metaphysical biology' with its own (partly Marxist-inspired) apparatus of practices, narratives and traditions, Solomon is clear that MacIntyre's core commitment is to a renewed Aristotelian ethics of virtue. He ends his chapter by expounding MacIntyre's call for new forms of community, in which individuals can both practise and protect an ethics of the virtues 'in the classical tradition'.

Notes

1 Situation ethics was propounded by Joseph Fletcher in Fletcher 1966; moral particularism is associated especially with the work of Jonathan Dancy (see, e.g., Dancy 2004).

2 The main source for John McDowell's concept of 'second nature' is McDowell 1994. For recent work on Aquinas and connaturality, see (e.g.) Alford 2010.

3 For recent work on the emotions, see (e.g.) Bagnoli 2011, Kirman et al. 2010 and Elster 1999.

4 For an excellent student's edition of Nietzsche's *Genealogy*, see Nietzsche 2007.

5 See Maritain 1964 (which supports Thomism), MacIntyre 1981 (an argument for Aristotelian virtue ethics) and Rist 2002 (which upholds a form of Platonism). Irwin's monumental narrative of Western ethics (Irwin 2011) is ultimately a defence of Aristotelianism.

References

Alford, F. (2010), *Narrative, Nature and the Natural Law: From Aquinas to International Human Rights*. London: Palgrave Macmillan.

Bagnoli, C. (2011), *Morality and the Emotions*. Oxford: Oxford University Press.

Dancy, J. (2004), *Ethics without Principles*. Oxford: Oxford University Press.

Elster, J. (1999), *Alchemies of the Mind: Rationality and the Emotions*. Cambridge: Cambridge University Press.

Fletcher, J. (1966), *Situation Ethics: The New Morality*. Louisville: Westminster Press.

Irwin, T. (2011), *The Development of Ethics* (3 vols). Oxford: Oxford University Press.

Kirman, A., Livet, P. and Teschl, M. (eds) (2010), *Rationality and Emotions*. London: The Royal Society.

MacIntyre, A. (1981), *After Virtue: An Essay in Moral Theory*. London: Duckworth.

Maritain, J. (1964), *Moral Philosophy: An Historical and Critical Survey of the Great Systems*. London: Geoffrey Bles.

McDowell, J. (1994), *Mind and World*. Cambridge, MA: Harvard University Press.

Nietzsche, F. (2007), *On the Genealogy of Morality* (ed. K. Ansell-
    Pearson, transl. C. Diethe). Cambridge: Cambridge University
    Press.
Rist, J. (2002), *Real Ethics: Reconsidering the Foundations of Morality.*
    Cambridge: Cambridge University Press.

1

Plato

Tom Angier

'**W**hat is the good life?' This question is fundamental both to ethical theory and to the work of Plato – the first systematic philosopher in the Western tradition (429–347 BCE). It is so largely owing to Socrates, who, as Plato's teacher and subsequently the hero of Plato's dialogues, brought about a significant turning point in the history of philosophy. For whereas the pre-Socratic philosophers, the *phusikoi*, had by and large concentrated on explaining the workings of *phusis* (the natural world),[1] Socrates turned instead, and decisively, to understanding the practical, human world. As he puts things in Plato's dialogue, the *Phaedo* (96ff.), as a young man he was 'wonderfully keen on that wisdom which they call natural science', for he thought it 'splendid to know the causes of everything'. But as he grew up, he realized that there is at least one kind of 'cause' that natural science is not well-equipped to discover: viz. what makes things *good*. It was this passionate concern with value and practice that encouraged Socrates to move beyond natural science to a more integral discipline, which he calls simply 'love of wisdom' – *philosophia*.

Inspired by Socrates, then, Plato sets himself the question: 'What is the good life?' This may appear a straightforward question, but is, on reflection, crucially ambiguous. For it can be read as asking either of two, seemingly very different things: either (a) 'What is the morally good, morally commendable life?' or (b) 'What kind of life makes for happiness, flourishing, fulfilment (or what the Greeks called *eudaimonia*)?' As twenty-first century readers, we are inclined to treat these questions as logically independent – why, after all, should living a morally commendable life be conducive to flourishing? Can't the virtuous be condemned to living the most miserable of lives? And we are confirmed in these thoughts by centuries of post-Enlightenment moral philosophy, for which the conjunction of virtue and *eudaimonia* is far from self-evident. Perhaps the paradigm disjunction between these is argued for by Kant,[2] who maintains that the desire for happiness is not itself a moral desire, and that we can (at best) hope for, but not expect some reward for moral goodness in a future life. This severance between moral goodness and leading a fulfilling life was dubbed by Henry Sidgwick 'the dualism of practical reason',[3] and we still live in its shadow.

Plato rejects this dualism wholesale. On the one hand, his dialogues assume that happiness is naturally and unproblematically desired by all human beings as their ultimate end.[4] On the other hand, his dialogues strongly suggest that virtue should always trump vice, no matter what (apparently) good things vice brings or the (supposed) costs of being virtuous.[5] Moreover, and vitally, these two views are internally related: as Gerasimos Santas puts matters, Plato presents virtue as 'absolutely *essential* to, and *dominant* in, human happiness' (Santas 2001, 20). Granted, issues of interpretation arise here, such as whether virtue is sufficient for flourishing, or merely necessary – an issue Julia Annas has devoted much attention to.[6] Furthermore, there is the issue of whether, in the *Republic*, Plato has to admit a tragic dissociation between virtue and flourishing, even in his ideal city (an issue I shall return to). But it is clear, nevertheless, that we are in a very different ethical universe from Kant: virtue and happiness are meant to be indissociable. All of which raises the question: what, according to the Platonic dialogues, *is* the good (*qua* virtuous) life which conditions a good (*qua* happy) life? Answering this question will be the task of this chapter. Before I embark on this task directly, however, I need to say something about a conception of virtue which was prevalent in fifth-century Athens, and to which Plato was implacably opposed.

Unlike the English word 'virtue', which has connotations of effete primness (deriving from the Victorian period), the Greek word *aretē* straightforwardly means 'character excellence', and in Plato's time was thought by many to pick out a series of qualities associated with the aristocratic, warrior class.[7] Central to the *aretai*, therefore, were qualities such as wealth, honour, strength, beauty or fineness and noble birth. These were the excellences celebrated throughout the Homeric epics and which found their highest embodiment in characters like Odysseus, Achilles and Hector. 'Most noble son of Atreus', 'Thebes the strong city of Eetion', 'Thyestes rich in flocks', 'Bellerophon, whom heaven endowed with the most surpassing comeliness and beauty': these are the kinds of accolade which punctuate the books of the *Iliad* and which influenced the social world in which Plato grew up and made his career. Key here is the assumption that the excellences or virtues are in vital respects dependent on family inheritance, on various endowments consequent upon social role and on what one happens to look like.[8] Faced with this barrage of worldly virtues, Plato set about questioning whether these were genuine *goods* at all.

This can be seen in the way his dialogues present true virtue as distinct from – and often as in tension with – the Homeric *aretai*. In the *Republic*, for instance, Cephalus asserts that 'Wealth can do a lot to save us from having to cheat or deceive someone against our will' (331a–b), but is shown to have little grasp of what justice actually requires. Successful sophists (so-called wise men) like Gorgias, Hippias and Protagoras gain popular esteem for their 'expertise' in virtue but are revealed as money-grubbing dealers in eristic (i.e. argument for the sake of winning, not of truth). Physical strength is also called into question by ruthless, violent characters like Thrasymachus,[9] just as good looks are impugned as valuable in and of themselves by physically attractive boys who grow up to be tyrants (Alcibiades in the *Symposium*, for instance, or Charmides in the *Charmides*). Finally, nobility is put in question as virtuous *per se* by characters like the aristocratic Lysis, who Socrates presents as in need of moral education no less than anyone else: he cannot simply inherit virtue from his noble lineage (*Lysis* 208–10; cf. *Meno* 93c–4e, *Protagoras* 319d–20b). Overall, then, we see in the Platonic dialogues a sustained assault on the idea that being good, *agathos*, is centrally a matter of inheritance: the virtues are properly voluntary, non-accidental and themselves condition other 'goods', rather than vice versa.

This revaluation of values clearly embodies a distinctive approach to virtue, no longer tying it to social role or personal physique but making it an 'absolute vantage-point' (Sayers 1999, 80) from which to criticize (or at least determine the proper use of) such endowments. And this, in turn, has two main upshots. First, virtue becomes something which can't simply be read off social appearances (rather in the way Socrates' beauty can't simply be read off his face – he was famously ugly).[10] Second, virtue becomes an all-determining good, without which other apparent goods lose their value.[11] Both these facets of Platonic virtue can be seen, moreover, in two of Socrates' most celebrated arguments. First, Socrates argues that 'a good man cannot be harmed, either in life or in death' (*Apology* 41d), a counterintuitive view, which nonetheless reflects and builds on the idea that virtue, and not external – including bodily – goods is the *sine qua non* of fulfilment. Second, Socrates argues that doing injustice is worse than suffering it (see *Gorgias* 472d–6e), another startling claim, which points up how virtue is worth preserving at all costs, even (as in his own case) at the cost of death. Evidently, human excellence or virtue – *aretē* – is Plato's ethical lodestar,[12] that on which human flourishing inextricably depends, and without which external goods are only dubiously goods at all. But this still leaves a vital question to be answered: namely what, exactly, does Platonic virtue consist in?

The traditional response to this has been to invoke a distinction between the early, middle and late dialogues[13] and to argue that Plato gives one answer in the early dialogues, but then changes his mind. Since this traditional account is still widely accepted, I shall deal with it in detail and go on to outline a more recent account, which is (I think justifiably) gaining ground. On the traditional or standard view, Plato's early dialogues propound an 'intellectualist' conception of virtue, according to which virtue is basically a form of knowledge. This is borne out in the *Euthyphro*, for example, where Socrates suggests that piety is a species of knowledge, and in the *Laches*, where he holds that courage is 'knowledge of the grounds of fear and hope' (196d). In the *Apology*, he speaks of virtue in general as a kind of knowledge, the human equivalent of expertise in horse-breeding (20a–c; cf. *Crito* 47c–d). And this points to a model of virtue found throughout the early dialogues, namely not knowledge *simpliciter* but specifically craft- or skill-knowledge, or what the Greeks called '*technē*'.[14] Virtue, in other words, is conceived of as akin to navigation, generalship, farming or shoe-making – as essentially a form of expertise. But why, one might ask, choose *technē*-knowledge as the paradigm for virtue?

Plato is attracted to the craft-model of virtue because, to begin with, it represents the *agathos* as highly reliable, just as a true craftsman [*technitēs*] is highly reliable, a certified master of his trade. As Polus says to Socrates, 'experience . . . causes our times to march along the way of *technē*, whereas inexperience causes it to march along the way of *tuchē* [chance, luck]' (*Gorgias* 448c). Craftsmen are reliable because their knowledge is secure: they have a rational grasp of an objective set of procedures of which they can provide an explanatory account.[15] So, likewise, courageous or temperate actions, for example, can be explained by the virtuous person as systematically conducing to a virtuous life. Lastly, because the *technitēs* has reliable knowledge of an organized, determinate set of procedures and goals, he can teach his craft to others. As Socrates notes in *Protagoras* 319b–c, 'When . . . the city has to take some action on a building project, we send for builders to advise us; if it has to do with the construction of ships, we send for shipwrights; and so forth for everything that is considered learnable and teachable' (cf. *Meno* 90b–c, *Phaedrus* 270d). Clearly, Socrates longs for virtue to be similarly teachable: 'I have had no teacher in this subject [of being virtuous]', he laments, '[and] . . . am unable to discover the *technē* even now' (*Laches* 186c).

Although this *technē*-model of virtue has undoubted appeal,[16] it arguably also has severe costs. I'll outline three of these. First, in the early dialogues, Socrates appears to downplay or even rule out any affective, emotional component to the knowledge that is virtue,[17] and this could be understood as owing to the inessential role emotion is thought to play in successfully practising a *technē*. Second, the early dialogues are notorious for their denial of *akrasia*, that is, they deny the possibility that one can know the good yet act against it. The *locus classicus* of this denial is in the *Protagoras*, where Socrates maintains that 'knowledge is a fine thing capable of ruling a person, and if someone were to know what is good and bad, he would not be forced by anything to act otherwise than knowledge dictates, and intelligence would be sufficient to save a person . . .' (352b). Many of Plato's readers are unsympathetic to this claim that 'no one does wrong willingly', and yet it too could be put down (at least in part) to the idea that those who possess *technē*-knowledge are paradigmatically reliable. Third, if virtue is knowledge of a strictly cognitive kind, the prospects of virtue being teachable look good – but at the cost of reducing such teaching to a form of rational instruction. This is plausibly to denature moral education, which requires a sustained shaping of the desires and emotions and not just learning a set of rules and procedures. Once again, the *technē*-model may be to blame, insofar as craft-learning is taken to involve primarily cognitive instruction in adulthood, with the affects relegated to a wholly secondary role – or even no role at all.[18]

In sum, virtue in the early dialogues, on the standard view, is conceived of intellectualistically, that is, as analogous to *technē*-knowledge – but this is seen to have the baleful consequence that the emotive component of virtue is denied, along with *akrasia*, and moral education is thereby denatured. The upshot, then, is that the early dialogues are deeply flawed. Nevertheless, the standard view also goes on to hold[19] that Plato sets about repairing the above problems in his middle dialogues – centrally in the *Republic* – and overcomes them. How so?

First, Plato leaves behind Socrates' idiom of referring simply to the *psuchē*, 'soul', as if it were a univocal, uniform centre of human agency, replacing this idiom with a picture of the soul as internally variegated and specifically as *including* desires and emotions. The *Republic* thus speaks in terms of a hierarchy of 'parts' of the soul, the rational, the spirited and the appetitive[20] – and this ensures against the error of presenting virtue as a straightforwardly cognitive, purely intellectual achievement. Another dividend of the *Republic*'s tripartite view of the soul is seen to be its admission of *akrasia* (or 'incontinence', 'weakness of will'). The evidence here centres on Leontius, a hapless figure who apparently knows where the good or virtuous course of action lies, but whose appetite 'forces [him] contrary to rational calculation' (440a): '[Leontius] had an appetite to look at [some corpses]', Socrates recounts, 'but at the same time he was disgusted and turned away. For a time he struggled with himself and covered his face, but finally, overpowered by the appetite, he pushed his eyes wide open . . .' (439e–40a). This episode is understood as overturning the *Protagoras*' view that desire or appetite is powerless against knowledge, together with the view that *akrasia* is no more than action in ignorance. Last but not least, *Republic* II, III and VII's lengthy disquisitions on how to habituate the emotional responses of the young, and shape the rational affections of the city's rulers, are taken successfully to displace the simplistic, cognitivist conception of moral education in the early dialogues.

As a whole, this traditional or standard account – which characterizes Platonic virtue as shifting from a purely cognitive, *akrasia*-proof achievement to one that centrally involves the 'passions' [*pathē*] and is vulnerable to them – is internally coherent and has dominated the secondary literature for a long time (perhaps owing largely to Aristotle's support – see note 17). For both these reasons, it needs to be taken seriously. But it is less clear that it has a firm foundation in Plato's texts. Perhaps the solidest aspect of the traditional view lies in its account of moral education, since in the early dialogues Socrates pays demonstrably little attention to the details of how virtue is learnt,[21] whereas in the *Republic* he spends most of Books II, III and VII on the topic. Here, he describes how the 'guardians' of his ideal city, *Kallipolis*, are to undergo a long and rigorous training, which covers everything from gymnastics, music and poetry[22] to astronomy, geometry and mathematics. But despite this lacuna in the early dialogues, they never positively deny that virtue requires a long period of moral (including affective) education. After all, Socrates acknowledges that 'virtue is teachable if it is knowledge' (*Meno* 89d), suggests that moral education is analogous to horse-breeding (*Apology* 20a–c) – which is hardly a paradigm of rational instruction – and spends most of his time engaging critically with the patrician youth of Athens, drawing on resources that are both ratiocinative and emotive.[23]

As to the claim that the early dialogues conceive of mature, achieved virtue as purely cognitive or devoid of affective components, the evidence is, I think, surprisingly slim. Indeed, as a growing number of commentators maintain, the early dialogues leave room for what Heda Segvic calls an emotive or desiderative intellectualism.[24] As Segvic notes, drawing on *Gorgias* 466a–8e, Socrates makes a distinction between doing as one sees fit and doing what one (truly) wants. The tyrant, for instance, may do what he sees fit, but does not do what he really wants, since what we all really want is to flourish, and his form of behaviour precludes this. In this way, Segvic holds,

Socrates is pointing to a special form of willing or wanting, which has both a *desiderative* and an *epistemic* aspect: it latches onto what is in fact good, through our deep desire to do well for ourselves, a desire which is 'hardwired' into our nature (Segvic 2009, 63). Now, clearly not all wanting is like this, since our desires often lead us astray, and we take things to be good for us which aren't (as in the case of the tyrant). But even here, cognition is at work (*qua* false belief), in and through our desires – as Segvic puts it, 'in every passion reason is in some way exercised' (ibid. 77).[25] It is just that reason can malfunction, given its close association with those desires. So even if dialogues like the *Protagoras* suggest that passion simply misleads reason, on closer inspection the early dialogues assume the two actually work together, whether in so doing they manage to discern the true good or not.

Moving on to the traditional interpretation of the *Republic* – as incorporating desire within the soul, and hence as allowing *akrasia* – this finds only dubious support in the text. To begin with, the Leontius passage is not probative. When Leontius rushes towards the corpses, opens his eyes and says 'Look for yourselves, you evil wretches, take your fill of the beautiful sight!' (440a), his heightened rhetoric suggests that his reason has already been misled into false belief by his base desires, spirit having given up the fight. Not only this, but we also have evidence that, however vulnerable reason is to being co-opted by the lower appetites, Plato remains as confident as ever that when reason finally attains *knowledge* – in virtue of its own desire for the good – it becomes invulnerable to those appetites. This is, I think, how we should interpret passages such as the following: 'the virtue of reason seems to belong above all to something more divine [than habituated desire], [something] which never loses its power' (518e); '[music and poetry] educated the guardians through habits. Its harmonies gave them a certain harmoniousness, not knowledge' (522a). Moreover and crucially, the *Republic* preserves the view that 'Every soul pursues the good and does whatever it does for its sake' (505e), indicating that when reason truly *knows* a course of action to be virtuous, as opposed to merely believing it to be so, such knowledge cannot (*pace* the devotees of *akrasia*) be countermanded.[26]

All in all, then, this threefold challenge succeeds in putting the traditional or standard account on the defensive. If it is cogent, it demonstrates how the early and middle dialogues are far more continuous with each other than has generally been thought. For according to the new account, the early dialogues make room for the educational theory of the *Republic*, along with its capacious, affectively rich view of the soul, and the *Republic* in turn upholds the early dialogues' ban on *akrasia*. And this changes the overall geography of Plato-interpretation substantially.[27] Even if this occurs, however, and a more 'unitarian', as opposed to 'developmentalist' account of Platonic virtue-knowledge gains acceptance, this still leaves an outstanding (and seminal) question to be answered: namely, what is the *content* of this cognitive-cum-affective knowledge? In short, what is virtue-knowledge *of*? In the remainder of this chapter, I will unpack two rival answers to this question – as elaborated in the *Protagoras* and *Republic* – and end by drawing some lessons for virtue theory in general.

The *Protagoras* is remarkable for being the only dialogue that develops, explicitly and at length, the notion of a virtue-*technē* which can be practised, in principle, by all. It has two central features: first, it is a 'measuring *technē*' (356d), and second, it measures pleasure. In short, it is a 'hedonistic art of measurement', which Socrates says is meant to constitute our 'salvation in life' (356d). How so, exactly? The idea that measurement and quantification can sort out seemingly intractable disputes goes back to the *Euthyphro*, where Socrates claims that 'if we differed about the larger and the smaller, we would turn to measurement and soon cease to differ' (7c). He then suggests that if this technique were applicable to disputes concerning 'the just and the unjust, the noble and the shameful, the good and the bad' (7d), these too could be resolved with relatively little strife. Where the *Protagoras* is innovative is in proposing a specifically hedonistic calculus, where pleasures and pains, summed over time without regard to when they occur, are taken to exhaust the good and the bad, respectively. This strikingly neat schema,[28] which anticipates Bentham's utilitarian calculus by millennia, thus supplies what looks like the perfect virtue-*technē*. It has a determinate *ergon* or product, namely the maximization of pleasure, which is conceived of as tantamount to happiness. And virtue is analysed, straightforwardly, as knowing how to produce this *ergon*. Is this, then, the virtue-*technē* which Socrates 'longed after . . . from [his] youth up' (*Laches* 186c)?

Although one major scholar has argued it is,[29] I think there are strong reasons to disagree. These centre on the fact that Socrates never directly affirms hedonism in the *Protagoras*. In the vast majority of instances, he attributes it to 'hoi polloi', 'the many', and/or to Protagoras himself (*vide* 353d, 354b–c, 356c).[30] Furthermore, dialogues beyond the *Protagoras* are very inhospitable to hedonism. The clearest attack on it comes in the *Gorgias*, where Socrates concludes that Callicles' pleasure-seeking leads him into contradiction (see 499a–b) – and we find hedonism being rejected even in the late dialogues. In the *Philebus*, for instance, we read that 'Socrates . . . affirms that . . . the good and the pleasant have a different nature' (60b), while in the *Laws* the Athenian holds that 'unhealthy instincts must be canalised away from what men call supreme pleasure, and towards the supreme good' (783a). When taken together with the fact that passages throughout the dialogues impugn the hedonistic assumption that all pleasures are evaluatively homogeneous, or even measurable at all,[31] there seems strong evidence for the view that – even if the hedonistic measuring *technē* serves certain of Socrates' dialectical purposes[32] – he never affirms it as a genuine virtue-*technē*.

In response to this, it might be objected that the *Protagoras*' hedonism does not conclusively scupper the idea of a virtue-*technē qua* 'art of measurement'. For one could replace pleasure with some other, less problematic *ergon*, thereby rescuing what seems an exceptionally economical, all-purpose decision procedure. But to respond to this objection, in turn, I would argue that it bypasses a central problem, which I will call the 'problem of guaranteeing goodness'. We have already seen that pleasure *per se* does not guarantee goodness, because pleasure can be taken in bad things – this being the core reason for Plato's systematic rejection of hedonism. Yet this raises the further, deeper question of whether *any ergon*, proposed by *any* putative virtue-*technē*, could rule out such misdirection. Plato treats this question most fully in the *Euthydemus* (279–81), where Socrates makes an analogy with the ordinary *technē* of carpentry. A person, Socrates holds, can possess many 'good things' – in this case, tools and plenty of wood – but he will derive no benefit from these without knowing how to use them properly. Indeed, without such knowledge (here, knowledge of carpentry), he is likely to do significant damage and end up more miserable than he was before. What conclusions does Socrates draw from this inevitable need for what he calls 'right use' (281a)?

The conclusions Socrates draws are already familiar from my brief excursus on external goods, except this time they arise not from a consideration of the Homeric virtues but from general reflection on virtue considered as a *technē*. As Socrates puts matters in 281d–e: 'it seems likely that with respect to all the things we called good in the beginning, the correct account is . . . that . . . if ignorance controls them, they are greater evils than their opposites . . .; but if good sense and wisdom are in control, they are greater goods. In themselves, however, neither sort is of any value'. This is a radical conclusion, since it appears to go against Socrates' previous distinction between 'the possession of good things' and 'the use of them' (280c, e), where 'good' is independent of and antecedent to 'use'. In other words, Socrates is apparently denying that virtue's *ergon* is in any way good *per se*, and this has sparked controversy over the exact force of this passage.[33] For present purposes, however, I think what the *Euthydemus* uncontroversially does establish[34] is that a virtue-*technē* cannot properly claim to guarantee goodness if it simply recommends (à la *Protagoras*) a specific *ergon*, or set of *erga*. Rather, it must also give real and determinate content to the knowledge that 'uses' or directs those *erga*. All of which brings us back to the *Republic*.

The *Republic*, Plato's most famous and philosophically wide-ranging dialogue, explores the prospects for a *technē* of justice or *dikaiosunē* (a virtue so all-encompassing it is tantamount to virtue itself).[35] On the one hand, as we have seen, the *Republic* argues that there is justice in the *psuchē* or soul, which Socrates characterizes as reason ruling the appetites with the help of spirit (see especially 442–3). When the three 'parts' of the soul are 'harmonized' in this way, they yield a kind of mental health: as Socrates puts it, 'Virtue seems . . . to be a kind of health, fine condition, and well-being of the soul' (444d; cf. 591b). On the other hand, justice exists also beyond the soul, namely in the city. This is justice in the usual sense, namely, a form of conduct or behaviour. As Socrates outlines it, it involves each class of citizen – guardians, soldiers and artisans – 'doing its own work [*ergon*]' (see especially 433). In the case of the artisans, this involves provisioning the city with things like shoes, shirts and ships, in the case of the soldiers, courageous protection of the city in line with the instructions of the guardians and in the case of the guardians themselves, ensuring the city as a whole is wisely and rationally ordered.

In response to this account, many commentators have accused Plato of fallaciously yoking two logically independent conceptions of justice, namely 'Platonic' (or soul-) justice and 'conventional' (or city-) justice.[36] What, they ask, is the connection between these? How has Plato shown that justice in the soul entails just achievements in the city or vice versa? But so far as I can see, these questions miss the mark. For as Iakovos Vasiliou has trenchantly argued, Plato simply relies here on an 'habituation principle' to correlate soul-justice with city-justice.[37] That is, he assumes that acting justly will, over time, generate a just, healthy soul, while a just, healthy soul will tend to act in right, appropriate ways. As Socrates maintains, 'when [a person] does anything, whether acquiring wealth, taking care of his body, engaging in politics . . . he believes that the action is just and fine that preserves [his] inner harmony and helps achieve it . . . and regards as wisdom the knowledge that oversees such actions' (443e; cf. 442a–3b, 444e). So even if it is true that harmony between parts of the soul does not *entail* just acts, or vice versa, Plato need not be fazed; he can just invoke the plausible psychological mechanism posited by his habituation principle and move on.[38]

In my view, the deeper and more salient question here is the following: what does reason *know*,[39] which guarantees the 'goods' of the city are properly directed, that is, the right trades practised and justly interrelated, the right people protected or attacked, etc.?[40] The *Republic*'s answer to this is beguilingly simple – namely, the 'Form of the Good'. The Form of the Good is said to be an absolutely superordinate Form,[41] which governs the goodness of all the other Forms, and thereby that of all worldly things as well. In this way, it is like the sun, since it conditions not only our cognitive relation to the world, but also the world's very essence – for everything seeks the good. It is therefore that without which nothing else is of benefit.[42] But what exactly, one wants to ask, affords such benefit? To this crucial question, Plato gives what I think is basically a mathematical answer. The Form of the Good, that is, is ultimately mathematical in content: through learning mathematics, geometry and finally 'dialectic' (see 532a, 533d, 537c), the guardians grasp how the city should be ordered and structured. And this mathematical vision of the good goes back at least to the *Gorgias*: 'justice', Socrates tells Callicles, 'hold[s] together heaven and earth, and gods and men, and that is why they call this universe a *world order* [*kosmos*] . . . You've failed to notice [this] . . . because you neglect geometry' (508a).[43]

Now this mathematical conception of justice may have been tantalizingly attractive for Plato, who was deeply influenced by the mathematical theories of the Pythagoreans (see Meinwald 1998 and Kahn 2001). But for us, it is difficult to acknowledge even a notional connection between justice, *qua* social harmony and order and number theory.[44] A large part of Plato's motivation here is grounded, I think, in his conviction that mathematics is the paradigmatically stable discipline, which deals with paradigmatically stable entities. And this holds immense appeal, of course, for his project of *guaranteeing* goodness. But it is worth asking whether Plato himself is not aware of the ultimate futility of this project. After all, the *Republic*'s metaphysics is relentlessly frank about the instability of the world: unlike the Forms, people and things are constantly changing, relative to time, place and perspective.[45] This makes justice a highly precarious achievement, which depends not only on maintaining a healthy soul, but also on continuing to inhabit a rightly ordered city and interacting with it in the right ways. And this is reflected in the brutally realistic account (in *Republic* VII) of how political regimes, together with their citizens, are in never-ending, anxiety-ridden flux.

In the end, then, I think Plato recognizes that, even in *Kallipolis*, with its putatively mathematically governed order, justice, virtue and thus happiness – in short, 'the good life' – is ineliminably fragile: its conditions are simply too manifold to be guaranteed.[46] And this explains why the guardians are tempted by a life of contemplating the Forms, as opposed to returning to the 'Cave' (i.e. political life; see 519c–21b) – they realize it is only by escaping the everyday world, together with its myriad injustices, that they can be truly happy. Of course, the implications of this are tragic. One cannot, on this view, attain true happiness in this world (even if political justice requires that one try).[47] However disillusioned this is, it is a powerful view, which many have found compelling. Aristotle, for instance, although he rejects Plato's Form of the Good, together with Plato's conception of the ideal city, seems equally given to locating ultimate happiness beyond the turmoil of politics (see *Nicomachean Ethics* X.7). And mediaeval thinkers like Thomas Aquinas, who led contemplative lives and set the bar for virtue as high as (if not higher than) Plato, locate true happiness beyond this life altogether. It is only with early modern philosophers, like Hume, that we begin to find the idea that the world is fundamentally hospitable to virtue and also to happiness.[48] The question is whether this idea, despite its attractions, depends on a profound (and very anti-Platonic) underestimation of what true goodness requires.

Notes

1 See Jonathan Barnes, *Early Greek Philosophy*, Penguin (Barnes 1987).

2 In the *Groundwork of the Metaphysics of Morals* and *Critique of Practical Reason*.

3 See Terence Irwin's chapter on Socrates in *The Development of Ethics* (volume 1) (Irwin 2007, 14).

4 N. B. 'Of one who wants to be happy there is no longer any point in asking, "For what reason does he want to be happy?" This answer is already final' (*Symposium* 205a). Cf. *Gorgias* 468b, *Euthydemus* 278e–82d, *Philebus* 60a–61a. Gregory Vlastos calls this the 'Eudaemonist Axiom' (see Vlastos 1991, 203–9).

5 N. B. '. . . the only thing we should consider is . . . whether we would be acting justly . . . or, in truth, unjustly' (*Crito* 48c–d) Cf. *Apology* 28b, 28d, *Gorgias* 470c–1a, *Republic* 444e–5a. Vlastos calls this the principle of the 'Sovereignty of Virtue' (see Vlastos 1991, 209–14).

6 Annas argues that Plato affirms the stronger doctrine, namely, virtue as sufficient for happiness. See Annas 1999, 2008, 270–1.

7 A trace of this conception remains in English, since the etymological root of 'virtue' is 'vir', the Latin for 'man' – as in 'virile'.

8 For more on these Homeric-type virtues, see Irwin 1977, 15–18, and Chapter 10 of MacIntyre 2007, entitled 'The Virtues of Heroic Societies' (121–30).

9 Socrates describes how Thrasymachus 'coiled himself up like a wild beast about to spring, and . . . hurled himself at us as if to tear us to pieces' (*Republic* 336b).

10 This is reflected in Plato's repeated privileging of the 'soul' over the body: see, e.g. *Phaedo passim.*, *Symposium* 211a, *Phaedrus* 250c, *Gorgias* 479a, 480b.

11 N. B. 'Wealth does not bring about virtue, but virtue makes wealth and everything else good for men' (*Apology* 30b).

12 '[V]irtue and justice', Socrates holds, 'are man's most precious possession, along with lawful behaviour and the laws' (*Crito* 53c–d).

13 These are commonly grouped as follows: early (or 'Socratic') – *Apology, Charmides, Crito, Cratylus, Euthydemus, Euthyphro, Gorgias, Hippias Minor* (and *Hippias Major*, if genuine), *Ion, Laches, Lysis, Menexenus, Meno, Phaedo, Protagoras, Symposium;* middle – *Phaedrus, Republic, Parmenides, Theaetetus;* late – *Sophist, Statesman, Philebus, Timaeus, Critias, Laws.* See Irwin 1977, 291–3 and Brandwood 1990, for details.

14 For confirmation of *technē* as Plato's model here – at least in the early dialogues – see Irwin 1977, 71–7, 94–7, Woodruff 1990, Roochnik 1996, Reeve 2003 and Angier 2010, Chapter 1.

15 N. B. Timaeus holds that the universe is 'a work of craft . . . grasped by a rational account [*logos*]' (*Timaeus* 29a), and Socrates asks rhetorically, 'does the medical craft . . . make people able both to have wisdom and to speak about the sick?' (*Gorgias* 449e–50a). Contrast Ion, the disorganized, unreflective and hence unskilled reciter of poetry, whose 'expertise' as a rhapsode Plato presents as no more than a 'knack': 'that's not a *technē* you've mastered', Socrates tartly remarks, 'it's a divine power that moves you' (*Ion* 533d).

16 *Intelligent Virtue* (Annas 2011) argues that we can and should construe the virtues as closely analogous to 'practical skills'.

17 Aristotle, for one, takes this view. Socrates 'used to make the virtues into sciences, and this is impossible', he adjures; 'The result is that . . . he does away with the nonrational part of the soul, and thereby does away also with passion and character; so that on this point he has not treated the virtues correctly' (*Magna Moralia* 1182a15–23; cf. *Eudemian Ethics* 1216b2–10, 1229a14–16, 1230a7–10, 1246b32–6). Irwin 1977, 7, 87 and Santas 1979 also take the view that, in the early dialogues, virtue-knowledge is purely cognitive.

18 Cf. Aristotle: character (including emotional) states are 'not reckoned in as conditions of the possession of the *technai*, except . . . bare knowledge; but as a condition of the possession of the *aretai*, knowledge has little or no weight, while the other conditions count . . . for everything' (*Nicomachean Ethics* 1105a33–b4).

19 Cf. Iakovos Vasiliou's nice summary at Vasiliou 2008, 10.

20 See especially *Republic* book IV, where Socrates divides the soul by analogy with the parts of the city. The parts of the soul should not be taken as strictly homogeneous, since the rational part has desires, and the appetitive or desiring part has certain (minimal) cognitive powers. On this, see Sayers 1999, 71–2, Lorenz 2008, 261, Annas 2008, 277 and Scott 2008, 361 n. 2.

21 As Aristotle remarks, Socrates 'enquired what virtue is, not how or from what it arises' (*Eudemian Ethics* 1216b9).

22 Book III makes clear how prescriptive and proscriptive is the *Republic*'s blueprint for the guardians' education in music and poetry. Not only is artistic content censored in line with Plato's revisionary conception of the gods and heroes, but also artistic form (or style) is dictated by what he considers the true canons of order [*kosmos*] and beauty [*kalon*]. For more on this, see Christopher Janaway's *Images of Excellence* (Janaway 1995).

23 It is worth noting here that the only account of moral education given in the early dialogues is given by Protagoras in a dialogue (the *Protagoras*) usually cited to justify the intellectualist view of Socratic virtue. Moreover, the account he gives is full of references to developing or habituating the pre-cognitive affects (see 325c f.)

24 See Segvic 2009, 48–9 (Segvic 2009 is a reprint of Segvic 2000). Cf. Carone 2004, Singpurwalla 2006 and Brickhouse and Smith 2010.

25 Brickhouse and Smith object to Segvic's claim that reason 'speaks through passion' (Segvic 2009, 79), accusing it of reducing desires to evaluative beliefs (see Brickhouse and Smith 2010, 86 n. 13). Segvic, however, explicitly denies that her view is reductive – all it denies, she claims, is that feelings and desires operate independently of reason (see Segvic 2009, 76–7). (N. B. Hendrik Lorenz – a scholar comparatively sympathetic to the traditional account – admits that even the *Protagoras* allows a 'joint working' of 'thought and affection'. See Lorenz 2008, 245, 249.)

26 Carone 2001 and Anagnostopoulos 2005 uphold this challenge to the interpretative *status quo*. N. B. Anagnostopoulos: 'Plato [in the *Republic*] . . . does hold that all desire is for the true good, in the completely virtuous soul governed by its optimally functioning rational element' (ibid. 168).

27 Including the idea that the craft-model is largely misleading. After all, many crafts depend on their practitioners' having the right desires and emotions, and it is partly in virtue of these that craftsmen are reliable. As Rachel Barney affirms, 'nothing in the idea of virtue as a *technē* entails dismissing nonrational factors such as habituation, discipline and natural aptitude: on the contrary, these are standard preconditions for acquiring any *technē* of importance' (see Barney (forthcoming)).

28 For more details, see Rudebusch 1999, Chapter 3, Reshotko 2006, Chapter 4 and Wolfsdorf 2008, 51–9.

29 Namely, Terence Irwin. See Irwin 1977, Chapter 4 and Irwin 1995, Chapter 6. Irwin is impressed by the measuring *technē*'s very economical formal features, but pays too little attention to its hedonism and the problems this generates.

30 Referring to these passages and others, Donald Zeyl has shown how Socrates' proposal of hedonism in the *Protagoras* is never more than oblique (see Zeyl 1980). David Wolfsdorf documents how most scholars have followed Zeyl (see Wolfsdorf 2006, 133–4 n. 38).

31 With regard to evaluative homogeneity, see *Phaedrus* 258e, *Republic* 582e, *Laws* 658e–9a (on noble versus slavish pleasures), *Philebus* 52c (on pure versus impure pleasures), and *Republic* 505b, 509a, 591c (on rational versus irrational pleasures). With regard to measurability, the *Gorgias* treats pleasure as an inherently changeable and unstable property (see 500b, 501a–b, 506d), while in the *Philebus*, Socrates asserts that 'one could [not] find anything . . . more outside all measure than pleasure' (65d; cf. 31a).

32 Wolfsdorf argues that Socrates uses the hedonistic hypothesis as a way of tarring Protagoras (and ultimately all sophists) with a populist brush, since to accept hedonism is, on Socrates' view, to enslave oneself to the arbitrary whims of the majority (see Wolfsdorf 2006, 134; 2008, 113–14). Not that Socrates repudiates taking pleasure in truly *good* things – something he endorses (N. B. *Republic* 582d, 583b, 585a, d–e). He merely rejects pursuing pleasure directly and *per se*.

33 Vlastos criticizes *Euthydemus* 281d–e, arguing that it contravenes not only previous passages in the same dialogue, but also similar passages in other dialogues (viz. *Lysis* 218e, *Meno* 78c; see Vlastos 1991, 224–31). Santas, drawing on Ferejohn 1984, argues that while neither virtue-knowledge nor its 'products' are 'self-sufficiently good' – since each requires the other for goodness to be realized – the former differs from the latter in being 'invariably beneficial' (see Santas 2001, 33–8).

34 Along with *Meno* 87–9, which also elaborates a distinction between possession and use.

35 See Irwin 1977, 22–3 and Vasiliou 2008, 2 n. 4 on the meaning of *dikaiosunē* (or *dikē*). *Contra* Irwin 1977, Plato does not straightforwardly drop craft as the model for virtue after the early dialogues. Justice is referred to as, or compared to a *technē* at *Republic* 332d, 374d–e, 495d and 496b.

36 First and foremost among these commentators is David Sachs: see his 'A Fallacy in Plato's *Republic*' (Sachs 1963).

37 See Vasiliou 2008, 17–18, 250.

38 This principle is adopted by Aristotle (see esp. *Nicomachean Ethics* II.1, *Eudemian Ethics* 1220a22–b20). For examples of scholars who nonetheless treat Sachs' 'fallacy' as genuine, see (e.g.) Irwin 1977, 210, Annas 1981, 160 and Scott 2000, 2.

39 That is, what do the guardians or rulers of the city know? In the case of other citizens, only true belief can be aspired to. (Below, I shall say a bit about why Plato places so much emphasis on the distinction between knowledge and belief.)

40 Clearly, the question I am raising here is the same one raised by the *Euthydemus* – namely, that of possession and right use – except this time it is being posed against the much broader canvas of the *Republic*.

41 See, primarily, Socrates' three analogies of Sun, Line and Cave (*Republic* 507–21). The literature on these is enormous, but I would particularly recommend Pappas 1995, Chapter 7, Sayers 1999, Chapters 10–11, Santas 2001, Chapter 5 and Santas 2010, Chapter 7.

42 As Socrates says, clearly recalling the *Euthydemus*' possession/ use distinction: 'if we don't know [the Form of the Good], even the fullest possible knowledge of other things is of no benefit to us, any more than if we acquire any possession without the good of it' (*Republic* 505a).

43 For more on the profound connection between goodness and number in the *Republic* (and also in other dialogues), see Burnyeat 2000, Denyer 2007 and Miller 2007.

44 Harmony is a pervasive value in the *Republic* – see (e.g.) 336b, 351d, 411e, 442c, 547a, 591d–e, 617b – which may be mathematical in essence (see 458d, 522e–3a).

45 See Fine 1999 on Plato's metaphysics. Most commentators agree that, according to the *Republic*, worldly particulars cannot be known, but only believed to have certain properties (in virtue of their unstable natures).

46 In *The Fragility of Goodness* (Nussbaum 1986), Martha Nussbaum criticizes Plato's longing for invulnerability and fear of fragility. But she underestimates the degree to which these arise from his longing for justice, and fear of injustice, respectively.

47 N. B. Socrates' claim that the guardians will agree to return to political life from 'the pure realm', because 'we'll be giving just orders to just people' (*Republic* 520d–e). At the same time, he implies this will not make them 'outstandingly happy' (519e).

48 The modern period also sees a systematic, deliberate severing of the connection between virtue and happiness. Perhaps the most famous instance of this is to be found in that great anti-Platonist, Nietzsche.

References

Anagnostopoulos, M. (2005), 'The Divided Soul and the Desire for Good in Plato's Republic', in G. Santas (ed.), *The Blackwell Guidebook to Plato's Republic*. Oxford: Blackwell. Pp. 166–88.

Angier, T. (2010), *Technē in Aristotle's Ethics: Crafting the Moral Life*. London and New York: Continuum Press.

Annas, J. (1981), *An Introduction to Plato's Republic*. Oxford: Clarendon Press.

—(1999), *Platonic Ethics, Old and New*. Ithaca: Cornell University Press.

—(2008), 'Plato's Ethics', in G. Fine (ed.), *The Oxford Handbook of Plato*. Oxford: Oxford University Press. Pp. 267–85.

—(2011), *Intelligent Virtue*. Oxford: Oxford University Press.

Barnes, J. (1987), *Early Greek Philosophy*. London: Penguin Books.

Barney, R. (forthcoming), 'Plato and the Intellectualist Hypothesis: A Prospectus for a Reading of the Early Dialogues'.

Brandwood, L. (1990), *The Chronology of Plato's Dialogues*. Cambridge: Cambridge University Press.

Brickhouse, T. C. and Smith, N. D. (2010), *Socratic Moral Psychology*. Cambridge: Cambridge University Press.

Burnyeat, M. (2000), 'Plato on Why Mathematics is Good for the Soul', in T. Smiley (ed.), *Mathematics and Necessity* (Proceedings of the British Academy, 103). Oxford: Oxford University Press.

Carone, G. R. (2001), '*Akrasia* in the *Republic*: Does Plato Change his Mind?', *Oxford Studies in Ancient Philosophy*, XX (summer): 107–48.

—(2004), 'Calculating Machines or Leaky Jars? The Moral Psychology of Plato's *Gorgias*', *Oxford Studies in Ancient Philosophy*, XXVI (summer): 55–96.

Denyer, N. (2007), 'Sun and Line: The Role of the Good', in G. R. F. Ferrari (ed.), *The Cambridge Companion to Plato's Republic*. Cambridge: Cambridge University Press.

Ferejohn, M. T. (1984), 'Socratic Thought Experiments and the Unity of Virtue Paradox', *Phronesis* 29 (2): 105–22.

Ferrari, G. R. F. (2007), *The Cambridge Companion to Plato's Republic*. Cambridge: Cambridge University Press.

Fine, G. (1999), *Plato 2: Ethics, Politics, Religion, and the Soul*. Oxford: Oxford University Press.

—(2008), *The Oxford Handbook of Plato*. Oxford: Oxford University Press.

Irwin, T. (1977), *Plato's Moral Theory: The Early and Middle Dialogues*. Oxford: Clarendon Press.

—(1995), *Plato's Ethics*. Oxford: Oxford University Press.
—(2007), *The Development of Ethics: A Historical and Critical Study. Volume 1 – From Socrates to the Reformation*. Oxford: Oxford University Press.
Janaway, C. (1995), *Images of Excellence: Plato's Critique of the Arts*. Oxford: Clarendon Press.
Kahn, C. H. (2001), *Pythagoras and the Pythagoreans: A Brief History*. Indianapolis: Hackett Publishing.
Kant, I. (1997), *Critique of Practical Reason* (M. J. Gregor, ed.) Cambridge: Cambridge University Press.
—(1998), *Groundwork of the Metaphysics of Morals* (M. J. Gregor, ed.) Cambridge: Cambridge University Press.
Lorenz, H. (2008), 'Plato on the Soul', in G. Fine (ed.), *The Oxford Handbook of Plato*. Oxford: Oxford University Press. pp. 243–66.
MacIntyre, A. (2007), *After Virtue: An Essay in Moral Theory* (3rd edn). London: Duckworth.
Meinwald, C. C. (1998), 'Prometheus' Bounds: *Peras* and *Apeiron* in Plato's *Philebus*', in J. Gentzler (ed.), *Method in Ancient Philosophy*. Oxford: Clarendon Press.
Miller, M. (2007), 'Beginning the "Longer Way"', in G. R. F. Ferrari (ed.), *The Cambridge Companion to Plato's Republic*. Cambridge: Cambridge University Press.
Nussbaum, M. (1986), *The Fragility of Goodness: Luck and Ethics in Greek Tragedy and Philosophy*. Cambridge: Cambridge University Press.
Pappas, N. (1995), *Plato and the Republic* (Routledge Philosophy Guidebooks), London and New York: Routledge.
Reeve, C. D. C. (2003), 'Plato's Metaphysics of Morals', *Oxford Studies in Ancient Philosophy*, XXV (winter): 39–58.
Reshotko, N. (2006), *Socratic Virtue: Making the Best of the Neither-Good-Nor-Bad*. Cambridge: Cambridge University Press.
Roochnik, D. (1996), *Of Art and Wisdom: Plato's Understanding of Techne*. University Park: Penn State University Press.
Rudebusch, G. (1999), *Socrates, Pleasure, and Value*. Oxford: Oxford University Press.
Sachs, D. (1963), 'A Fallacy in Plato's Republic', *The Philosophical Review* 72 (2): 141–58.
Santas, G. (1979), *Socrates (Arguments of the Philosophers)*. London and New York: Routledge.
—(2001), *Goodness and Justice: Plato, Aristotle, and the Moderns*. Oxford: Blackwell.
—(2005), *The Blackwell Guidebook to Plato's Republic*. Oxford: Blackwell.
—(2010), *Understanding Plato's Republic*. Oxford: Wiley-Blackwell.

Sayers, S. (1999), *Plato's Republic: An Introduction*. Edinburgh: Edinburgh University Press.

Scott, D. (2000), 'Plato's Critique of the Democratic Character', *Phronesis* 45 (1): 19–37.

—(2008), 'The Republic', in G. Fine (ed.), *The Oxford Handbook of Plato*. Oxford: Oxford University Press. pp. 360–82.

Segvic, H. (2000), 'No One Errs Willingly: The Meaning of Socratic Intellectualism', *Oxford Studies in Ancient Philosophy*, XIX: 1–45.

—(2009), *From Protagoras to Aristotle: Essays in Ancient Moral Philosophy* (M. Burnyeat, ed.) Princeton: Princeton University Press.

Singpurwalla, R. (2006), 'Reasoning with the Irrational: Moral Psychology in the *Protagoras*', *Ancient Philosophy* 26 (2): 243–58.

Vasiliou, I. (2008), *Aiming at Virtue in Plato*. Cambridge: Cambridge University Press.

Vlastos, G. (1991), *Socrates: Ironist and Moral Philosopher*. Cambridge: Cambridge University Press.

Wolfsdorf, D. (2006), 'The Ridiculousness of Being Overcome by Pleasure: *Protagoras* 352 B 1 – 358 D 4', *Oxford Studies in Ancient Philosophy*, XXXI (winter): 113–36.

—(2008), *Trials of Reason: Plato and the Crafting of Philosophy*. Oxford: Oxford University Press.

Woodruff, (1990), 'Plato's Early Theory of Knowledge', in S. Everson (ed.), *Epistemology – Companions to Ancient Thought: 1*. Cambridge: Cambridge University Press.

Zeyl, D. J. (1980), 'Socrates and Hedonism: *Protagoras* 351b – 358d', *Phronesis* 25 (3): 250–69.

Recommended reading

Two excellent collections of essays on Plato (multi-authored):

Fine, G. (ed.) (1999), *Plato 2: Ethics, Politics, Religion, and the Soul*. Oxford: Oxford University Press.

Fine, G. (ed.) (2008), *The Oxford Handbook of Plato*. Oxford: Oxford University Press.

Three subtle, book-length treatments of Plato (single-authored):

Kahn, C. H. (1996), *Plato and the Socratic Dialogue: The Philosophical Use of a Literary Form*. Cambridge: Cambridge University Press.

Santas, G. (2001), *Goodness and Justice: Plato, Aristotle, and the Moderns*. Oxford: Blackwell.

Vlastos, G. (1991), *Socrates: Ironist and Moral Philosopher*. Cambridge: Cambridge University Press.

Two impressive volumes on Plato's Republic:

Ferrari, G. R. F. (ed.) (2007), *The Cambridge Companion to Plato's Republic*. Cambridge: Cambridge University Press.
Santas, G. (2010), *Understanding Plato's Republic*. Oxford: Wiley-Blackwell.

2

Aristotle

Timothy Chappell

It seems odd to say that Aristotle's *Ethics*,[1] written c. 330 BCE, has been particularly influential in the last few decades. Odd, but right. Relatively recently, Aristotle's exceedingly ancient work has begun to change the thinking about ethics within Anglophone philosophy in fundamental and far-reaching ways, nearly all of them improvements.

It is a remarkable phenomenon, and one that needs explanation,[2] this new engagement with what is in one sense the first treatise ever written on ethics in the Western tradition and what is in another sense (to be explained shortly) not a treatise about *ethics* at all. Another phenomenon that needs explanation is the general absence of Aristotle's visible influence from modern moral philosophy before – at the earliest – the late nineteenth century.[3] However, my focus here is the content of Aristotle's ethics, not historical explanation; though since ideas can and do change the world, perhaps that content is itself part of the explanation.

Let us begin with the very word 'ethics'. Consider *NE* 1103a14–20, which I translate as follows[4]:

Excellence[5] is of two kinds: intellectual excellence (*tês dianoêtikês*), and excellence of character (*tês êthikês*).[6] Usually, intellectual excellence gets both its beginning and its growth from teaching; that is why it requires experience and time. But excellence of character (*hê d'êthikê*) arises from habituation (*ethos*) – whence it gets its name, by a small change [viz. from *ethos* to *êthos*]. From which it is also clear that none of the excellences of character comes about in us by nature (*physei*); for nothing that is [as it is] by nature can be altered by habituation (*allôs ethizetai*).

Those encountering the *Nicomachean Ethics* for the first time often report a feeling of bafflement at Aristotle's apparent bland common sense. I remember the feeling well. 'What is he actually *saying* here?' I wondered on my own first reading of *NE* as an undergraduate. 'Why would anyone bother to state such truisms, let alone argue for them?'

Sometimes (e.g. 1097b22, 1103b32, 1144b22) Aristotle really is propounding or discussing what he takes to be truisms; there are interesting reasons, to which we will come, why he thought that was worth doing. It is not what he is doing here. The words I quote are characteristically dry and understated, but in them two points of cardinal importance emerge.

The first cardinal point is terminological or at least begins from terminology. In the entire extant corpus of the classical Greek language, the above quoted is the second occurrence ever of the adjective *êthikê*. The first occurrence ever is only a few lines before (*NE* 1103a6); all the other 35 occurrences of the word that Liddell and Scott's Greek lexicon lists are also in Aristotle's *Ethics*. Aristotle does not say that he invented the term: he reports it as if it were an already established usage (*legomen*, 'we use the word . . .', 1103a5). But his introduction of it at the end of what we call[7] *NE* Book 1 is carefully staged. To cover intellectual excellence, Aristotle has the adjective *dianoêtikê*, from *dianoia*, 'the understanding'. *Dianoêtikê* is to *dianoia* exactly as *êthikê* is to *êthos* – and *êthos* is the ordinary Greek for 'character'. So *êthikê aretê* means 'excellence of character', and a book called *êthika nikomakheia* is a book about the nature of character edited by Nicomachus.

These remarks are not just harmless antiquarianism. Their upshot is that, in Aristotle's usage, and as he himself originally intended the word,[8] *êthika does not mean 'ethics'; a fortiori, êthikê aretê does not mean 'moral virtue'*. If you ask any typical student of philosophy today what the *NE* is about, the reply will very likely be 'It's about ethics, or moral philosophy'. But if Aristotle himself could answer (in English) our question what his book is about, his reply would be 'civic society (the *polis*)', or 'the good (*to agathon*)', or 'happiness (*eudaimonia*)', or 'excellence of character (*aretê*)'. If he has a single name for the subject matter of the *Ethics*, it more often seems to be *hê politikê* (*tekhnê? epistêmê?*), political craft or science, than *ta êthika or hê êthikê* (*NE* 1095a3, a16, 1099b30, 1102a8).

This is a great difference between Aristotle and modern moral philosophy that has not (yet) felt his influence. Aristotle does not have the modern concept of a distinctive subject-area, property-type or layer of reality called 'the ethical' or 'the moral'.[9] The nearest he has is the notion that certain excellences, such as courage and justice, are distinctively excellences of a person's *character*, not of his or her *intellect*. But if Aristotle takes this to be (so to speak) of any – ical importance, he takes it to be not of *eth*ical but of *poli*tical importance. That people's characters are affectable for better or worse matters, on his view, because it contributes to the well-being or otherwise of the *polis*. Likewise, the position in Aristotle's thought of the question 'What is *eudaimonia*?' is well marked by the fact that he takes *eudaimonia* to be the objective of *politics*. It is not for nothing that the last word of the *Nicomachean Ethics*, pointing us forward to the *Politics*, is 'let us begin' (1181b24).

In not believing in any distinctively moral 'layer of reality', and in seeing quite different (and much closer) connections between moral and political philosophy from those we typically see today, is Aristotle missing something that we moderns have got? Or is our modern thinking about practical philosophy[10] hampered and tainted, as his is not, by a terminology of 'ethical', 'moral' and the like that appears to mean something but in fact introduces nothing but gratuitous obscurity and mystery? Elizabeth Anscombe (1958) and others have suggested that we might do better to stop using terms like 'the moral' altogether in practical philosophy and simply concentrate on questions about what is good, what is beneficial, what happiness or excellence is, how character is constituted, how people should live together, what exculpates and what inculpates and the like. If we do so, we are following Aristotle. We are also leaving behind a whole web of supposed problems produced by insisting on the 'ethical'/'moral' terminology; the questions, for instance, of how there can be a layer of reality, or again a layer of motivation, which is the *specially moral* layer.

To see a second cardinal point that emerges from *NE* 1103a14–20, we need to understand the dialectical background. Aristotle's remarks are a contribution to, perhaps even the resolution of, at least one famous and long-running Greek ethical dispute. Protagoras, Socrates, Plato and others had shared an interest in whether virtue or excellence is a matter of nature (*physis*) or convention (*nomos*) and whether it can be taught. Aristotle replies, as good philosophers often do, by making some distinctions. If intellectual excellence is meant, then (he says) of course *that* can be taught; it hardly ever appears 'naturally', that is, without any teaching, and it is nearly always improved by further teaching. If, on the other hand, excellence of character is meant, then it is misleading to say that this is *taught*, at least if that means 'taught in the same way as intellectual excellence'. However, it doesn't follow that excellence of character arises by nature. The familiar nature/convention dichotomy is (Aristotle holds) misleading, because there is at least one other possibility, which he spends most of the *NE* developing. This is the possibility that excellence of character (*êthos*) arises neither from nature nor from (directly rational, discursive) teaching but from good habituation (*ethos*) – and in the quotation above from *NE* 1103a14–20, Aristotle gratefully exploits this apparent verbal connection.

When Aristotle says that excellence of character arises from habituation, *ethismos*, what does he mean by *ethismos*? At least part of what he means is something that Plato had discussed in *Republic* 401e–402a and *Laws* 653a ff. – our 'sentimental education', our training in what gives us pain and pleasure:

> The pleasure or pain that accompanies our deeds is bound (*dei*)[11] to provide a measure of our dispositions . . . In fact pleasure and pain is what excellence of character is about. For it is because of pleasure that we do ignoble deeds, and it is because of pain that we fail to do noble ones. That is no doubt why, as Plato says, people need (*dei*) to be habituated from childhood on to take pleasure and pain in the right things (*hois dei*); that is what correct education *is*. (*NE* 1104a4–14)

In the *Protagoras* and elsewhere, Socrates presents[12] arguments implying that the function and the method of education are both alike purely cognitive. The point of education is simply to train people to reason well about both theoretical and practical matters; the method for training them is simply to reason with them. This method is strikingly on display in a famous passage in the *Meno* (82b–85c), where Socrates no sooner meets an illiterate slave-boy than – albeit with an ulterior motive besides the educational one – he is reasoning with him about geometry.

Aristotle and Plato are in at least rough agreement with these arguments of Socrates' about the *point* of education. As they would say, the point of education is to develop excellence (*aretê*) of character and intellect: this *aretê* certainly entails the ability to reason well, though it is less obvious that the converse entailment also holds. But Aristotle and Plato unreservedly reject the rationalistic view of the *method* of education. Before a teacher can reason with his pupils, those pupils have to get to be reasonable in the first place. Wittgenstein famously emphasizes, in the *Philosophical Investigations*, that 'the teaching of language is not explanation, but training' (PI I, 5): much 'stage-setting', as Anscombe's translation calls it, is needed before even such a basic thing as naming can happen (PI I, 257). Similarly Aristotle and Plato both think that much stage-setting is a prerequisite for the learning of *aretê*; that the stage-setting in question is not rational explanation, but non-cognitive or pre-cognitive training and that this aspect of our education in excellence is completely overlooked by Socratic rationalism. (In a sense, then, Aristotle takes up the second alternative presented at *Meno* 72a1–4: that virtue should be a matter of training rather than of teaching. So, in a different sense, does Plato in the *Republic*.)

This emphasis on the importance of the pre-cognitive in any effective education in excellence comes out in a number of ways. One is that, as Hallvard Fossheim has argued, there is a place in Aristotle's account of the education of character for a notion which is often supposed to be of purely aesthetic importance to him: *mimêsis*, imitation.[13]

To relate *mimêsis* as a factor in the habituation of character to the more or less professionalised poetic *mimêsis* which is the main topic of the *Poetics*, we need to understand poetic *mimêsis* in reverse. The poet creates an action from the resources of who he already is; habituation involves establishing a character by first performing its characteristic actions.[14] Habituation does not mean activating a formed character and thereby realising something out there in the world; it means realising something in the world and thereby forming a character . . . The child does as others do, and learns to become a certain sort of person by emulating the actions and manners of others. (Fossheim 2006: 111)

'Practical *mimêsis*', as Fossheim calls it, is not just for children. Adults too have much to learn ethically from, and by imitation – as we see if we adopt the plausible interpretation of Aristotle that Linda Zagzebski has developed under the name 'exemplarism':

> Aristotle has quite a bit to say about what the virtue of *phronêsis* [practical wisdom] consists in, but he clearly is not confident that he can give a full account of it. [However,] he thinks that . . . this does not matter, because we can pick out people who are *phronimoi* [practically wise] in advance of investigating the nature of *phronêsis*. The *phronimos* can be defined, roughly, as a person *like that*, where we make a demonstrative reference to a paradigmatically practically wise person . . . Just as competent speakers can successfully refer to water or gold, and make appropriate assertions about these natural kinds whether or not they know any chemistry, so competent speakers can successfully talk about practically wise persons . . . The phronimos is a person *like that*, just as water is a substance *like that*. (Zagzebski 2006: 58)

On Zagzebski's reading, Aristotle believes that we typically learn to pick out exemplars of the human excellences well before we learn (if we ever do) to say with full explicitness *why* they are exemplars. (Cf. *NE* 1098b3: 'The primary thing and the first principle is the *that*'.) If this is true of excellence, what should we expect to be true of learning to be excellent? Imitation seems bound to have some role to play; if excellence means 'being *like this*', then the obvious way to try and learn excellence is to try and be 'like this' for yourself.

For another sign of the importance of the pre-cognitive to Aristotle's account of how we learn to be virtuous, consider his remark, quoted above, that 'pleasure and pain is what excellence of character is about' (1104a9; cf. 1121a4, 'It belongs to excellence to take pleasure and pain in the right things in the right way').

Suppose someone, Alcibiades perhaps, enjoys drunken orgies and gladiatorial contests but hates bracing walks or applying himself to reading philosophy; suppose he gets pain from seeing his friends do well in life, and pleasure from seeing them come a cropper. As Aristotle says, these pleasures and pains are an indicator (*sêmeion*) of Alcibiades' character. It is because these are Alcibiades' pains and pleasures that we call him intemperate, lazy, envious and malicious; 'what is pleasant to those with bad characters is not necessarily pleasant as such' (*NE* 1173b23); 'badness of character destroys the first principles' (*NE* 1140b20). Hence Aristotle's thesis that 'the real pleasures are the pleasures of the good man': 'In all cases [to do with pleasure], what appears to the good man *is*' (*NE* 1176a16; cf. *NE* 1113a30–34, *NE* 1144a33–5).

For Aristotle, there is a fundamental connection between virtue and pleasure: between what we find enjoyable or not and whether we are to be called good people or not. 'What the dissolute man enjoys most, the temperate man does not enjoy at all; in fact, he positively dislikes it' (*NE* 1119a13–14). But it would be absurd, Aristotle thinks, to suppose that you could *reason* a man like Alcibiades out of getting more fun from drunken orgies or the spectacle of cruelty than from intellectual discovery or innocent exercise. That is one reason why our education in *aretê* has to proceed, at least initially and in childhood, not by rational argument but by training, habituation and imitation. Perhaps as adults we can come to a complete, or at least less incomplete, understanding of the reasons underlying the kind of sentimental education that we have already been given; no doubt that is part of what the *Ethics* itself has to offer. But this rational understanding is not, on its own, the kind of thing that can overturn bad dispositions that have already taken root. Having a rational understanding of what is good without a properly operational affective training to incline towards it is not the condition of the *agathos*, the good person, but of the *akratês*, the akratic or weak-willed person (see *NE* VII). To say it again, what Aristotle takes to be the crucial thing for excellence of character will already be in place or not in place, before any such rationalizing discussion of it is so much as possible. That is why 'it makes no small difference whether one has been habituated one way or the other from the very beginning of childhood; rather it makes all the difference, indeed every kind of difference there is' (NE 1103b23).

Here three questions arise. The first we may call the 'Owl of Minerva' question.[15] Aristotle conjoins sayings like the last quotation with ones like the passage where he says, much to the resentment of undergraduates (including me), that 'young men are not in their element listening to lectures on the political craft' (1095a2–3, cf. 1142a13–16). What use can it be (we may ask) for Aristotle to advance a conception of aretê, which entails that by the time we are competent to consider it, it is already too late for us to do whatever is most important for the development of our own aretê? The answer is, as before, that Aristotle does not think of his typical reader as concerned principally to secure just his own excellence, but rather that of the society he lives in. Certainly the Ethics comes too late to secure the virtue of its immediate readers. It does not come too late for those readers to secure the virtue of the upcoming generation in their own polis. (So when Aristotle famously says that we study what the Ethics studies 'not in order that we may know the essence of virtue, but in order that we may become good' (NE 1103b26–9), we should give the plural, we, its full weight.)

Hence the second question about the understanding of the reasons underlying our sentimental education that we might derive from a study like Aristotle's Ethics. Why shouldn't this understanding take the form sketched in Plato's Protagoras 354e–8e – the form of a 'Socratic hedonism', or indeed of Socratic hedonism's direct contemporary descendant, hedonistic utilitarianism? The answer is obvious by now: hedonism presupposes that there is something neutrally identifiable that we can all agree to call pleasure, no matter whether we are ourselves sublimely good in character or abysmally bad. Aristotle rejects this presupposition. So far from thinking, as a hedonistic utilitarian will, that a good character is one that tends to produce what we all agree is pleasure, Aristotle thinks that the key differences between those of good character and those of bad are revealed precisely where they disagree about what is pleasure.

But (to pose a third question) doesn't Aristotle have *anything* specific to say about what we ought to do? If he isn't a hedonistic utilitarian, what kind of ethicist *is* he? Contemporary moral theory is obsessed by the contest of the theories, in which consequentialists, contractarians, Kantians and indeed virtue ethicists – the last group at least allegedly inspired by Aristotle – set different accounts of 'the right' in competition, exploring their explanatory powers and exposing their unwelcome consequences by reference to ever more far-fetched imaginary cases. Doesn't Aristotle have anything to contribute to this burgeoning industry? Given his alleged practical emphasis – 'not for the sake of theory, but so as to become good' – *mustn't* he have something to contribute to it?

The answer is No, and the tag just quoted has no tendency to undermine this negative answer. Aristotle does not say 'so as to do the right (action)' but 'so as to become good (people)', and this for good reason: because he thinks that becoming good people is both necessary and sufficient for our knowing how to do the right action, and hence that there is no point in trying, as moderns usually do, to identify the criterion of the right independently of goodness of character. There is no formula for right action, such as contemporary moral theory typically seeks. While there are a few things which are very obviously the things *not to* do (1107a9–26), finding the thing *to* do is generally a matter of judgement, of practical wisdom (*phronêsis*). And the reason why there is no such formula is a generalization of the point just made about pleasure against hedonistic utilitarianism: because any such formula would have to be built around some essentially contested term. Ask yourself which actions or principles for action 'maximize pleasure', or 'are universalizable', or are such that 'they could not be reasonably rejected', or are such that they 'accord with virtue'. Good people and bad people will probably come up with different answers to all these questions; so will the proponents of different moral theories. It is not just the perception of pleasure that divides good from bad characters.

Aristotle gives no formula for right action because he thinks that right action will follow from good character. Then won't he give us a formula for good character? Not exactly. Aristotle has plenty to say about good character. Even on the narrowest construal, the discursive and descriptive enterprise of telling us in detail what good character is like fills the whole of *NE* 3.6–6.13; in a wider sense, it fills the entire book. But he never offers us a formula – a *logos* – for good character or for that matter for happiness, of the kind that moderns so often want to offer.

For example, he does not – despite what is sometimes read into 'the *ergon* argument' of 1097b29–1098a30 – offer the notion of *ergon*, proper function, as a formula for human happiness or goodness. In John McDowell's words (1998: 35–6):

> To many commentators [the *ergon* argument] suggests that Aristotle envisages an external validation for his ethic, starting from the facts about human nature. [But] in fact there are only two substantive points on which Aristotle suggests that facts about human nature constrain the truth about the good human life, in a way that might be supposed to be independent of inculcated propensities to value this and despise that. First, a good human life must be an active life of that which has *logos* (1098a3–4) . . . Second, human beings are naturally social (1097b11, 1169b18–19) . . . Obviously these two points fall a long way short of purporting to afford a validation of Aristotle's ethic in full.

This conclusion has important further consequences. Most notably, it implies that there is little or no substance in Bernard Williams' well-known charge that Aristotle's ethics depends on and presupposes a superannuated teleological worldview.[16] Aristotle undoubtedly held such a worldview, and he has distinguished followers today, most notably Philippa Foot in her *Natural Goodness*, who seem intent on replicating it. But Aristotle's strictly *biological* teleology drops out of the picture almost immediately when he gets down to serious ethical work: so, for example, at 1141a30–34, he explicitly denies that the wisdom that concerns him has much to do with the self-preserving 'wisdom' whereby each species pursues its own interests. His ethical views are certainly teleological in a broad sense (broad enough not to entail consequentialism) and in that respect consistent with his teleological view of the life sciences. But his ethics in no way entails his biology nor is even – at any level of detail – much influenced by it.

This logical independence is strikingly illustrated by what Aristotle has to tell us about the relation of the human to the divine. Aristotle certainly sees humans, for much of the time, as animals in nature, living the lives of a particular kind of animal, fulfilling the functions of their biological nature and capacities just like any other Aristotelian species. But this picture of what it is to be human is overlaid by another entirely different picture in which the central good for us is not a human good at all but a divine one – the good of *theôria*, contemplation.

> Such a life would be superior to human capacities; no one will live like this insofar as he is human, but insofar as he has something divine present within him. To the degree that this divine something differs from his composite nature, to that same degree its fulfilment will differ from the fulfilment of what is virtue in the rest of him. For if pure mind (*nous*) is divine as compared with what is human, so the life of the mind is divine compared with human life. But we should not do what the proverbs tell us to, and 'think human things being human', or 'mortal things being mortal'. Rather, we should live the life of the immortals so far as that is possible, and do everything we can to live according to the supremest part of our being. (*NE* 1177b27–37; cf. *Politics* 1325b17–22)

Aristotle is so far from thinking that the human good is defined by the human biological function as to claim that the best thing for human beings is to *go beyond* any good that could conceivably be dictated for us by our place in nature. As we might also say (if we like to be paradoxical), Aristotle thinks that the human good consists ultimately in transcending the human good.

Aristotle, then, is not offering a formula for virtue when he talks of the human function. Nor would Aristotle endorse the modern indirect utilitarian formula for virtue, which says that the virtues are by definition those character-traits that promote overall well-being. Not that Aristotle would reject the idea that virtues must, in general, promote well-being; it is the words 'by definition' that he would reject. No such form of words can be a *formula* for good character, a way of deducing the nature of the virtues from something that is theoretically prior to them and can be identified independently of them. Aristotle would deny the possibility of a virtue-neutral specification of well-being as surely as he would deny the possibility of a virtue-neutral specification of pleasure. If pleasure is nothing other than what virtue says it is, then *a fortiori* so is well-being.

The different character-virtues that Aristotle lists and discusses in *NE* 3.6–6.1 are the heart of his depiction of excellence of character. Each of them is a disposition of voluntary and deliberate choice (*hexis prohairetikê, NE* 1106b36), a power of acting which does not force or compel the agent but does shape his actions. Thus, temperance being a virtue, the explanatory 'He did it (or didn't do it) because he is temperate' is the kind of claim that can be true, and so is the predictive 'He will do it (or won't do it) because he is temperate', and similarly for the vice of intemperance. Aristotle disagrees with those moderns – such as Harman (1999) – who say that only circumstances can be used to explain or predict actions, and hence that there *are* no virtues or vices. He equally disagrees with anyone who says, as someone might, that some virtue – justice is perhaps the most tempting case – is not really a single disposition at all but a misleadingly unitary name for a variety of disparate causes; though he also makes it clear (*NE* 1129a27) that he sees why someone might think this.

The fact that Aristotelian character-virtues are in this way causal powers raises an obvious yet rather delicate question. How does their being causal relate to their being voluntary, which Aristotle also says they are? The question is delicate because we often think of dispositions not as subserving voluntariness, but as opposed to it. If an object has a disposition to poison humans, that means that in the right circumstances the object is *bound* to poison humans, not *free* to poison them. If I have a disposition to be just (or for that matter unjust), won't that mean that, in circumstances where justice is called for, I will have no choice but to be just (or unjust)?

The best answer to this understands the virtues and the vices as what we may, in a metaphor of Aristotle's own, call *ways of seeing* circumstances and actions (*NE* 1143b5, b14, 1144a30). To be temperate entails perceiving another glass of wine as a glass too many, and hence not-to-be-taken; to be just entails perceiving an expedient political murder as an outrage, and hence to-be-deplored-and-punished; to be gentle entails perceiving your new pupil as nervous, and so to-be-put-at-her-ease – and so on indefinitely.[17]

From such ways of seeing as the virtues and vices produce in their possessors, there arise both liberties and necessities.[18] Someone who has a given virtue will, in line with that virtue, see himself as free to do some things but bound to do others – while other things again he will be bound not to do; at the extreme, some things may be unthinkable.[19] It will not even occur to a just man to procure an expedient political murder; if the murder is proposed to him, his response will be 'But I *can't* do that'. This might seem to make the just man less free than the unjust man who is, as they say, relaxed about political murder, and so apparently has a wider range of actions open to him.[20] But either the unjust man has his own way of seeing, in line with which he will recognize, not murder, but other options as unthinkable ('But we can't let Jones take office; we *must* get rid of him!'). Or else, if the man we call unjust is really someone who has *no* particular 'way of seeing', someone for whom *nothing* is unthinkable (as the Greeks would call him, a *panourgos*, a do-anything: *EE* 1221a12) – then he is no doubt the kind of character that a lot of modern moral theory likes to deal with: someone who will unblinkingly reason out the pros and cons of every available alternative from first principles upwards.[21] But anyone like this who had no particular 'way of seeing' would not really be a character at all. He would be dispositionally shapeless. There would be no saying what he values or what he might do. If he resembled anyone, perhaps he would resemble Camus' *étranger*. According to Aristotle, there are no such blankly insubstantial characters; even if there were, there would be no such 'first principles' for them to reason from and no such reasoning for them to do either. Character, as he sees it, is the first principle for virtue, and it is virtue's mode of reasoning too.

Understanding a virtue as a way of seeing – a disposition to frame situations and to deliberate about them in a particular way or ways – clarifies how actions can be caused by that virtue and yet also be voluntary and deliberate. But – to turn to an objection that Aristotle himself states and rejects at 1114a32–b26 – what about the voluntariness, not of the action but of the virtue? Aristotle says that if I see and respond to situations 'under the aspect of' temperance, I will act temperately. But are we to be praised because we see and respond a given way, or blamed if we do not? Perhaps it is not, to use a phrase that Aristotle himself coined, 'up to us' (eph' hêmin, 1112a31) if we see and respond to things under the aspect of temperance. Perhaps we do so simply as a matter of nature. Aristotle's reply (1114b12–26) is a little oblique; it seems a few steps of argument away from the objection itself. He says that even if our natural end – eudaimonia – is set by nature, still it is up to me to articulate the detail of that natural end as it is to be realized in my own life: it is up to me to settle what it means for me, here and now, to act 'towards' eudaimonia. Even if eudaimonia-in-itself is a 'given', still eudaimonia-for-me is something I need to work out for myself. Now (to fill in the missing steps), such reflection on the meaning and the shape of eudaimonia for me is a voluntary activity, and it proceeds by reference to the virtues. The life of virtue is the same thing as the life of eudaimonia. So thinking out what eudaimonia is, is thinking out what the virtues are, in detail. It means understanding what each virtue demands, recommends and allows in particular situations. It is by this sort of reflection that we develop our own ability to see things under the aspect of the various virtues. But plainly, such reflection is voluntary. So, therefore, are the articulations of the virtues in which it results.

Thus we can be held responsible for the ways in which we see, or fail to see, the situations that confront us under the aspect of the relevant virtues: 'we are, in a way (pôs), co-authors (synaitioi) of our own dispositions, and it is because we have particular characters that we take the end (telos) to be what we take it to be' (1114b33–4). Or at least, we can be held responsible to an extent: note the 'co' in co-authors. Here as elsewhere, Aristotle is sensitive to the importance of the pre-cognitive and the pre-voluntary in the shaping of character: we come back here to the importance of having (already) had the right education.

Aristotle lists the virtues; but as noted before, he has no general formula of the indirect utilitarian's kind from which he might logically deduce this list. On the contrary, Aristotle simply assumes it. At NE 1107a33, he says, rather puzzlingly, 'So let these things be taken from the diagram (diagraphês) . . .', and begins without further explanation to talk about courage. It is only at Eudemian Ethics (1220b38 ff.) (where his word is hypographê) that we find out what sort of a diagram he has been talking about:

Excess	Deficiency	Virtue
Irritability	Flaccidity	Gentleness
Rashness	Cowardice	Courage
Shamelessness	Bashfulness	Modesty
Intemperance	Lack of feeling	Temperance
Envy	[Apathy?]	Righteous anger
Profit	Loss	Justice
Wastefulness	Meanness	Liberality
Boastfulness	Self-deprecation	Truthfulness
Ingratiatingness	Surliness	Friendship
Stiff-neckedness	Subservience	Dignity
Brutishness	Submission to evils	Endurance
Vanity	Smallness of soul	Greatness of soul
Ostentation	Mean-spiritedness	Magnificence
Unscrupulousness[22]	Naivety	Practical wisdom

Aristotle is very taken with the idea that each of these virtues – each of the excellences in the right-hand column – is a mean between a corresponding defective disposition (in the middle column) and a corresponding excessive disposition (in the left-hand column). Aristotle, no doubt, sometimes pushes this 'doctrine of the mean' too hard: why think, for example, of friendship as a virtue rather than a human good or of justice as a mean between profit and loss (as if a just man could never do more, or less, than barely break even)?[23] Still, overall the idea is an attractive one. It is also a philosophically interesting way of cashing out two well-known Greek proverbs: Solon's *mêden agan*, 'nothing to excess', and Cleobulus' *metron ariston*, 'moderation is best'.[24]

Modern writers have sometimes pounced on Aristotle here, as if he were offering the doctrine of the mean as a formula for right action. We have seen that Aristotle is not in the business of offering any such formula: 'there *is* no precise formula for particular actions' (*NF* 1104a7). What he says about the mean is supposed to be true-to-life phenomenological description of how it is with a wide range of excellences of character. Which it is; but it is no more than that, and not meant to be. Aristotle himself emphasizes that the mean he has in mind is 'relative to us' and not 'arithmetical' (1106a27 ff.) He also denies that, for any action-type whatever, there is a virtuous mean of that type (1107a9 ff.): unlike some recent practical ethicists, Aristotle does not think that there is a virtuously moderate way of committing adultery, bestiality or murder.

Aristotle qualifies the doctrine in a third way, too: he observes that some of the 'extremes' are more opposed to (*antikeitai mallon*) the mean than others are; for example, cowardice is more opposed to courage than rashness is (1108b35 ff.) Every Aristotelian virtue compensates for some human weakness; as Aquinas was later to say, the virtues are *circa difficilia*, about things we find difficult.[25] In the sort of difficulty that fear and danger cause us, the hard thing is to be courageous, the weak and easy thing is to be a coward. The person who is rash is, typically, at least *trying* not to be cowardly; that is why rashness is the extreme that is 'less opposed' to courage. We need to come to the list of the virtues with a degree of self-knowledge – remembering, perhaps, another Greek proverb: Chilon's *gnôthi seauton*, 'know yourself' (Diels-Kranz I, 63). Then with the list's help, we can identify our own characteristic weaknesses in respect of each of the virtues and learn to correct for these ourselves (1109b2–3).

A lot like this can be learned from Aristotle's list. What we will not learn from it, as Aristotle himself is careful to remind us, is any way of computing the actions of the virtuous man from a virtue-neutral standpoint:

> Virtue is a disposition of voluntary choice, lying in the mean relative to us, which is defined by reason, *and in the way that the man of practical wisdom would define it.* (1106b36–1107a2)

Here, as elsewhere, Aristotle's key determinant of virtue is practical wisdom, *phronêsis*. The whole point about *phronêsis* is that, unless you have it yourself, you cannot understand *how* it acts as a determinant of virtue.

Not only does Aristotle present his remarkable list of virtues at *EE* 1220b38 ff. without the slightest attempt to derive it from any deeper level of analysis, such as the indirect utilitarian's 'overall well-being', but he also offers no justification at all even of the large claim that this *is* a list of virtues (or perhaps *the* list of virtues). Why not?

Probably he thinks no such derivation is possible, because there *is* no deeper level of analysis at which we can see why these and just these are the virtues. Here we come to Aristotle's method of consensus in ethics:

> The right procedure [in all enquiries] is to take hold of what seems to be true and begin by exploring the difficulties about it, in order thus to establish as true all of the reputable views (*endoxa*) about the subject-matter; or if not all, then as many as possible of the most important of these views. For if the difficulties can be resolved and the reputable views preserved, then we will have a sufficient proof of their truth. (1145b2–7)

> What seems [true] to everyone, we say that this *is* [true]; the person who takes away *this* conviction, can have nothing *more* convincing to put in its place. (1173a1–2)

Rather like G. E. Moore, Aristotle is less sceptical about our commonsense beliefs, including our ethical beliefs, than he is about any scepticism that might be marshalled to assail them. Of course there may be inconsistencies, conflicts and anomalies within the fabric of our commonsense beliefs. We cannot resolve these by looking, as Plato did (see *NE* I.6), for deeper foundations; rather, we must deploy the method of coherence to try and see how our various beliefs, or as many of them as possible, can hold together. The only way to be competent in this method is, once more, to be or become *phronimos,* practically wise.

This should not be made to sound too conservative a conclusion. Mightn't someone challenge Aristotle's list of virtues, either by saying that it includes something it shouldn't or that it excludes something it shouldn't? Of course they might, and Aristotle is entirely open to the possibility of such a challenge. Indeed, he apparently put this challenge to himself, since the *Nicomachean Ethics* discusses an importantly different list of virtues from the Eudemian list given above. Some of the virtues that were in the *EE* list are now said to be nameless, while others are omitted – most notably 'nobility', *kalokagathia*, which is the topic of the whole of *EE* Book 8, and seems in that work to approach, but not quite stably attain, the status of a 'kingpin' virtue; rather as *megalopsykhia* (greatness of soul) seems to do in *NE*. Other virtues again are discussed for the first time in the *NE*, in some cases at very great length. The *NE* list is: courage (3.6–9; cf. *EE* 3.1), temperance (3.10–12; *EE* 3.2), liberality (4.1; *EE* 3.4), magnificence (4.2; *EE* 3.6), greatness of soul (4.3; *EE* 3.5), the (nameless) proper attitude to honour (4.4), gentleness (4.5; *EE* 3.3), friendliness (4.6), the (nameless) proper mean between boasting and self-deprecation (4.7), wit (4.8), the proper mean between shame and shamelessness (4.9), justice (Book 5), the intellectual virtues (including practical wisdom) (Book 6) and friendship (Books 8 and 9; *EE* Book 7). The greater fullness of the *NE*'s discussion of the virtues is one reason for taking it to be a later and more authoritative treatise.

Aristotle never insists that there must be exactly one way to individuate all the virtues. He is entirely open to the idea that what we may call the 'minor' virtues that he lists – virtues like friendliness and wit – can be described or schematized in more than one reasonable way. It is, after all, his innovation to discuss these virtues at all. The tradition that he inherits from Plato spoke of just four virtues – justice, temperance, courage and wisdom;[26] evidently, it is a new idea of Aristotle's to ask what else we might count as a virtue alongside these, the principal virtues.[27] Aristotle is neither surprised nor alarmed by the thought that there might be some theoretical looseness in this area. As for the sceptical suggestion that *everything* in his list of virtues might be mistaken, his response to that, I think, will be the same as before. He will just challenge the sceptic to produce a credible alternative list (1173a1–2); here too, he will say that 'anyone who takes away these beliefs will hardly have anything *more* believable to tell us'.

Notes

1 There are two works by Aristotle named the *Ethics*, called the *Nicomachean* (*NE*) and the *Eudemian* (*EE*) after their original editors, Nicomachus, Aristotle's son, who died young (in battle, it seems), and Eudemus, one of Aristotle's pupils, who apparently outlived Nicomachus. (A third work, usually called the *Magna Moralia* in English [Greek *êthika megala*], is apparently school-of-Aristotle rather than Aristotle, and despite its name, rather short.) Confusingly, the *NE* and *EE* overlap, having three books in common: *NE* V, VI, VII = *EE* IV, V, VI. For over a century, scholars have debated which of the two is historically primary and more representative of Aristotle's most considered teachings. I prefer the *NE*, but I say little about this here.

2 Probably relevant is the pre-eminence in twentieth-century philosophical training of Oxford's *Literae Humaniores* syllabus, to which Aristotle's *Ethics* was and is central.

3 Of course, Aristotle is influential in Western ethics if you go back far enough. In mediaeval philosophical ethics, Aristotle – alongside the Bible – was not *an* influence but *the* influence. To Dante, the greatest philosophical poet since Homer, he was *il maestro di color che sanno*, 'the master of those who know'; to Dante's contemporary Aquinas, he was simply *Philosophus*, 'the philosopher'. Luther's and Calvin's rejection of Catholicism was also a rejection of the Christianized Aristotelianism taught by Aquinas, Scotus and their followers; Renaissance humanists such as Erasmus and More rejected that scholasticism too. The Reformation's and the Renaissance's contempt (the word is not too strong) for Aristotelianism was still influential up to the late nineteenth century. John Locke was rather exceptional, as he so often is, in having a high respect for Aristotle; David Hume was entirely unoriginal, as he so often is, in barely considering him at all.

4 I use my own translations throughout.

5 Or as *aretê* is most often translated, 'virtue'. For convenience, I shall sometimes use 'virtue' myself, but 'excellence' is better; it lacks 'virtue's' ideological taint. (More about ideological taint later.)

To translate *aretê* as '*human* excellence' would be over-translation, but it would bring out the essentially relative nature of the concept: *aretê* is always the excellence *of* something.

6 Grammatically, *tês êthikês* is an adjectival phrase qualifying the understood noun *aretês*. It occurs here in the genitive case because the clause it comes in is a genitive absolute.

7 The division of *NE* into ten books, and of *EE* into eight books, is ancient and often supported by verbal and thematic features of the text, but it is not Aristotle's.

8 It may of course have been that, in or shortly after Aristotle's own time, *êthika* came to mean something like what we today mean by 'ethics': consider how the Stoics use *êthika*, as the name for one of the three principal divisions of philosophy alongside logic and physics; or consider the classifications added to Plato's dialogues by later editors (e.g. 'peirastic', 'logical', 'apotreptic', 'maieutic' and '*ethical*': cf. Sedley 2010: 64). It may also have been that Aristotle's own *êthika* were one of the main reasons why this semantic development occurred. If so there was – I am suggesting – a certain irony about that process.

9 I can say this without committing the lexical fallacy. It is one thing for a writer to have a concept N without having a word for it, 'N'. It is quite another for a writer to discuss a range of concepts A–M without so much as mentioning concept N. The former may be only weak evidence, but the latter is pretty strong evidence that the writer has no such concept.

10 This name for the subject area of the *NE is* ideologically innocent, in a way that 'ethics' and 'moral philosophy' are not. It is also much more nearly sanctioned by Aristotle's own text than those names: see, for example, how he uses *ho peri tôn praxeôn logos* and *en tais praxesi* at 1104a. However, 'moral' and 'ethical' are too well-entrenched for me to be able to do entirely without them here. (Cf. Haldane 2009.)

11 Large claims are sometimes made about *dei*, for example, that it is the classical (or at any rate Aristotelian) Greek for the special moral ought. The casualness and variety of the three uses of *dei* marked in my translation of this passage is part of the large body of evidence that undermines such claims.

12 The usual caution is necessary: an argument that Socrates presents in a Socratic dialogue by Plato is not necessarily one that the historical Socrates endorsed, or one that Plato's character Socrates endorsed, or one that Plato endorsed.

For a different reading of Socrates' ethics from the one presented here, see Chapter 1.

13 Aristotle is deeply interested, like Plato before him, in the educative power of music: see *Politics* 8.5.

14 This also clarifies Aristotle's remark that the just or temperate person is not merely he who does the appropriate deeds but does them *as* the just or temperate man does them (*NE* 1105b7–8). A key part of this 'as' involves, as before, taking pleasure in those deeds: cf. 1120b30.

15 See G. W. F. Hegel, *Grundlinien der Philosophie des Rechts*, Vorrede (p. 16 in 1972 Frankfurt am Main edition): *die Eule der Minerva beginnt erst mit der einbrechenden Dämmerung ihren Flug* – 'The owl of Minerva only takes wing at dusk'.

16 See Williams 1985: 43–5, Nussbaum 1995 and Williams 1995: 201: 'in leaving behind Aristotle's cosmology, the modern world has left behind elements necessary to making his style of ethical theory as a whole plausible, however many useful thoughts we can, quite certainly, gain from it'.

17 This does not saddle Aristotle with a special faculty of moral intuition. As already argued, Aristotle has no notion of a special moral anything. Aristotle himself in effect observes (1142a27–8) that there need be nothing more unitary to these acts of 'seeing' than there is to the things that can all be grouped under the English word 'realizing'.

18 Augustine scholars may recognize an affinity between this paragraph's discussion and the discussion of the distinction between *posse non peccare* and *non posse peccare* at *de Civitate Dei* 22.30.

19 With this argument, compare Williams 1993.

20 A possibility which Morton 2011 explores: 'I shall argue that there is a blinkering effect to decency. Being a morally sensitive person, and having internalised a code of behaviour that restricts the range of actions that one takes as live options for oneself, constrains one's imagination . . . it limits one's capacity to understand those who perform atrocious acts'.

21 For a critique of the very idea of such reasoners and such reasoning, see Chappell 2001.

22 Aristotle's word is *panourgia* on which cf. my remarks above. Comparison with *NE* 1144b23–7 suggests that his word for the same thing in *NE* is *deinotês*, 'cleverness' or 'craftiness'.

23 Despite his use of *philia* in this list, Aristotle cannot seriously think that friendship is a virtue, rather than a human good, full enjoyment of which involves virtues (*Rhetoric* 1362a10–20). For (a) Aristotle does not claim that friendship lies in a mean; (b) Aristotle takes virtue-friendship to be just one kind of friendship; (c) *NE* 1126b23ff. distinguishes friend*ship* from friend*liness* and discusses the latter, which intuitively *is* a virtue. (Friendship cannot reasonably be required of anyone; friendliness can.)

24 See Diels-Kranz, *Die Fragmente der Vorsokratiker*, vol. 1, p. 63. For another nod towards these *endoxa* (respected and/or common opinions) in a different context, see *Politics* 1295b4–5.

25 Aquinas, *Commentary on the Sentences,* Book 2, Section 29, Article 4.

26 That tradition also often spoke of a fifth principal virtue, piety or holiness (*hosiotês*). Piety seems, in Plato's early dialogue the *Euthyphro*, to drop out of the discussion by becoming simply the application to the case of the gods of the broader virtue of justice, which 'renders to each his due'. Aristotle does not restore piety to its earlier place in the catalogue, but that is not because he is uninterested in the divine and our relation to it: cf. his above-quoted remarks about *theôria*.

27 The principal virtues were later, for example, in Aquinas's discussion, to be named the cardinal virtues – the virtues on which everything else hinges (Latin *cardo*, a hinge; it seems to have been St Ambrose who invented the term *virtus cardinalis*). H. Diels and W. Kranz, Die Fragmente der Vorsokratiker. Berlin: Weidmann, 1952.

References

Aristotle, *Nicomachean Ethics, Eudemian Ethics, Magna Moralia.*
Broadie, S. J. and Rowe, C. J. (2002), *Aristotle: Nicomachean Ethics.* Oxford: Oxford University Press.
Diels, H. and Kranz, W. (1952), *Die Fragmente der Vorsokratiker.* Berlin: Weidmann.
Greek: *Aristotelis Ethica Nicomachea, Ethica Eudemia, Magna Moralia* in the Oxford Classical Texts series, ed. Ingram Bywater (Clarendon, Oxford, many editions).
Parallel text: *Aristotle: Nicomachean Ethics, Eudemian Ethics, Magna Moralia,* with a translation by Harold Rackham (Cambridge, MA: Harvard University Press, Loeb Classical Library, 1926). [An old and highly moralized translation which needs to be handled with care: e.g. Rackham consistently gives *logos* ('reason') the extremely misleading translation 'principle'.]

Recommended reading

Anscombe, Elizabeth (1958), 'Modern moral philosophy', *Philosophy* 33: 1–19.
Chappell, Timothy (2001), 'Option ranges', *Journal of Applied Ethics,* 1–17.
Foot, Philippa (2001), *Natural Goodness.* Oxford: Oxford University Press.

Fossheim, Hallvard (2006), 'Habituation as Mimesis', in T. Chappell (ed.), *Values and Virtues: Aristotelianism in Contemporary Ethics*. Oxford: Oxford University Press.

Haldane, John (2009), *Practical Philosophy*. Aberdeen University Press: St Andrews Studies in Philosophy and Public Affairs.

Harman, Gilbert (1999), 'Moral Philosophy Meets Social Psychology: Virtue Ethics and the Fundamental Attribution Error', *Proceedings of the Aristotelian Society* New Series, 99, 315–31.

Hegel, G. W. F. [1821], *Grundlinien der Philosophie des Rechts*. Frankfurt am Main: Suhrkamp, 1972.

Liddell, H. G., Scott, R. and Jones, H. *Greek-English Lexicon*. Oxford: Clarendon Press.

McDowell, John (1998), *Mind, Value, and Reality*. Oxford: Oxford University Press.

Morton, Adam (2011), 'Empathy for the devil', in A. Coplan and P. Goldie, eds., *Empathy*. Oxford: Oxford University Press.

Nussbaum, Martha (1995), 'Aristotle on human nature and the foundations of ethics', in J. Altham and R. Harrison, eds, *World, Mind, and Ethics*. Cambridge: Cambridge University Press.

Sedley, David (2010), 'The *Theaetetus* as an ethical dialogue', in D. Sedley and A. Nightingale, *Ancient Models of Mind*. Cambridge: Cambridge University Press. Bernard Williams (1985), *Ethics and the Limits of Philosophy*. London: Harmondsworth.

Williams, Bernard (1993), 'Moral Incapacity', *Proceedings of the Aristotelian Society* New Series, 93, (1993), 59–70.

— (1995), 'Replies', in J. Altham and R. Harrison, eds., *World, Mind, and Ethics*. Cambridge: Cambridge University Press.

Wittgenstein, Ludwig (1953), *Philosophical Investigations*. Oxford: Blackwell.

Zagzebski, Linda (2006), 'The admirable life and the desirable life', in T. Chappell (ed.), *Values and Virtues: Aristotelianism in Contemporary Ethics*. Oxford: Oxford University Press.

3

The Stoics

Jacob Klein

Introduction

The Stoic school of philosophy was founded by Zeno of Citium (modern-day Lacarna in Cyprus), who arrived in Athens some twenty years after Aristotle's death.

Stoicism's origin corresponds roughly, therefore, to the beginning of the Hellenistic period, conventionally dated from the death of Alexander the Great in 323 BC. The term 'Stoic' itself derives from Zeno's practice of teaching in the painted portico (*stoa poikilê*) of Athens, one of several colonnades clustered in the marketplace at the foot of the Acropolis. The Stoa continued as one of the main philosophical institutions of Athens until about the beginning of the first century, remaining at the philosophical centre of the ancient world for nearly 200 years. During this period, successive heads of the school elaborated and defended the teachings of its founder, producing an impressive body of writing on a range of philosophical topics, including logic, ethics and physical theory. These treatises would have been available to the philosophical community in Athens during the second and third centuries BC, and some of them probably circulated widely throughout the Mediterranean world.[1]

Despite their wide circulation, we are in a very different position with respect to these early Stoic writings than to the works of Plato and Aristotle, for numerous and influential as they were, none of the treatises of the original Greek Stoics has come down to us intact. This does not make it impossible to study Stoic philosophy as it was taught and practised in Athens, but it does mean that this study presents special challenges, and a number of preliminary cautions should be borne in mind. It should be remembered, first, that almost everything we know about the Greek Stoics is based on the second-hand reports of later authors. With few exceptions, we are at one or more removes from the earliest Stoic writings, and the discussions of Stoic doctrines that survive frequently reflect the biases and assumptions of later thinkers. Second, it should be remembered that Stoic philosophy is not a homogeneous whole but a body of thought developed and elaborated by various individuals over time. Though the main lines of Stoic thought remain fairly constant, it is clear that some of the leading Stoics disagreed with one another on finer points of doctrine. Since the picture of Stoicism that we are able to recover is not always sensitive to these differences, it is best thought of, perhaps, as a kind of composite image, rather than a snapshot of the system as articulated by any particular Stoic thinker. In speaking of Stoic thought as though it were a unified whole, we are doing our best to extract a coherent doctrine from many later, incomplete accounts.[2]

Fortunately, we are in a better position with respect to Stoic ethics than to most other facets of Stoic philosophy, and for two reasons. First, partly by accident, and partly due to the preoccupations of later writers, a number of continuous expositions of Stoic ethical theory have survived, and from authors who have no particular motives (so far as we know) for distorting the views they report.[3] Second, it is arguably in the field of ethics that Stoicism came to exercise its most enduring influence. Much of the work produced by Stoic writers during the time of imperial Rome – by Seneca, Epictetus and Marcus Aurelius, for instance – is primarily concerned with ethical matters. Though these authors are not always accurate guides to the complexities of Stoic theory as articulated by earlier thinkers, their treatises provide us with an indispensable view of much that has been lost. They also allow us to see, at first hand, the very considerable influence that Stoic ethics came to exercise on the Roman world.

Foundations and influences

Like other philosophers of the Hellenistic period, the Stoics are indebted to their classical inheritance. In the realm of ethics, their deepest debt is to Socrates and to a body of Socratic thought current when Zeno arrived in Athens. Indeed, as we shall see, Stoic ethics may be usefully viewed as an elaboration and defence of key Socratic claims. It is clear, in particular, that many of the earliest Stoic writings, such as the *Republic* of Zeno, were shaped by a close interaction with Platonic texts. A number of Stoic doctrines appear to build on claims Plato himself associates with Socrates in the early dialogues, while others derive from a largely independent tradition of Socratic teaching.[4] Zeno is said to have spent a considerable time as the pupil of the Cynic Crates, who was himself associated with a line of teachers reaching back, through Antisthenes, to Socrates himself. Some of the central features of early Stoic thought were almost certainly inherited from the Cynic tradition.[5]

The Stoics' relationship to Aristotle is less clear. Though Aristotle's published treatises were probably available in Athens during the lifetime of his successor, Theophrastus, Aristotle is rarely mentioned by name in Stoic texts, and many elements of Stoicism that initially seem to recall Aristotle can also be explained as independent developments of Platonic thought.[6] One central element of Stoic ethics may reasonably be thought of as Aristotelian, however, for it is arguably Aristotle who, in Book One of the *Nicomachean Ethics*, gives it its most explicit formulation. This is the thesis that a rational agent will be guided by a conception of *eudaimonia* or happiness, by an account of the kind of human life that is best overall. Like most Hellenistic philosophers, the Stoics adopt the framework of eudaimonism as a basis for the requirements that an ethical theory enjoins.[7] They assume with Aristotle that each of our actions, insofar as it is rational, will be directed towards the overarching end of happiness, and that the job of an ethical theory is to say what this end consists in and how it may be achieved. As Aristotle puts it, if there is a highest good for human beings – and Aristotle thinks there is – it is of the greatest importance to understand what it is, so that, like archers, we will have a target to aim at.[8]

Such a concern with happiness may seem an objectionable starting point for an ethical theory. Ethics, after all, seems centrally concerned with questions about our obligations to others. How can a theory that regards self-interest as the foundation of rational action purport to be an *ethical* theory? Those sympathetic to the ancient tradition of ethical theorizing sometimes provide an answer along the following lines.[9] They point, first, to differences between the concept expressed by *eudaimonia* and that expressed by the popular notion of happiness. Though 'happiness' is probably the best way to render the Greek term, this translation can be misleading, for it may seem to suggest an episodic or fleeting condition of the agent, one dependent on the satisfaction of transient desires. By contrast, the Greek conception is more closely associated with the idea of a human life conceived as an ordered whole. Though *eudaimonia* may certainly include the satisfaction of desire, the Greeks tend to take it for granted that an agent who is *eudaimôn* must also have the *right kinds* of desires. This point helps us to see why eudaimonism need not amount to a narrowly self-interested theory, for the right kind of desires, the kind that go to make up the best form of human life, will plausibly include concern for others. This does not conclusively show that eudaimonism can supply an adequate basis for ethics, but it does help to show that it is not obviously deficient in this respect.[10]

By itself, however, the framework of eudaimonism imposes a largely formal constraint. It is compatible, for instance, with the Epicurean claim that the highest good consists in pleasure and the absence of pain, or with a view that came to be associated with both Plato and Aristotle during the Hellenistic period: that it consists in the exercise of virtue together with the possession of additional goods such as health or wealth.[11] On the Epicurean view, the traditional virtues are no part of happiness at all; they are means to securing the good life, but the good remains distinct from virtue. According to Hellenistic accounts deriving from Plato and Aristotle, though virtue is a necessary part of happiness and perhaps its most important ingredient, it is not all that a successful human life requires. The virtuous agent who is wholly unfortunate in his or her external circumstances will find his or her happiness marred, as Aristotle says. He or she will need the cooperation of fortune to secure the goal of happiness.[12]

What especially distinguishes Stoic ethics from the rival Hellenistic theories is the Stoics' defence, from within the framework of eudaimonism, of two theses closely associated with Socrates and the Socratic tradition. First, the Stoics follow Socrates insofar as they regard virtue or human excellence (*aretê*) as the *sole* ingredient of the happy human life and, in fact, as the only unqualified good.[13] This fits with the Socratic claim that no evil can befall a good individual and implies that happiness is fully within an agent's control, invulnerable to circumstances and the whims of fortune.[14] Second, the Stoics develop and defend the Socratic view that virtue is a kind of technical knowledge, the *technê tou biou* or *ars vitae*, the skill required to live one's life well. As such, Stoic theory rejects out of hand the Epicurean claim that virtue is valuable only for the results it secures. And although they agree with Plato and Aristotle that virtue is an intrinsic good and an essential component of the good life, the Stoics maintain, as Plato and Aristotle arguably do not, that happiness is available to an agent in even the worst external circumstances.

Nature

The Stoics' effort to elaborate and defend these claims explains some of the most distinctive features of their ethical system. It also requires them to deal with a basic difficulty implicit in the Socratic view. In Plato's early dialogues, when Socrates asks his interlocutors to define one of the conventional virtues, such as justice or temperance or piety, he frequently insists that the definition must not appeal to any one of the other virtues or rely on any prior, unanalysed notion of what is just or right. In the *Meno*, for example, Meno is not permitted to define virtue in terms of one of its parts or, more generally, in ethical terms of the sort he and Socrates are investigating.[15] Instead, Socrates wants Meno to provide a non-circular analysis, one that identifies the basic property or properties in which virtue consists in terms he and Meno already understand.[16] Socrates seems to suppose that to possess such an account of one of the virtues would be to possess the virtue itself, that to know the properties on which justice or piety depends would enable an agent, with perfect consistency, to identify the just or pious course of action.[17] Yet most of the early dialogues represent Socrates' interlocutors as failing to provide a reductive definition of the sort Socrates wants, and Socrates famously denies that he possesses any such knowledge himself.

In developing the Socratic claim that virtue is knowledge, then, the Stoics need to develop an account of its content, of what one must know in order to possess the virtues. Early Stoic definitions of the *telos*, or human end, indicate the Stoics' general line of response to this difficulty. The Stoic answer to the Socratic question is, roughly, that virtue consists in knowledge of a rational pattern implicit in the natural order. Zeno himself is said to have defined the *telos* simply as *homologia*, a Greek term indicating consistency or agreement. Later Stoic formulations of the end imply, however, that *homologia* should not be understood primarily as a matter of internal consistency – of consistency in one's reasoning or one's actions, say – but of agreement between the content of one's beliefs and the order of nature itself.[18] According to Chrysippus of Soli, the most important and influential Stoic to follow Zeno, the human good consists in 'living in accordance with experience of what happens by nature'. Chrysippus' use of the term 'experience' (*empeiria*, from which our word 'empirical' derives) is important, for it strongly suggests that when the Stoics speak of conformity to nature they are not thinking, in the first instance, of an individual who *acts* in certain ways that are more natural than others but of an individual who possesses an accurate and secure knowledge of nature's ends. As it happens, the Stoics do believe that an agent who possesses this knowledge will act in some ways rather than others. The emphasis in their definition of the good life falls not on an agent's actions, however, but on the knowledge that precedes and explains them.[19]

Later formulations of the Stoic *telos* elaborate the notion of agreement with nature in a distinctive way. They maintain, in particular, that the end consists in reasoning well in the selection (*eklogê*) and rejection (*apeklogê*) of things in accordance with nature (*ta kata phusin*). We will need to consider the significance of these formulations more carefully, for they help to explain how (on the Stoic view) knowledge of nature's purposes is connected with virtuous motivation and action. It is worth pausing, however, to consider a prior question with which commentators on Stoic ethics have been concerned: when the early Stoics speak of agreement with nature, which features or aspects of nature do they have in mind? Many references to nature in later Stoic works, such as those of Epictetus and Marcus Aurelius, associate nature with the order of the cosmos as a whole. By contrast, Cicero's summary of Stoic ethics, which antedates these writings, gives central place to an account of human nature and of ethical progress in the human case. Commentators have wondered whether one of these conceptions of nature plays a more fundamental role in early Stoic theory. Some have concluded that, as in Aristotle, the dominant appeal in early Stoic ethics is to human nature in particular, while others have argued that an understanding of cosmic nature is foundational to Stoic ethics, and that the notion of agreement the Stoics defend centrally requires knowledge of the cosmic order.[20]

On balance, the evidence suggests that the early Stoics would have rejected a rigid distinction between human and cosmic nature, which the question seems to presuppose. As a fragment from Chrysippus emphasizes, human nature is part of the cosmos in such a way that one cannot live in agreement with human nature without also conforming to the rational principles expressed in the cosmos, and vice versa.[21] *Homologia* requires knowledge of what is essential to human nature, certainly, but also knowledge of the order of which human nature is a part. For the Stoics, such knowledge appears to include some of the facts that today we would regard as theoretical and scientific in nature. Seneca speaks, for instance, of knowing the causes of natural phenomena (*causas naturalium*), while according to Posidonius, the end is 'living as a student of the truth and order of the whole, and helping to promote this as far as possible'.[22] Here it is not simply knowledge of the processes that occur throughout the cosmos that is essential, on the Stoic view, but knowledge of how they contribute to an overarching set of rational ends that structure the natural world.[23] The surviving Stoic sources tell us far less about this teleological framework than we would like. They do say, however, that the highest end, with a view to which Zeus has ordered the physical world in the way that he has, is the manifestation of every sort of excellence and beauty.[24]

On the Stoic account, then, the knowledge that underpins right action is knowledge of the normative properties exhibited in the cosmos itself, properties that are ultimately to be analysed in naturalistic and aesthetic terms.[25] A similar solution to the Socratic search for ethical knowledge is suggested in some of Plato's dialogues, most notably, perhaps, in the programme of philosophical education proposed in the *Republic*, which includes a long and searching study of science and mathematics as part of the ascent to knowledge of the Form of the Good. Though the Stoics reject Plato's doctrine of transcendent Forms, they agree that knowledge of nature's ends is an explicit and foundational part of ethical theory. Such a view implies a distinctive meta-ethical account, one that treats central forms of value as both natural and objective, independent of an agent's psychological state and which regards evaluative judgements as true or false depending on whether they correctly represent these independent, axiological facts.[26]

Ethical progress

In adopting the core of Socratic ethics, the Stoics place epistemology at the centre of their ethical theory. Virtue, in their view, is an essentially cognitive achievement, a systematic form of knowledge directed towards the end of living well, and one that arises through a grasp of nature's principles. According to one of the Stoics' formal definitions, virtue is 'a disposition and faculty of the governing principle of the soul brought into being by reason, or rather: reason itself, consistent, firm, and unwavering'.[27] This condition is built up from a form of representational cognition the Stoics characterize as *katalêpsis*, a mental grasp or grip on the world. As the Stoics describe it, *katalêpsis* is a mental state with propositionally structured content that is both true and justified. By itself, however, *katalêpsis* does not amount to virtue. The Stoics draw a clear distinction between *katalêpsis* and *epistêmê*, the highest form of cognition, and the form on which virtue depends. In isolation, none of the *katalêpseis* or mental grasps on the world is constitutive of knowledge in this more demanding sense, but only when it is anchored by a system (*systêma*) of beliefs that has been entirely purged of error and cannot be undermined by further experience or argument. Since on the Stoic account even a single false belief is sufficient to undermine the stability of the whole, virtue turns out to be an all or nothing affair, an ironclad cognition of the world consisting in a thoroughly secure system of true and justified beliefs.

It goes without saying that virtue, so conceived, is an exceptionally demanding and difficult condition to achieve. In practice, this conception of virtue came to function in Stoic ethics as something of a regulative ideal: to specify the virtuous course of action is to say what someone who has achieved an epistemic condition of this sort (a *sophos* or sage) would do. In principle, however, virtue is a condition available to every rational agent. A central task of Stoic theory is to show how it is possible for human beings to achieve the epistemic relation to the world the Stoic analysis of virtue requires. The Stoics defend this possibility, in part, by arguing for an epistemological account according to which agents are able to discriminate between true and false impressions and to assent only to those which are true and justified.[28] Because each of the cognitive steps on the road to virtue is in our power in this way, the responsibility for virtue and vice lies wholly with the agent. But the Stoics also offer a theory of psychological development in both rational and non-rational animals, one designed to show that correct or appropriate action is everywhere the result of accurate perception and that, in animals and humans alike, teleological success depends on an accurate representation of the world. The latter theory is worth considering, for it is central to some of the most important extant accounts of Stoic ethics, and it seems clear that the Stoics appealed to it to support some of their most basic ethical claims.

Reports of the Stoic theory of *oikeiôsis* (as commentators tend to call it) are woefully incomplete, but the fragments that survive are fascinating, for they begin from a series of empirical claims about a range of phenomena readily observable in the animal kingdom. Every animal, the Stoics maintain, is born with an array of motivational tendencies given to it by nature, including, most saliently, the desire to preserve and care for itself. Some of these motivations are present immediately upon birth, while others, such as the desire to care for its offspring, are manifested as the animal matures. All of these impulses, however, arise only in virtue of a more fundamental capacity it possesses, namely, the capacity to perceive its own disposition and, more strictly, to perceive the correct orientation of its disposition to a range of elements in its environment. Without any instruction, the Stoics observe, animals perceive their vulnerability or superiority in relation to a variety of predators and prey and know, as it were, how to make use of the faculties nature has given them. A chicken flees from the shadow of a hawk, while a bull by nature employs its horns as weapons against other animals. Stoic texts provide a range of further examples to support this account, each calculated to show that animals are born with an awareness of what their constitutions are like and of what their physical dispositions are for.[29]

Some of the elements of this theory seem to have originated in dialogue with the Epicureans. The Stoics share with the Epicureans the view that the earliest forms of behaviour manifested by animals constitute a criterion of what is natural to the animal and constitutive of its *telos* as such. The Epicureans, however, deploy this assumption in support of their hedonism: what animals pursue from birth, they argue, is pleasure or the absence of pain, and an animal's *telos* depends on the achievement of this goal. The Stoic theory seems intended to counter this analysis on the grounds that it misdescribes the case. A turtle on its back, writes Seneca, does not struggle to right itself because it is in pain but because it possesses a representational awareness, however vague or inarticulate, of its correct relation to the world.[30] Indeed, the Stoics argue that in a range of cases animals do not appear to act with a view to pleasure at all, but pursue various goals even in the teeth of pain and discomfort. This complex of goal-directed activities is made possible, they hold, only by a mode of perception with which animals are born: immediately from birth an animal *perceives*, in a teleologically informed way, the actions that are appropriate to it in virtue of the kind of animal it is and the environment in which it finds itself.

The Stoic term for this innate, reflexive awareness is *oikeiôsis*, while the motivation to which it gives rise is called *hormê*, a term mediaeval philosophers sometimes render as *instinctus naturalis*.[31] Central to the Stoic theory of *oikeiôsis*, then, is something recognizably similar to later notions of animal instinct: *oikeiôsis* depends on an innate capacity that enables the animal to structure its behaviour in ways conducive to its own preservation and to that of the species as the whole. Though most of the surviving discussions of *oikeiôsis* begin with examples from the animal world, it is clear that an analysis of animal behaviour is not the central import of the

Stoic theory. In each of the main accounts, this initial focus shifts to an analysis of psychological development in humans and, finally, to conclusions about the character of the human good. It is not easy to tell from the fragments that survive precisely how the Stoics applied their theoretical observations about animal behaviour to the human case. In general, however, the theory of *oikeiôsis* seems intended to support the Stoic account of the human *telos* in two respects.

First, the theory functions as a kind of inductive argument for the Stoic claim that human excellence depends, first and foremost, on a cognitive grasp of the natural order. Importantly, on the Stoic account, the capacity for *oikeiôsis* is an essentially perceptual capacity. What animals do by nature on the basis of non-rational perception, human beings do on the basis of rational or conceptually structured perception. Just as the appropriate behaviour of animals – the preservation of themselves or their offering, cooperation within and across species – depends on a rudimentary form of cognition, so appropriate action in human beings is explained by a form of rational cognition. In contrast to various ancient and modern models of action, and particularly that associated with Hume, the Stoic account assumes that cognitive states can also be motivating states, capable of generating action in virtue of their representational content. This assumption is a central legacy of the Stoics' Socratic inheritance and one fully integrated, within the Stoic system, with the claim that virtue consists in conformity to nature.[32]

Second, the *oikeiôsis* theory seems intended to support the claim that knowledge, because it is sufficient for right action, is also sufficient for achieving the human *telos*. What an animal pursues is not the experience of pleasure but a fixed pattern of behaviour determined by its nature and place within a wider order. Though pleasure may supervene on a correct pattern of action, it is incidental to the achievement of the pattern itself. The Stoics describe these patterns of actions in both animals and humans as *kathêkonta,* a word Cicero translates as *officium* and which has often been rendered in English by the word 'duty'. In the human case, the actions appropriate to human beings in virtue of their nature and place in the world, and which are known through rational cognition, are the actions that a fully virtuous agent will perform. When these actions arise from the system of cognitive grasps or *katalêpseis* in which virtue consists, they are called not simply correct or appropriate actions (*kathêkonta*) but right actions (*katorthômata*). *Katorthômata* are actions that, as Cicero says, are correct and complete in every respect.[33] They are appropriate actions done in the right way, from the stable and consistent disposition in which virtue consists.[34]

A basic aim of the *oikeiôsis* theory, therefore, is to make a cognitive analysis of motivation central to the Stoic account of ethical development. The examples of animal behaviour support a wider, perception-based account of action the Stoics also apply to the human case. Just as an animal exhibits appropriate modes of behaviour through the perceptual capacities that nature has given it, so also human beings achieve the virtues through a form of perception that includes a teleological or evaluative component. In human beings, perception is governed by the faculty of reason, a sophisticated set of conceptions built up from experience of the natural order. This faculty supervenes as the craftsman of impulse on human experience, as one source puts it, structuring motivation through an accurate representation of the world. Its fullest development leads both to the perfected expression of the actions appropriate to human agents, and to the recognition that this pattern of action, and the knowledge from which it flows, is the central goal of human existence. Cicero describes the final stages of this process as follows:

> But as soon as [one] has acquired understanding, or rather, the conception which the Stoics call *ennoia*, and has seen the regularity and, so to speak, the harmony of conduct, he comes to value this far higher than all those objects of his initial affection; and he draws the rational conclusion that this constitutes the highest human good which is worthy of praise and desirable for its own sake.[35]

Cicero does not tell us as much as we would like about the final transition to virtue in human beings. It is clearly accompanied, however, by the agent's recognition, in the fullest possible sense, that the human good does not depend on external conditions or circumstances, on the presence or absence of pleasure or pain, but simply on an understanding of the harmony implicit in the natural order and expressed in the actions of a virtuous agent. It is this condition, the outcome of a developmental process in which an agent's beliefs are gradually freed from error, which the Stoics characterize as *homologia*, the defining excellence of a human being. It is one that enables an agent to determine the appropriate course of action in every instance, and to structure her actions by the same rational principles that order and inform the natural world.

Virtue and indifferents

The claim that virtue is the only good and sufficient for human happiness may strike us, as it struck the Stoics' critics, as an extreme view. It seems clear that throughout Stoicism's history this thesis remained a basic target of criticism from rival schools. Though the theory of *oikeiôsis* may have been intended to provide some inductive support for the sufficiency thesis, it is not the only ground on which the Stoics defend it. Two other forms of argument are worth mentioning. On the one hand, some of the Stoic arguments for the claim that virtue alone is good appear to have been offered in the spirit of conceptual analysis. For example, the Stoics accept the claim, which Plato sometimes puts forward, that every good thing is intrinsically beneficial. They argue, however, that resources like health or wealth may be used both well and badly, and so cannot be intrinsically beneficial, and so cannot be goods. Though a number of variations of this argument are attributed to the Stoics, it seems unlikely that they gained much traction with the Stoics' critics. Cicero describes one argument of this sort as a 'dagger of lead', noting that the Stoics' opponents will simply deny the first premise, that all good things are essentially beneficial and therefore beneficial in every circumstance.[36] Such arguments were probably not intended to bear the weight of the Stoic view by themselves, but rather to confirm a set of claims rooted in the teleological framework I have described.

A deeper rationale for the sufficiency thesis, I suspect, depends on a very different form of argument, one already suggested by the *oikeiôsis* account and ultimately bound up with Stoic physics and the Stoic vision of the cosmos as a whole. The thesis that health and wealth, pain and poverty are indifferent is a fundamental consequence of the Stoics' attempt to reconcile their understanding of nature as a rational order with the fact that this order has not been arranged in such a way that rational agents may infallibly attain these things. Accordingly, the Stoics draw the conclusion that the attainment of these things cannot be essential to the human good.[37] This direction of argument puts a tremendous amount of weight on the Stoic supposition that the cosmos exhibits a providential structure and that, in consequence, teleological success and happiness are within our power. The Stoics' critics were fully prepared to reverse the direction of argument, arguing that since goods such as health and wealth are not universally available to human agents, the cosmos is not, after all, such a providentially ordered place. The cosmological premises from which this argument begins may sound implausible to modern ears. From the ancient perspective, however, the attribution of reason and intelligence to the cosmos plays an important role in explaining the order, symmetry and beauty that (as both the Stoics and their critics agree) are present within it.[38]

We may wonder how far Stoic arguments for the sufficiency thesis succeed and whether the claim that virtue is sufficient for happiness can be defended adequately. A deeper challenge for the Stoic position, however, is to show that the sufficiency thesis can be squared with the framework of rational eudaimonism. This brings us to a second central difficulty with which the Stoics must deal in their effort to defend the Socratic claims I have outlined. Rational action, it seems, aims essentially at some objective worth achieving. Yet on the Stoic hypothesis, there are no goods or rational ends distinct from virtue itself. The Stoics' commitment to rational eudaimonism seems to threaten their identification of virtue with happiness, for in order to give content to the notion of virtue it appears that something other than virtue must be a worthwhile end in its own right. Most of us suppose that health and physical well-being are genuine goods and that the endeavour to secure these goods for ourselves and others is an important part of a virtuous life. Yet if such outcomes are not good and if virtue, as the whole of happiness, is the only final object at which a rational agent may aim, what exactly is the virtuous Stoic agent to *do*? Since the Stoics deny that objectives such as health or wealth are an appropriate focus of rational desire, it may seem that the Stoic agent has no reasonable basis at all for acting in one way rather than another.

The Stoics reply to this difficulty by drawing a distinction within the class of objects and conditions they regard as indifferent to virtue and happiness. Though they maintain that external circumstances cannot disturb the happiness of the fully rational agent, they argue that one is rationally required to pursue some outcomes and avoid others, and that a failure to do so constitutes a failure of virtue and rationality. Those indifferent outcomes that one is rationally required to pursue, the Stoics call 'preferred' (*proêgmena*), while those outcomes that an agent is rationally required to avoid, they call 'dispreferred' (*apoproêgmena*). It is just this pursuit and avoidance, they maintain, that comprises the actions that are appropriate to a human being.[39] Later formulations of the Stoic *telos* emphasize this process of rationally selecting and rejecting preferred and dispreferred indifferents. Though the Stoics argue that it is no part of our good that we actually *succeed* in securing or avoiding indifferent things (whether for ourselves or for others), they insist that virtue requires us to manage them rationally, and, indeed, that virtuous activity *consists* in managing them rationally. Indifferents are, in this sense, the material with which virtue must work. Even though one may be happy without indifferents, 'the manner of using them is constitutive of happiness or unhappiness', as one source puts it.[40]

Such a reply may seem like an enormous cheat, and it is clear that many of the Stoics' ancient critics regarded it as such. The Stoics argue that although it makes no difference to our good whether or not we actually secure or avoid various indifferent outcomes, we are rationally required to act so as to secure or avoid them. Yet, this reply seems merely to push the problem back a step. For how can it be good and rational to *pursue* or even *make use* of a thing if having it does not in some way contribute to a good and rational objective? The Stoics seem to embrace two incompatible theses. On the one hand, they hold that preferred indifferents contribute nothing to happiness, the final goal of rational action. On the other, they hold that the effort to achieve these things is somehow constitutive of rational agency. If the Stoics acknowledge that it is rational to pursue a given outcome, it seems they should also acknowledge that the outcome is good, that it is an appropriate focus of rational motivation and that a human life is better for including it. Such criticisms have been urged against the Stoics by both ancient and modern commentators.[41]

I think that the tendency to charge the Stoics with incoherence in this respect is due, in part, to a tendency to conceive of practical rationality in different terms than do the Stoics themselves. The key to understanding the Stoic view is to recognize that because they defend a cognitive account of motivation, according to which beliefs play the role of motivating states, the Stoics are not working with any sharp distinction between theoretical and practical rationality, or even, indeed, with a distinction between practical and epistemic norms. A rational action is not one calculated to secure an intrinsically good outcome, on their account, but one that arises from a cognitive state that is itself justified and which is itself an intrinsically good state of affairs. On such an analysis, actions will be rationally justified just in case and insofar as they result from a rationally justified cognitive condition. Because the value of a virtuous action derives from its origin in this way, to show that an agent has acted for good reasons is not to show that he or she has acted for the sake of securing an independently valuable end but to show that he or she has acted on the basis of true and reliable beliefs.

Preferred and dispreferred indifferents play an important role in practical reasoning, therefore, but not as practical objectives independent of virtue and happiness. Rather, their justificatory role is epistemic. Because the Stoic classification of indifferents codifies the states and conditions that rational nature allots to human agents usually or on the whole, it constitutes part of the grounds on which an agent's beliefs about the natural order are based.[42] All else being equal, a rational agent will select health because she truly believes that, in the usual order of things, the rational pattern of nature assigns this condition to human agents.[43] His or her final objective, however, is simply to reason well, where this consists in forming true and unshakeable beliefs about the structure of nature. The actions of the virtuous agent will follow on these beliefs automatically, as it were, but they will not be good because they are aimed at valuable outcomes. They will be good because they arise from an understanding of the place these things have within a broader order.

The axiology implicit in this account is quite clearly expressed in the Stoics' metaphors for virtuous activity. Virtue, the Stoics maintain, is like the skill expressed in the motions of an actor or a dancer.[44] These motions are not valuable because of any further result they secure but simply because of the pattern or order they exemplify. The point of these analogies is to help the Stoics' critics understand why health and wealth, though they are indeed indifferent, are not irrelevant to the concerns of the virtuous agent. Their status as preferred or dispreferred is a reflection of the rational pattern exhibited by nature, and a consideration of this status will figure in a justification of the beliefs that explain and motivate the virtuous agents' actions.[45] In treating rationally justified action as a product of true and justified belief, the Stoics effectively treat the norms of practical justification as epistemic norms and indifferents as a source of epistemic reasons. The difficulties that arise in understanding the place of indifferents in Stoic theory arise, in part, from a failure to appreciate that Stoic theory applies cognitive standards in its appraisal of actions.

The legacy of Stoic ethics

I have so far focused on some of the foundational features of Stoic ethics, on the Stoic conception of virtue, on the fundamental role of nature and on the claim that virtue is sufficient for happiness. The Stoics have much more to say about a range of narrower normative issues, including political matters, human sexuality and obligations to self and others. Some of the Stoics' most striking ethical claims are related to their cosmopolitanism, to the view that the cosmos as a whole has the character of a city and that, as a result, many of our obligations are universal in scope, comprising duties to humanity as such.[46] These claims are worthy of study in their own right. Attention to the foundations of Stoic ethics, however, helps to bring out some of the respects in which Stoic theory has had an enduring influence on Western ethical thought and prefigures later ethical views.

Two features of Stoicism are especially salient in this respect. The first is one I have not yet mentioned: the Stoic characterization of the natural order and of reason itself as a kind of law (*nomos*). This is a striking characterization, in part, because it is a clear departure from the opposition between nature and law articulated by many earlier thinkers in the Greek intellectual tradition. In identifying law with a rational structure implicit in nature, the Stoics are arguably committed to a quite extensive form of ethical naturalism: they regard the facts that fix the ethical facts as part of the natural order and, indeed, as a consequence of cosmic teleology. There are important differences between the Stoic account and later theories of natural law, yet the Stoic theory, particularly as transmitted through the work of Cicero, has played an important role in the natural law tradition in ethics.[47]

A second important feature of Stoicism, less often remarked, is the axiology of virtue the Stoics defend and the account of moral motivation it implies. Other Hellenistic thinkers agree that virtue is good, at least in part, because of the good results it secures. The Stoic theory reverses this order of priority, holding that actions are good only as expressions of a virtuous character. This point is reflected in many Stoic texts, but the easiest way to see that the Stoics are committed to the claim that virtue's value is wholly intrinsic is to note that this thesis is a consequence of two of the Stoic commitments I mentioned earlier. Since happiness is that for the sake of which every rational action is undertaken and is not itself sought for the sake of anything further, and since happiness and virtue are extensional equivalents, nothing that falls outside the scope of virtue can supply the justificatory ground of virtuous character and action.[48] Together with the identification of virtue and happiness, the acceptance of rational eudaimonism effectively commits the Stoics to a view sometimes attributed to Kant: that the intentional features of a virtuous action exhaust the ground of its value.[49]

This axiological point has a further, psychological corollary, one that goes to the heart of the difference between the Stoics and their critics. For the Stoic position, like the Kantian, concerns more than the source of virtue's value. It has corresponding implications for the character of appropriate motivation. Since the single end of rational desire consists in virtue alone, and since virtue is wholly up to the agent, no desire for any final end that cannot be realized through one's own agency will be rational, according to the Stoics. Seneca puts this point with characteristic flare:

> I have, says [a good conscience] what I wished (*volui*), what I strove for. I do not regret it, nor shall I ever regret it, and no injustice of Fortune shall ever bring me to such a pass that she will hear me say, what was it I wished? What profit have I now from my good intention (*bona voluntas*)?[50]

As Seneca here makes clear, there is no room in the Stoic account for rational regret so long as an agent has acted virtuously. Such an account reverses the axiology of consequentialism and strongly anticipates elements of the deontological tradition, including Kant's claim, in the beginning of the *Groundwork*, that nothing is intrinsically good, either in this world or out of it, other than a good will.[51] Many Stoic images express a similar point. Virtue is to be chosen, on the Stoic account, not because of a further outcome it enables the agent to achieve but because it imposes on a human life the same orderly structure exhibited in the cosmos as a whole.

Notes

1 On Zeno of Citium, see J. Brunschwig (2002), 'Zeno between Kition and Athens', in T. Scaltsas and A. Mason (eds), *The Philosophy of Zeno*. Lacarna: The Municipality of Lacarna, pp. 13–27. For the school's history during the Hellenistic period, see D. Sedley (2003), 'The school, from Zeno to Arius Didymus', in B. Inwood (ed.) *The Cambridge Companion to the Stoics*. Cambridge: Cambridge University Press, pp. 7–32.

2 For an overview of the surviving source material, see especially, J. Mansfeld (1999), 'Sources', in K. Algra, J. Barnes, J. Mansfeld, and M. Schofield (eds), *The Cambridge History of Hellenistic Philosophy*. Cambridge: Cambridge University Press, pp. 3–30. The standard collection of Greek and Latin fragments is H. von Arnim (1903–5), *Stoicorum Veterum Fragmenta*. Leipzig: Teubner (hereafter SVF). An outstanding translation of and commentary on many of the most important passages is provided in A. Long and D. Sedley (1987), *The Hellenistic Philosophers Vol. 1*. Cambridge: Cambridge University Press (hereafter LS).

3 The most extensive and systematic accounts of Stoic ethics are Cicero, *On Ends* Book 3; Diogenes Laertius, *Lives of Eminent Philosophers* 2.7; Stobaeus, *Eclogues* 2.57–2.116. The summaries of Cicero and Diogenes are available in the Loeb Classical Library series. The summary preserved by Stobaeus, along with an English translation and commentary, may be found in Arthur Pomeroy (1999), *Arius Didymus: Epitome of Stoic Ethics*. Atlanta: Society of Biblical Literature.

4 These distinctions presuppose a conventional division of Plato's dialogues into early, middle and late (on which cf. Chapter 1, note 13). For discussion of the Socratic background to Stoic ethics, see

especially G. Striker (1994), 'Plato's Socrates and the Stoics', in
P. Vander Waerdt (ed.), *The Socratic Movement*. Ithaca: Cornell, pp.
241–51; S. Menn (1995), 'Physics as a virtue', *Proceedings of the
Boston Area Colloquium in Ancient Philosophy*, 11, 1–34.

5 The Cynic influence on Stoicism is most clearly reflected, perhaps,
in the Stoic doctrine that virtue depends on conformity to nature.
Though the Stoics develop this doctrine in a way that differs from
the ideals of Cynicism, it may well have originated in Zeno's early
association with Crates.

6 The view that Aristotle exercised any significant influence on the
early Stoics is comprehensively criticized in F. H. Sandbach (1985),
Aristotle and the Stoics. Cambridge: Cambridge Philological Society.
For a more moderate view, see B. Inwood (1986), 'Review of
Sandbach', *The Philosophical Review*, 95, 470–73.

7 According to one important summary of Stoic views, the Stoics
'say that being happy is the end, for the sake of which everything
is done but which is not itself done for the sake of anything' (LS
63A = SVF 3.16, trans. Long and Sedley). Happiness, says another
fragment, is the final object of rational desire (*orexis*), desire that
is informed by considerations about what is good (SVF 3.3). When
he sets out to explain the Stoic view, Cicero assumes that each of
the central philosophical schools of his time shares the conviction
that one should always pursue the sort of life that is beneficial
to the agent, and which renders the agent happy in Aristotle's
sense. Ethical theorists who take the eudaimonist perspective for
granted during the Hellenistic period include the Stoics, Epicureans,
Academics and Sceptics. The Cyrenaics are a notable exception.
Rational eudaimonism, it should be noted, is also compatible with
various forms of immoralism, such as that of Thrasymachus (Plato's
Republic, Book I), according to whom *injustice* is one of the virtues
essential to the good life, and that of Callicles (Plato's *Gorgias*),
who argues that some of the traditional virtues (e.g. courage) but
not others (e.g. justice) are required for happiness. For discussion
of this framework, see especially, J. Annas (1993), *The Morality of
Happiness*. Oxford: Oxford University Press, pp. 27–46.

8 *Nicomachean Ethics* 1094a23–5. Cf. Plato, *Symposium* 205a1–8.

9 See, for example, R. Kraut (1979), 'Two conceptions of happiness',
The Philosophical Review, 88, 167–97; Vlastos G. (1991), 'Happiness
and virtue in Socrates' moral theory', in G. Vlastos, *Socrates, Ironist
and Moral Philosopher*. Ithaca: Cornell University Press, pp. 200–35;
J. Annas (2004), 'Happiness as achievement', *Daedelus*, 138, 44–51.

10 Later thinkers, most notably Kant, reject the framework of
eudaimonism on the grounds that it cannot accommodate the
form of motivation essential to morality. For recent criticism of

eudaimonism along these lines, see T. Nagel (1989), *The View from Nowhere*. Oxford: Oxford University Press, pp. 195–7.

11 As some of the Hellenistic thinkers appear to interpret Aristotle, these goods will not merely supply the agent with the means or scope for exercising his or her virtue; they also comprise independently necessary and valuable components of happiness. See, for example, Cicero, *On Ends* 2.19: 'Many and great philosophers have made these ultimate goods a composite, as Aristotle conjoined the exercise of virtue with prosperity in a complete life'.

12 See, for example, *Nicomachean Ethics* 1100b ff.

13 The claim that virtue is identical to happiness has been associated with the Socrates of Plato's early dialogues on the strength of passages such as *Crito* 48b4–10, but it remains controversial as an interpretation of Socrates' considered position. Terence Irwin argues at length that although Socrates regards virtue as a sufficient condition of happiness, he does not regard it as *constitutive* of the happy human life. Such an interpretation aligns the Socratic position more closely with the Epicurean view. See, especially, T. Irwin, *Plato's Moral Theory*. Oxford: Oxford University Press, Chapter 4; T. Irwin, *Plato's Ethics*. Oxford: Oxford University Press, Chapter 6. For some criticisms of Irwin's interpretation, see J. Cooper (1982), 'The *Gorgias* and Irwin's Socrates', *The Review of Metaphysics*, 35, 577–87. Cf. also Vlastos (1991).

14 Thus, Cicero (*On Ends* 3.29) describes the Stoic sage as 'holding that no evil can happen to a wise man'. Cf. Plato, *Apology* 41d.

15 *Meno* 79a–d.

16 Cf. *Meno* 75c–d.

17 Socrates provides examples of the kind of reductive definition he is seeking at *Meno* 75b–c and 76d.

18 The Stoic notion does not approximate neo-Kantian views of procedural rationality. See, especially, T. Brennan (2005), *The Stoic Life*. Oxford: Oxford University Press, pp. 138–41.

19 Cf. especially, Cicero, *On Ends* 2.34, 3.31, 4.14. In Stoic theory, actions themselves are analysed as a kind of cognitive performance. See Seneca, Letter 113.23 (= LS 53L).

20 For an example of the former approach, see, especially, J. Annas (1993), pp. 159–79; for the latter, see A. Long (1970), 'The logical basis of Stoic Ethics', *Proceedings of the Aristotelian Society*, 71, 85–104; N. White (1979), 'The basis of Stoic ethics', *Harvard Studies in Classical Philology*, 83, 143–78.

21 LS 57A.

22 Trans. Long and Sedley. Cf. Seneca, Letter 88.26; LS 63J. Cf. also
G. B. Kerford, 'What does the wise man know?' in J. Rist (ed.) (1978),
The Stoics. Berkeley: University of California Press, pp. 125–36.

23 It seems clear that the early Stoics developed a comprehensive
teleological framework that included an analysis of the ends
appropriate to various biological species. According to Cicero (*On
Ends* 4.28), Chrysippus composed a treatise in which he surveyed
a range of animal species and offered an account of the final
good of each. It is likely that this is the treatise *On Ends* cited in
Diogenes Laertius' report of the Stoic theory of *oikeiôsis* (Diogenes
Laertius 7.85–6 = LS 57A). Other fragments indicate that the Stoics
attempted to say how the realization of these ends serves a broader
cosmic purpose.

24 Cicero, *On the Nature of the Gods* 2.57–8. Cf. SVF 2.1027 (= LS 46A).

25 The latter terms also have a normative valence for the Stoics.
Though the Stoics offer a broadly naturalistic account of morality,
there is little reason to suppose that they succeed in eliminating
normative terms from their analysis of basic moral properties or
that they take themselves to have done so. In this respect, their
answer to the Socratic question is one Socrates himself might
well have rejected. Stoicism reduces moral properties to those
properties in virtue of which nature itself is orderly and rational.
Given the state of the sources, it is impossible to say how the
Stoics attempted to characterize these features of nature at the
most fundamental level, if indeed they attempted to do so. It
seems clear, however, that they regard the cosmos as rational in
part because they regard it as an aesthetically perfect whole. There
is some reason to suppose that their account of moral properties
ends with an appeal to aesthetic properties. See, for example,
Cicero, *On the Nature of the Gods* 2.35. Cf. M. Frede (1999), 'On
the Stoic conception of the good', in K. Ierodiakonou (ed.), *Topics
in Stoic Philosophy*. Oxford: Oxford University Press: pp. 71–94;
R. Bett (2010), 'Beauty and its relation to goodness in Stoicism',
in D. Sedley and A. Nightingale (eds), *Ancient Models of Mind:
Studies in Divine and Human Rationality*. Cambridge: Cambridge
University Press, pp. 130–52.

26 The Stoics agree with Plato and Aristotle in treating moral norms as
objective and accessible to reason. Yet their theory is more explicitly
naturalistic than that of Plato, who has been regarded as a non-
naturalist in ethics because of his commitment to transcendent,
immaterial Forms. At the same time, Stoic naturalism is arguably
more extensive than that of Aristotle. Like Aristotle, the Stoics
regard the goal-directed functions of individual organisms as a
basis for norms that, in the human case, partly determine the
requirements of virtue. But the Stoics also incorporate this account

(as Aristotle arguably does not) within a more comprehensive teleological framework, treating the organization of the cosmos itself as an expression of substantive principles of rationality that play a role in fixing the character and scope of moral obligation. The wider scope of Stoic naturalism is apparent, for instance, in the Stoic doctrine that the cosmos itself has the character of a city, citizenship of which imposes duties of mutual concern upon its members.

27 Plutarch, *On Moral Virtue* 441c (= SVF 1.202), trans. A. Long.

28 The best discussion of these features of Stoic epistemology is Michael Frede (1987), 'Stoics and Skeptics on clear and distinct impressions', in M. Frede, *Essays in Ancient Philosophy*. Minneapolis: University of Minnesota Press, pp. 151–78.

29 The classic account of the Stoic theory is S. Pembroke (1971), '*Oikeiôsis*', in A. Long (ed.), *Problems in Stoicism*. London: Athlone, pp. 114–49. For a discussion of the cognitive dimensions of *oikeiôsis*, see, especially, A. Long (1991), 'Representation and the self in Stoicism', in S. Everson (ed.), *Companions to Ancient Thought 2: Psychology*. Cambridge: Cambridge University Press, pp. 101–20; A. Long (1993), 'Hierocles on *oikeiôsis* and self-perception', in K. J. Boudouris (ed.), *Hellenistic Philosophy Vol. 1*. Athens, pp. 93–104; C. Brittain (2002), 'Non-rational perception in the Stoics and Augustine', *Oxford Studies in Ancient Philosophy*, 22, 253–88.

30 Letter 121 (= LS 57).

31 Cf. Pembroke (1971), p. 117, 141 n. 10.

32 For a systematic discussion of these and other details of Stoic moral psychology, see Tad Brennan (2003), 'Stoic moral psychology', in B. Inwood (ed.) *The Cambridge Companion to the Stoics*. Cambridge: Cambridge University Press, pp. 257–94.

33 *On Ends* 3.32 (= LS 59L).

34 For a discussion of the theory's ethical import, see, especially, B. Inwood (1984), 'Hierocles the Stoic: theory and argument in the second century A. D.', *Oxford Studies in Ancient Philosophy*, 2, 151–84; G. Striker (1983), 'The role of *oikeiôsis* in Stoic ethics', *Oxford Studies in Ancient Philosophy*, 1, 145–67; T. Brennan (2005), Chapter 10.

35 *On Ends* 3.21 (= LS 59D), trans. Long and Sedley.

36 *On Ends* 4.48.

37 For a further discussion of this mode of argument, see J. Cooper (1996), 'Eudaimonism, the appeal to nature, and "moral duty" in Stoicism', in S. Engstrom and J. Whiting (eds), *Aristotle, Kant and the Stoics: Rethinking Happiness and Duty*. Cambridge: Cambridge University Press, pp. 261–84.

38 Cicero's *On the Nature of the Gods* records a number of Stoic arguments for the claim that the cosmos exhibits a rational structure, together with ancient criticisms of the Stoic view. See, especially, 2.29–39, 3.20–28.

39 Here, a clarification is perhaps in order. In speaking of the selection and rejection of indifferents, the Stoics are not thinking simply of selection or rejection for oneself but, much more broadly, of disposing of indifferents in the way that reason as expressed in nature requires. So understood, the appropriate pattern of selection and rejection may well be guided by other-regarding principles. The best accounts of the role of preferred and dispreferred indifferents in Stoic deliberation are R. Barney (2003), 'A puzzle in Stoic ethics', *Oxford Studies in Ancient Philosophy*, 24, 273–302 and T. Brennan (2005), Chapters 11–13.

40 Diogenes Laertius 7.104–5 (= LS 58B), trans. Long and Sedley.

41 Some of the ancient criticisms are preserved by Plutarch (*On Common Conceptions*) and Alexander of Aphrodisias (*Supplement to 'On the Soul'*). For a recent criticism of the Stoic doctrine, see C. C. W. Taylor (1987), 'Hellenistic ethics', *Oxford Studies in Ancient Philosophy*, 5, pp. 235–45 (especially 239).

42 On this point, see, especially, B. Inwood and P. Donini (1999), 'Stoic Ethics' in K. Algra, J. Barnes, J. Mansfeld, and M. Schofield, *The Cambridge History of Hellenistic Philosophy*. Cambridge: Cambridge University Press, pp. 675–738 (especially 690–99).

43 Cf. Epictetus, *Discourses* 2.6.9 (= LS 57J).

44 Cicero, *On Ends* 3.23–5.

45 According to the summary of Stoic ethics preserved by Stobaeus, natural states and conditions are variously preferred and dispreferred in virtue of their relation to a set of generative principles (*spermatikoi logoi*) by which the cosmos as a whole is ordered (*Eclogues* 2.82). How the Stoics themselves conceived of these principles, or what reductive account they may have given of them, is a matter of debate. That the principles by which Zeus structures the cosmos have an aesthetic character is suggested by Cicero's discussion in *On the Nature of the Gods* (cf. n. 24–5 above). Very little material that bears on these questions survives.

46 On Stoic cosmopolitanism, see M. Schofield (1991), *The Stoic Idea of the City*. Cambridge: Cambridge University Press. For Stoic views on more specific normative issues, see, for example, Seneca, Letters 94–5; Cicero, *On Duties* 1.15–161. Fragments of Hierocles' ethical treatises are collected in Ilaria Ramelli (2009), *Hierocles the Stoic: 'Elements of Ethics', Fragments, and Excerpts*.

Atlanta: Society of Biblical Literature. Accounts of Musonius Rufus' lectures are collected in C. Lutz (1947), *Musonius Rufus: The Roman Socrates*. New Haven: Yale University Press. Important selections from Musonius, Epictetus and Seneca are included in B. Inwood and L. Gerson (2008), *The Stoics Reader*. Indianapolis: Hackett, pp. 177–205.

47 The work of Thomas Aquinas (A. D. 1225–74) is central to this tradition. See Chapter 4 of this volume.

48 This point needs to be spelt out. I am here assuming an essential connection between intrinsic value and objective normative reasons, that is, that as Scanlon puts it, 'to claim that something is valu*able* (or that it is "of value") is to claim that others also have reason to value it, as you do'. Cf. T. Scanlon (1998), *What We Owe to Each Other*. Cambridge: Harvard University Press, p. 95. Since the Stoics regard *eudaimonia* as the only source of ultimate reasons for acting, and since they identify *eudaimonia* with virtue, they cannot consistently regard anything other than virtue itself as a source of value that could supply a rational agent with normative reasons that regulate her desires and actions.

49 Cf. G 4:399: 'an action done from duty has its moral worth not in the purpose attained by it but in the maxim in accordance with which it is decided upon' (trans. H. J. Paton).

50 *On Benefits* 4.21 (trans. Basore).

51 G 4:393. Cf. Chapter 6 of this volume.

Recommended reading

The best and most accessible general account of Stoic ethical theory:

Brennan, Tad (2005), *The Stoic Life*. Oxford: Oxford University Press.

A comprehensive, groundbreaking study of Stoic moral psychology:

Inwood, Brad (1985), *Ethics and Human Action in Early Stoicism*. Oxford: Oxford University Press.

Two recent, detailed studies of Stoic political theory and the Stoic account of natural law:

Schofield, Malcolm (1999), *The Stoic Idea of the City*. Cambridge: Cambridge University Press.
Vogt, Katja Maria (2008), *Law, Reason and the Cosmic City*. Oxford: Oxford University Press.

A comprehensive study of Hellenistic Ethics generally:

Annas, Julia (1993), *The Morality of Happiness*. Oxford: Oxford University Press.

Accessible, shorter overviews of Stoic ethics:

Inwood, Brad and Donini, Pierluigi (1999), 'Stoic Ethics', in K. Algra, J. Barnes, J. Mansfeld, and M. Schofield (eds), *The Cambridge History of Hellenistic Philosophy*. Cambridge: Cambridge University Press, pp. 675–736.

Schofield, Malcolm (2003), 'Stoic Ethics', in B. Inwood (ed.), *The Cambridge Companion to the Stoics*. Cambridge: Cambridge University Press, pp. 233–56.

Some especially important papers on Stoic ethics are collected in:

Long, Anthony (1996), *Stoic Studies*. Berkeley: University of California Press.

Striker, Gisela (1996), *Essays on Hellenistic Epistemology and Ethics*. Cambridge: Cambridge University Press.

4

Aquinas

Vivian Boland O. P.

The moral teaching of Thomas Aquinas (1225–74) is both original and unique. He is the first and only theologian to develop a Christian ethics that takes its conceptual apparatus, for the most part, from Aristotle's *Nicomachean Ethics* and that presents much of its applied morality in recognizably Aristotelian terms. A full Latin translation of Aristotle's work was available only from the 1240s and Albert the Great had already begun to use it in his teaching. But there is no project comparable to what Aquinas attempts in his *Summa Theologiae*: a comprehensive and systematic presentation of moral theology that is, in effect, a Christianization of Aristotle's ethics. How successful this project was is a moot point: if philosophers hesitate because of the theological context and orientation of Aquinas's work, theologians hesitate because of its obvious dependence on Aristotle's philosophy. While the philosopher may be tempted to rule it out as an ethics or as moral philosophy, the theologian may be tempted to rule it out as a Christian ethics or as moral theology.

Although Aquinas's best known work, the *Summa Theologiae*, is now often regarded as the only one of his works that needs to be consulted in order to understand his thinking, any engagement with his thought quickly shows such a restriction to be seriously mistaken. In the area of ethics alone, important sets of *Quaestiones Disputatae* – for example, those on evil, on the virtues in general and on the cardinal virtues – contain much more extensive treatments of many of the moral themes summarily presented in the *Summa*. His commentary on Aristotle's *Ethics* shows us how he received that work – composing it perhaps even after he had finished the *Summa* – and sought to understand it on its own terms. His commentaries on various books of the Bible are further relevant sources for his thinking about morality and show his indebtedness to Jewish, Greek and Roman traditions of moral teaching. With this caveat, it is nevertheless convenient, in presenting his ethical thought, to follow the structure of the *Secunda pars* of the *Summa Theologiae* while drawing on the full range of his works.

Eudaimonia – beatitudo

Aquinas begins with the notion of *eudaimonia*, familiar from Aristotle. Translated into mediaeval Latin as *beatitudo*, it linked easily with earlier biblical and Christian teaching about what makes human life blessed or fulfilled. The structures of Aristotle's eudaimonistic ethics are combined with the eschatological orientation that is fundamental to Jewish and Christian moral thinking. Every human act is towards an end: this is what gives meaning to an act, Aquinas says. Within every human act there are at least two levels of finality, that of the immediate purpose or goal for which the act is done and that of the ultimate purpose or goal for which the totality of human acts is done. In seeking any particular good one is also always seeking an ultimate good, whether one is conscious of this or not, and whether one identifies this ultimate good in terms of power, pleasure or possessions, in terms of living according to nature or according to reason, in terms of fulfilment, flourishing or happiness, in terms of union with the divine or becoming like God.

The fullest possible flourishing of the human being is found in appropriating this ultimate purpose or goal: it is, we can say, 'what the human being is for'. Aristotle's text provides different accounts of the ultimate purpose or goal of human life. At some points it seems to him to consist in the moderate enjoyment and use of all the good things that can come the way of a human being. At other points it is identified as 'the highest act of the highest faculty [namely reason]', what Aristotle calls *theoria* (or 'contemplation'). Aquinas accepts this starting point and believes that Aristotle comes closer to the truth when he speaks of *theoria* as the activity in which human beings find their fullest happiness. Once again, the mediaeval Latin translation of this term as *contemplatio* facilitated Aquinas's use of Aristotle's work, since *contemplatio* also had a distinguished pedigree, not only in interpretations of Plato's philosophy but also in the monastic and other spiritual traditions of Christianity.

James Doig argues that Aquinas's commentary on the *Ethics* is a work of moral philosophy whose essential principles are properly philosophical and not at all dependent on theological convictions.[1] Doig's argument, however, depends on accepting Aquinas's reading of Aristotle's philosophy as itself more substantially 'theological' than most interpreters of Aristotle would now allow – including, for example, divine creation and providence, personal immortality and God as the supreme good. Aquinas is clear that Aristotle cannot have been fully aware of the experience in which human fulfilment is to be found, in the supernatural vision of God which is Aquinas's own definition of *beatitudo*.[2] Nevertheless, Aristotle provides him again and again with insights that facilitate his own explication of the good human life.

The human act

The goals and purposes of human beings are achieved and appropriated through 'acts', and this is what Aquinas considers next. He gives a detailed analysis of the human act, of which the most striking aspect is how intellect and will cooperate in its production. These two aspects of rationality always go together for Aquinas: there is no knowing power that does not inform an appetitive or desiring power, and there is no appetitive or desiring power that does not depend on a knowing power, and this is true also at the level of rational powers. The material found in what seems like a simple psychology of human action (*Summa Theologiae* I.II qq.6–17) has already been treated in his consideration of the first principles of practical reasoning (*Summa Theologiae* I q.79, aa.11–13) and will figure again in his considerations of law (*Summa Theologiae* I.II q.94, aa.1–2) and of prudence (*Summa Theologiae* II.II q.47, aa.1–8). In fact,

Aristotle's comment about prudence in *Nicomachean Ethics* VI.2 that it may be described either as 'desiderative reason' or as 'reasoning desire', clearly rings true for Aquinas, at the heart of whose moral psychology is this interplay of intellect and will, of knowing and desiring, of perception and response.

If human goals and purposes are achieved through human acts, and only what is done with understanding and freedom can be regarded as a properly human act, then the morality of acts comes not just from the integrity with which they are performed – what we might call their procedural integrity – but depends also on what they are for, the goals and purposes to which they are directed. Human acts are fully human when they are intentional, having a finality that is not just recognized, but is consciously chosen, by their agent. That they be properly human in this sense is essential for what we may call their 'subjective' moral character, but that they be for goals and purposes that really do fulfil human beings is essential for what we may call their 'objective' moral character. Aquinas himself does not use these terms but their use is justified in the way he summarizes what is required for the goodness of a human act. In appealing to a description of the moral good that comes from Pseudo-Dionysius the Areopagite, a sixth-century Syrian monk whose theology is of great importance for his, Aquinas spells out that this means an act is good only when its object, end and circumstances are all good (*Summa Theologiae* I.II q.18, a.4, ad 3). This was to become an axiom frequently appealed to by moral theologians: *bonum ex integra causa, malum ex quocumque defectu*; an act is good when it has this integrity, evil if it is defective in any aspect of it.

Just as his account of human action identifies a dynamic interplay between intellect and will, so Aquinas's account of human freedom presupposes the same dynamic interplay. Although Aquinas does on occasion use the phrase 'free will', it is not sufficient, and may indeed be misleading, to speak of his understanding of human freedom simply in those terms. In the vast majority of places in which he speaks about freedom, he prefers 'free judgement', *liberum arbitrium*, an expression that already implies that judgement or decision requires the action of both intellect and will, perception and choice.

The fullest presentation of his arguments in support of freedom is found in *Quaestiones Disputatae de Malo* q.6, where he speaks of it as *libera electio* [free choice]. After two 'appalling scenario' arguments (from what are clearly absurd consequences if human beings are not free), he develops an argument based on the relationship of intellect and will in the activation and specification of the rational powers of judgement and decision. Because the will is not specified by any all-fulfilling good, it remains free in relation to any of the goods by which it is now specified. If it were to be specified by such an all-fulfilling good, it would no longer be free as regards its specification since it would be in the presence of its own deepest fulfilment. On the other hand, the activation or awakening of the will to want anything at all – 'what wills the will to will?' – is given a theological answer by Aquinas, in terms of God's creating power and presence which, far from threatening human freedom, actually establishes that freedom in the first place. For this theological answer, he finds support in Aristotle, in what he knew as *Liber de Bona Fortuna*, a mediaeval Latin translation of parts of Aristotle's *Magna Moralia* and *Eudemian Ethics*.[3]

Principles of human action

For Aquinas, there are interior and exterior principles of human acts. The interior principles are, in the first place, psychological powers or capacities, in particular the rational powers of intellect and will. They are called interior because they are resources of the individual human agent. 'This individual human being thinks and decides', is how Aquinas puts it in response to philosophical psychologies that would assign some of the responsibility for human action to supra-individual causes. He will allow, of course, some determining influence to such causes but not to the extent that they would be the complete explanation of human action: that would be to deny human moral agency altogether. Aquinas's famously holistic account of the union of body and soul means the rational powers are always dependent on the powers of exterior sensation (perception in its various modalities of seeing, hearing, etc.) as well as on the powers of interior sensation (the common sense that synthesizes different kinds of perception, as well as memory, an evaluative sense and imagination). The rational powers, and therefore human acts, are also inextricably involved with *passiones animae*, the emotions or passions, which are a kind of 'raw material' of human action. These powers or capacities are directed and developed by interior principles called *habitus*, skills or dispositions, that an agent can generate in himself or herself or otherwise receive. When concerned with matters of moral significance (and in practice, for Aquinas, that means all human behaviour) such dispositions are called virtues.

Passion

A striking aspect of Aquinas's account of morality is the space he gives to the passions. Drawing on the experience of many ancient and earlier Christian thinkers, he provides a masterly summary of practical wisdom and concrete advice. He accepts Aristotle's distinction of passions into two kinds. The concupiscible, or desiring, passions are activated in the presence of pleasurable or painful things, things experienced as 'good' or 'evil' in a straightforward way. Things experienced as good will be loved, desired and eventually enjoyed. Things experienced as evil will be hated, avoided if possible, and cause sorrow where they cannot be avoided. The other kind of passion is described as irascible or contending. Here, there is an element of difficulty which renders these passions less straightforward than the first kind. So we have the passions of hope and despair, confidence and fear: clearly these are also about things experienced as good and desirable or as evil and to be avoided. But the strength required is greater here because of the note of difficulty, whatever the source or nature of that difficulty may be.

So he speaks of six concupiscible passions – love, desire and joy; hate, aversion and sorrow – and of four irascible passions – hope and confidence; fear and despair. There is a fifth irascible passion, anger, or *ira*, which gives its name to the second group. But it is a complex passion, Aquinas says, whose object cannot easily be identified as simply 'good' or 'evil'.

Augustine sharply contrasted Stoic and Aristotelian approaches to passion and his view on this, as on so many things, was influential in the Middle Ages. Aquinas faithfully records it: the Stoics regarded all passion as in some way evil: agitations and distractions, they are even a kind of disease according to Stoic philosophers such as Cicero, disturbing the human being and making rational action more difficult, perhaps even impossible. Aristotelians, on the other hand, took what seems a far more sensible approach, regarding irrational passion as evil, but rational passion not just as good, but as essential if an act is to have its full strength and significance as a human act. A superficial contrast between texts from, say, Cicero and Aristotle, seems to support Augustine's point. Aquinas clearly agrees that the ideal of human action is not *apatheia*, passionlessness, but is a fully passionate engagement, at all levels of human response, with the goods that are desirable and with whatever evils threaten those goods.

Aristotle writes as follows in the *Nicomachean Ethics*:

I believe it to be an error to say that acts occasioned by anger or desire are involuntary. For in the first place if we maintain this we shall have to give up the view that any of the lower animals, or even children, are capable of voluntary action. In the second place, when we act from desire or anger are none of our actions voluntary? Or are our fine actions voluntary, our ignoble actions involuntary? It is an absurd distinction, since the agent is one and the same person. It is surely paradoxical to describe as 'involuntary' acts inspired by sentiments which we quite properly desire to have. There are some things at which we *ought* to feel angry, and others which we *ought* to desire – health, for instance, and the acquisition of knowledge. Thirdly, people assume that what is involuntary must be painful and what falls in with our own wishes must be pleasant. Fourthly, what difference is there in point of voluntariness between wrong actions which are calculated and wrong actions which are done on impulse? Both are to be avoided; and the further reflection suggests itself, that the irrational emotions are no less typically human than our considered judgement. Whence it follows that actions inspired by anger or desire are equally typical of the human being who performs them. Therefore to classify these actions as 'involuntary' is surely a very strange proceeding.[4]

And Aquinas writes about good human anger as follows:

Since human nature means being composed of soul and body, as well as of an intellectual and a sensual nature, the good of the human being requires that he be totally subject to virtue, namely in his intellectual part, and in his sensual part, and in his physical part. So for human virtue it is required that the desire for due retribution should be present not only in the rational part of the soul, but also in the sensitive part, and in the body itself, so that even the body is moved to serve virtue.[5]

Aquinas's distinction between acting *out of* emotion and acting *with* emotion is helpful and true to experience. The first refers to what he calls *antecedent passion*, where emotion precedes the judgement of reason and clouds that judgement. The second refers to what he calls *consequent passion*, where one is so convinced in one's judgement that the intensity of that conviction redounds, as it were, in one's heart, imagination, emotions and flesh. Our judgement, he says elsewhere, is hindered by passion, whereas our execution of an act is helped by it.[6]

Consequent passion also refers to the situation where one chooses to be affected by an emotion, so as to act more promptly. This is a bit puzzling: if one chooses to be affected by an emotion how can 'passion' have its full meaning, since it refers to something suffered, in other words something more or less unchosen! Antecedent passion, Aquinas concludes, diminishes the goodness (or indeed evil) of an act because it renders it less fully human and so less fully free. Consequent passion increases the goodness or evil of an act because it is more fully under our control and therefore falls more under our conscious responsibility.

Aquinas carried this line of thought to its logical conclusion. Not only are the passions of the human being part of the total moral subject and part of what is involved in the virtuous life, but they are also 'graced'. They remain and become part of the Christian reality of loving God and loving other people, not in the austere and rationalistic way that has sometimes been regarded as the desired ideal for Christians (and indeed was often labelled 'stoic'), but in a way that engages the whole person, imaginatively, passionately and leading to concrete action. The Christian, on Aquinas's account, ought to be filled with hope, enthusiasm, joy, love, anger and pleasure, all at the service of God's love.

Such comments ought to be enough to show that any kind of Stoic or Cartesian interpretation of Aquinas on the passions is wide of the mark. There is much practical wisdom in how he distinguishes pain and sorrow or in the remedies he recommends for depression. There is sanity and balance in his understanding of anger. Some of this has to do with his eirenic approach to earlier thinkers and with what those earlier thinkers taught him, some of it perhaps with his own famously balanced and serene temperament. Aquinas even raises a question about Augustine's contrast between Stoic and Aristotelian understandings of passion: it may actually be a simple matter of terminology, he writes, the Stoics' meaning by 'passion' what the Aristotelians meant by 'disordered passion'.[7] Nevertheless, he warns against thinking that reason can exercise any kind of despotic control over the passions. It is more like a constitutional than an absolute monarch, which is why the virtues that manage and guide the energies of passion are so important.

Aquinas's moral psychology has sometimes been interpreted and presented as if it were a post-Cartesian psychology, and much effort is often still required to show that such interpretations fail to do justice either to the intellectual context in which he worked or to the distinctiveness of his own account. Herbert McCabe is one of the most important recent interpreters of Aquinas's thought to engage significantly with this set of questions. His work *On Aquinas* includes two important chapters on the interior senses that help to position Aquinas in relation to later 'philosophies of mind'.[8] These chapters show how, for Aquinas, the good life is a passionate life because human goodness requires emotional commitment. The good life is achieved not by the repression of emotion but by emotion guided by virtues. The intimate co-involvement of intellect and will in human action is once again emphasized, as is the importance of the virtue of prudence, or 'good sense', which consists in an intimate co-involvement of sense and sensibility, of the rational and the emotional.

McCabe shows how for Aquinas the virtue of prudence involves the senses, not so much the exterior senses as the four interior senses.

Practical reason requires good dispositions of the interior senses. He disagrees with Anthony Kenny (for whom these are not senses at all) and says that 'a great deal of what post-Renaissance philosophers have attributed to the "mind" as organizing our perceptions of the world is attributed by Aquinas to the interior senses'.[9] For Aquinas, the imagination is always involved in human knowing, which cannot happen without 'turning to phantasms'. In discussing the common sense, McCabe makes interesting links between Gestalt-psychology, the sensitivity of the skin as the organ of the common sense, and Aquinas' view that such sensitivity is linked essentially with intelligence: increased sensitivity means increased awareness and freedom. The common sense coordinates the data of the exterior senses and is also the source of the animal's self-awareness. Descriptions of the effects of LSD, says McCabe, witness to a suppression of the common sense: sensations become interchangeable (seeing sounds and hearing colours), and self-awareness is lost in an experience of merging into the environment. If the body is the metaphysical basis for our individuation, he concludes, the interior senses are the psychological basis of our awareness of individual identity.

A full account of interior sensation requires a consideration also of the 'evaluative sense' and of the sense-memory. Although he might have said a lot more about the interior senses and their contribution to the functioning of prudence, McCabe has at least restored this aspect of Aquinas' philosophical psychology to the agenda of the philosophy of human nature. Because it is about the kind of animal the human being is – one who has not only a lifetime but also a life story, as McCabe puts it – this philosophical psychology is fundamental to Aquinas' understanding of the human being as a moral agent.

Disposition – virtue

The interior principle of human action given significant treatment in *Summa Theologiae* I.II is *habitus*, which we can translate (with Anthony Kenny) as 'disposition'. Aquinas does some fresh thinking about this notion in *Summa Theologiae* I.II qq.49–54. As he writes these questions, he is working his way through a newly acquired Latin translation of Simplicius' commentary on Aristotle's *Categories*, and what he says about dispositions is significantly informed by that earlier text. These questions are of particular interest, therefore, for the history of philosophy, although most readers tend to move quickly to what he has to say about virtues, a particular class of dispositions and the ones of most interest to the ethicist.

Habitus, disposition, is between potentiality and actuality. To have a power or capacity for some action or realization is to have a passive potentiality for it. To perform the action is to actualize it. To have a disposition for that action is to be between pure potentiality and simple actuality: knowing how to speak German or to play the harp does not imply that one need be actually speaking German or playing the harp. Neither does it mean that one must start again from scratch if one wants to speak German or play the harp. The capacity is already developed, and easily made actual, something that is not true where a person has never started on either activity.

For Aquinas, dispositions are necessary where a nature or capacity is other than that to which it is disposed, so that there is a potentiality/ actuality 'gap' to be bridged. This gap may be bridged in a number of ways, because what is in potency can be determined in a variety of ways and to different things, and many factors combine to dispose the subject to one of the things to which it is in potency. 'Because, therefore', he concludes, 'there are many beings whose natures and actions cannot be brought to completion without the presence of many elements which can be combined in various proportions, it follows that it is necessary that there should be such things as dispositions'.[10]

So dispositions belong to the rational powers of the human being, which are not determined to one thing but hold themselves undetermined towards many things. It is by means of dispositions that such powers, poised before a variety of determinations, are actually determined to one thing rather than another.[11] Our desire is inclined to many different things, Aquinas continues, but human life is not possible unless our desire fixes itself on actual goals and purposes. Hence the need, in our will and in other desiring powers, for certain 'inclining qualities', *qualitates inclinantes*, which are called dispositions.[12]

Aquinas considers which powers are capable of 'hosting' dispositions, how dispositions are generated and strengthened, and how they might diminish and be lost. Dispositions are distinguished as good and bad. A good disposition is appropriate to the nature of its agent and a bad disposition is inappropriate to the nature of its agent. Virtues are appropriate to human nature because they are in accordance with reason. Vices are discordant with human nature because they are against reason, *contra rationem*. Aquinas adds a further distinction between human virtue (reason guiding the other powers) and divine or heroic virtue (grace giving human beings a higher 'nature' and enabling them to act in accordance with it). What is in question in either case is determinate good, the good appropriate to a determinate nature.[13]

In thus introducing the notion of virtue, Aquinas appeals to concepts that have always attracted substantial philosophical interest, namely 'nature' and 'reason'. What is worth stressing is how, for Aquinas, the realities to which these concepts refer are not contrasting or contradictory in the case of the human being. Dispositions to activity are not, strictly speaking, innate, he says.[14] Some dispositions seem to be almost innate to human beings – for example, the understanding of first principles (such as 'a whole is greater than its parts') – but their actuation requires stimulation from without. So too the first seeds of common morality seem to be innate, though he adds that this is not disposition in the strict sense. Some individuals may be gifted with certain dispositions or be temperamentally more disposed to some virtues. He counters an objection which depends, he says, on the term 'nature' being understood over against reason and will, for 'reason and will pertain to the nature of the human being'.[15] Thus a disposition to come about partly *a natura* and partly *ab exteriori principio* may still be natural for the human being. There is no easy contrast of reason over against nature, then, just as the artificial is not, *ipso facto*, unnatural.

There has been a revival of interest in virtue ethics in recent decades and Aquinas is well known as a contributor to that tradition. It is a point on which philosophical and theological interpreters of his work may once again differ: is his interest in the notion of virtue purely psychological and philosophical and so a matter on which his ethics may be brought directly into conversation with the work of philosophers before and after him? Or is his real interest the theological question of grace and theological virtue for which his consideration of *habitus* is partly a necessary philosophical prolegomenon, but partly also necessary in order to highlight the difference between 'acquired skills' and 'infused virtues', between the cardinal or political virtues of antiquity and the theological virtues of mediaeval Christendom? Grace and the supernatural already figure in the philosophical questions in which, with Simplicius' help, Aquinas develops his understanding of *habitus*. In his *Quaestiones Disputatae de Veritate*, he says that dispositions are needed when the activity required of a capacity is beyond its natural condition. For human nature to be joined to God in friendship, our affective power requires the *habitus* of charity. When a capacity receives as a passion, *per modum passionis*, what is received is not immanent to the receiver nor does it become a quality of the receiver. But when a capacity receives as a disposition, *per modum habitus*, then what is received is, as it were, 'connatural' with the receiver. A disposition is not easily lost, and the capacity operates promptly, easily and with delight since the effects proceeding from dispositions are 'second nature' to it. The intellectual powers are added to in this way, he says (referring to intellectual virtues), and the rational creature becomes 'mistress of her own activity', prompt to act because it can operate whenever it wishes (referring to moral virtue).[16] Now the elevation of natural capacities by grace is received as disposition rather than as passion. Hence, Paul's highest gifts are described as theological virtues and charity means a real participation by us in God's own power of loving. As any human virtue becomes 'connatural' – so much part of ourselves and our behaviour that it might as well be innate – in a similar way divine or heroic virtue is connatural because it flows from a new level of being, which is in us by grace.

This may seem like an adventitious contamination of moral philosophy by extraneous theological concerns but, once again, it is Aristotle who provides Aquinas with conceptual resources for thinking the issues through. In arguing that the human being cannot attain happiness by his natural powers, Aquinas says that just as nature is not failing us by neglecting to equip us with weapons and clothing, since it gives us reason and hands with which we can get these things, neither is it failing us because it does not give us happiness – 'for this it could not do'. Nature gives us free will, with which we can turn to God that he might make us happy, for, as Aristotle says, 'what we do by means of our friends is done in a sense by ourselves'.[17] As friendship is at the heart of Aristotle's ethics, so charity is the life of that wider communion between God and people which is, for Aquinas, the full human world in which we are called to live, to act and to flourish.

Law

When he considers the exterior principles of human action, Aquinas names just two. God moves us towards the good, instructing us with law and helping us with grace. The devil, a creature infinitely less powerful, seeks to turn us to evil by interfering with human perception, desire and action. It is within his treatment of law that we find the part of Aquinas's moral theory that has generated most interest and controversy: his account of natural law.

On this, Aquinas inherits a wealth of traditions coming from the Bible, from early Greek philosophy and Stoicism, and from civil and canon lawyers. Sophocles' Antigone famously appeals to 'the unwritten, unalterable laws of God and heaven' that cannot be overwritten by human rulers (*Antigone*, lines 546–57). For Cicero, true law is right reason in agreement with nature. There is one eternal and unchangeable law, he says, of which God is the author, promulgator and enforcing judge. This, the *lex gentium*, is valid for all nations and all times. Roman jurists developed the idea of *ius naturale*, natural 'right' or 'law'. Much of the *Corpus Iuris Civile*, the body of civil law systematized under the sixth-century Emperor Justinian, was extracted from the writings of Ulpian, a third-century Roman jurist. For Ulpian, *ius naturale* is 'what nature has taught all animals', whereas *ius gentium* applies only to human beings and is established by custom. Gaius, another Roman jurist, developed the distinction between civil law, *ius civile*, which applied to Roman citizens, and the law of nations, *ius gentium*, which applied to foreigners also and which is established by the natural reason of all humankind. Gratian (fl. 1140 AD) is the most important of the mediaeval canon lawyers. *Lex naturalis* is what is contained in the Law and the Gospels, he says, dictating that each person do to others what he wants done to himself. It has its origins in nature and not in any constitution, and is about rendering justice and administering equality. There are many texts in the Bible that presuppose that people ought naturally to know what is right and wrong: see, for example, *Amos* 5 and *Romans* 2:14–15.

Although he offers a definition of law, *lex*, as a promulgated rational ordering for the common good by one who has responsibility for the relevant community, it is clear that Aquinas uses the term *lex* analogically. Thus, the treatise on law begins with an account of eternal law, *lex aeterna*, and ends with an account of the new law, *lex nova*, which is primarily the grace of the Holy Spirit in the hearts of believers. Between these two theological notions, we find Aquinas's consideration of natural law and of positive laws.

The eternal law is the ordering of creation by the One who has responsibility for it, the plan of divine wisdom as it directs all actions and movements. All things created by God fall under eternal law, and so too all laws are derived from eternal law insofar as they participate in right reason.[18] Natural law is how human beings participate in eternal law. Where other creatures are passive under that law, fulfilling its requirements through instinct, human beings are active under it, and fulfil its requirements intelligently and freely. They participate in providence by providing for themselves and for others.[19] Human beings collaborate as subjects, as persons, in the working out of the divine plan.

So, for Aquinas, natural law has to do with that whereby the human being is distinct from the other animals. Just as the first principle of our speculative reasoning is based on what is – something cannot simultaneously both be and not be, and we see this immediately – so the first principle of our practical reasoning is based on good, understood in Aristotle's sense as 'what all things seek'. So the first command (*praeceptum*) of natural law is that 'good is to be sought and done, evil is to be avoided' (*bonum est faciendum et prosequendum et malum vitandum*).[20]

Reason naturally apprehends as good those things towards which the human being has a natural tendency, and therefore these are to be actively pursued. It apprehends their contraries as bad and therefore to be shunned. The order of precepts in natural law corresponds to that of our natural tendencies: first, towards the good of what we have in common with all beings; second, towards the goods we have in common with other animals; third, towards the good of human nature as rational. These tendencies support a set of secondary precepts of natural law concerning respect for life and its elementary requirements, the coupling of male and female, the rearing of young, living in society, and knowing about God. The interpretation of this account is much disputed. Is the first precept, as Aquinas expresses it, prescriptive in a strict sense, or is it merely descriptive of how in fact practical reasoning is undertaken? If it is thought to be prescriptive in a strict sense, from where does it get its imperative force? How specific can the requirements of natural law become in what is derived from the primary and secondary precepts? Aquinas considers some of these questions but not always with a clarity and rigour to satisfy later philosophers. Thus he contrasts the kind of certainty one can expect from theoretical reasoning with what practical reasoning can offer. Theoretical reason deals with truths that cannot be otherwise and draws particular conclusions from its premises without error. Practical reason deals with contingent matters, the domain of human acts, and although there is some necessity in general principles, the closer we come to the particular, the more mistaken we can be. Something true 'in the majority of cases', *ut in pluribus*, may not apply in a particular case,[21] since the more you descend into the detail, the more the general rule admits of exceptions, so that you have to hedge it with cautions and qualifications. Whether *ut in pluribus* can itself be turned into an absolute principle (i.e. there is no exceptionless norm in ethics – except this one!) is another disputed point. Aquinas merely gives examples of situations where a norm that would usually apply is suspended because of some particular circumstance.

For some, natural law is a general orientation towards morality, which identifies some general values or goods to be pursued and protected. Some believe that Aquinas's account, properly understood, supports concrete moral prescriptions (a traditional view among 'Thomists'). Others believe that it can do so only when supplemented by some other principle or principles. Alan Donagan, for example, says specific moral precepts may be derived from the first precept of natural law through the Kantian notion that the human being exists as an end in himself, one form of the categorical imperative.[22] The 'new natural law theorists' John Finnis and Germain Grisez also believe that Aquinas's account needs to be supplemented. The first principle proposed by

Grisez – *in voluntarily acting for human goods and avoiding what is opposed to them, one ought to choose and otherwise will those and only those possibilities whose willing is compatible with a will towards integral human fulfilment* – includes a reference to choice which is lacking in Aquinas's first precept. The basic human goods they identify are not merely diverse possible fields of action, but together comprise the stuff of integral human fulfilment.[23] They develop an account of what they call 'modes of responsibility' which, added to the first principle of natural law, establish the norms that protect and defend the 'basic human goods' that fulfil persons. John Bowlin argues that this is not an issue at all because such concrete moral prescription is not what Aquinas himself was trying to establish.[24]

Finnis and Grisez are concerned also to interpret and develop Aquinas in such a way that he cannot be accused of the naturalistic fallacy, i.e. an unwarranted move from 'is' to 'ought'. However, a recent study, Lichacz (2010), argues that these concerns are misplaced and that efforts to 'save' Aquinas from this fallacy are unnecessary. Such efforts are not just anachronistic, Lichacz argues, but they inevitably distort the context and meaning of Aquinas's moral theory.[25]

Grace

Aquinas's account of the human being as a moral agent ends with a treatment of grace. In this he may seem to have decisively gone beyond philosophical ethics, but that is a conclusion one ought not to draw too quickly. It is true that with his account of the new law, law becomes grace. Following Augustine, he builds his account of the new law from biblical texts of the Old and New Testaments. Jeremiah 31:31ff. speaks of a new covenant written on human hearts. People will no longer need to be taught about justice and goodness from without, but will be taught interiorly by the Holy Spirit. People will no longer need encouragement to seek justice and goodness through fear of punishment but will be moved to seek them as what they have come most deeply to desire. Many texts in Paul speak of this new law of freedom in which the one who has received the Spirit is attuned to goodness, instinctively recognizing and desiring it.

Philosophers too, however, might well be open to considering such themes as 'luck', 'fortune', 'transcendence' and 'inspiration', themes that are given extensive treatment in Aquinas's moral teaching in relation to 'grace', 'providence', 'the supernatural' and 'the gifts of the Spirit'. For much of this, Aquinas follows explicitly religious and Christian moral thinkers such as Paul, Augustine, Ambrose and Gregory the Great. But even the pagan thinkers he uses, such as Aristotle, Cicero and Seneca, are religious thinkers contributing in important ways to his working out of these themes. Stoic accounts of natural law are theological in the sense that they view that law as an expression of the divine ordering of things. Aquinas's treatment of the gifts of the Holy Spirit is facilitated by comments of Aristotle and others, and may be compared with how contemporary and modern philosophers speak of inspiration and spontaneity in human action. A way of classifying virtues, found in Plotinus and transmitted to the Middle Ages by Macrobius, is known to Aquinas.[26] It distinguishes ascending levels of virtue – political, of the soul being purged, of the purged soul, and exemplar virtue – and although it does not play a significant part in Aquinas's own theory, the kind of natural transcendence it expresses serves as a counterpoint to Aquinas's properly theological ethics.

Conclusion

In modernity, interpreters of Aquinas were keen to present his thought with an eye especially on Kant and Hume. More recently, there has been a fresh appreciation of the historical and theological context in which Aquinas's moral theory is set. The current revival of interest in Aristotle has opened the way for a fresh reception also of Aquinas. Themes such as virtue, passion, prudence, nature, friendship and even grace, which could never be completely ignored by interpreters, are once again at the centre. In highlighting the limitations of modern moral philosophy, thinkers such as Elizabeth Anscombe and Alasdair MacIntyre opened the way for reconsiderations of earlier thinkers, in particular of Aquinas. Among theologians, the increasingly valued work of Servais Pinckaers[27] shows how appreciating Aquinas as, in the first place, a Christian theologian, encourages rather than excludes robust philosophical evaluation of, and engagement with his thought.

Notes

1 Doig (2001).

2 There has been a persistent argument about the interpretation of Aquinas on the twofold end of the human being, natural and supernatural (see, e.g., *Summa Theologiae* I.II q.3, a.8; q.5, a.5; q.62, a.1). The most recent, and comprehensive, consideration of this argument is to be found in Feingold (2010).

3 Valérie Cordonier has been working on *Liber de Bona Fortuna* and is preparing *Ethica Eudemica (fragmenta), Liber de bona fortuna, Translatio Moerbeckana*, which will be volume XXVIII of *Aristoteles Latinus* and is expected in 2012.

4 *Nicomachean Ethics* III, 1 (Penguin translation (2004), pp. 81–2).

5 *Quaestiones Disputatae de Malo* 12,1. See also his view that 'carnality', or the passion of love (*amor*), when it accompanies affection (*dilectio*), is not bad but actually belongs to the 'fervour of charity' (*caritas*): *Quaestiones Disputatae de Veritate* q.26, a.7 ad 7.

6 *Quaestiones disputatae de veritate*, q.26, a.7 ad 3.

7 *Summa Theologiae*, q.24, a.2. There continues to be considerable interest in Aquinas's account of the passions. Among a number of recent books presenting and explaining his thought, Lombardo (2010) is particularly clear and helpful. See also Gondreau (2002), Fritz-Cates (2009) and Miner (2009).

8 McCabe (2008).

9 McCabe, op.cit., pp. 111–12.

10 *Summa Theologiae* I.II q.49, a.4.

11 *Summa Theologiae* I.II q.55, a.1.

12 *Summa Theologiae* I.II q.50, a.5 ad 1.

13 *Summa Theologiae* I.II q.54, a.3.

14 *Summa Theologiae* I.II q.51, a.1.

15 *Summa Theologiae* I.II q.51, a.1 ad 1.

16 *Quaestiones disputatae de veritate* q.20, a.2.

17 *Summa Theologiae* I.II q.5, a.5 ad 1, referring to *Nicomachean Ethics* III.3.

18 See *Summa Theologiae* I.II q.93.

19 *Summa Theologiae* I.II q.91, a.2.

20 *Summa Theologiae* I.II q.94, a.2.

21 *Summa Theologiae* I.II q.94, a.4.

22 See Donagan's paper in Kenny (1976).

23 See Grisez (1983), pp. 134, 184–5, and for the modes of responsibility pp. 189–92, 205–16, 222–3.

24 Bowlin (1999), Chapter 3.

25 Lichacz (2010). Note also the ongoing work of Jean Porter, most recently Porter (2010).

26 *Summa theologiae* I.II q.61, a.5.

27 For Pinckaers' work, see, especially, Pinckaers (1995) and Berkman and Titus (2005). A helpful collection of essays introducing Aquinas's ethics is Pope (2002).

References

Aristotle (2004), *The Nicomachean Ethics* (transl. J. A. K. Thomson and H. Tredennick). London and New York: Penguin Books.

Berkman, J. and Titus, C. S. (2005), *The Pinckaers Reader: Renewing Thomistic Moral Theology*. Washington DC: The Catholic University of America Press.

Bowlin, J. (1999), *Contingency and Fortune in Aquinas's Ethics*. Cambridge: Cambridge University Press.

Doig, J. C. (2001), *Aquinas's Philosophical Commentary on the Ethics: A Historical Perspective*. Dordrecht/Boston/London: Kluwer Academic Publishers.

Feingold, L. (2010), *The Natural Desire to See God According to St. Thomas Aquinas and His Interpreters* (second edn). Ave Maria FL: Sapientia Press of Ave Maria University.

Fritz-Cates, D. (2009), *Aquinas on the Emotions: A Religious-Ethical Enquiry*. Washington DC: Georgetown University Press.

Gondreau, P. (2002), *The Passions of Christ's Soul in the Theology of St. Thomas Aquinas*. Scranton PA: The University of Scranton Press.

Grisez, G. (1983), *The Way of the Lord Jesus, Volume I: Christian Moral Principles*. Chicago IL: Franciscan Herald Press.

Kenny, A. (1976), *Aquinas: A Collection of Critical Essays*. Notre Dame IN: The University of Notre Dame Press.

Lichacz, P. (2010), *Did Aquinas Justify the Transition from 'Is' to 'Ought'?* Warsaw: Instytut Tomistyczny.

Lombardo, N. (2010), *The Logic of Desire: Aquinas on Emotion*. Washington DC: The Catholic University of America Press.

McCabe, H. (2008), *On Aquinas*. London and New York: Burns & Oates Ltd.

Miner, R. (2009), *Thomas Aquinas on the Passions: A Study of Summa theologiae Iallae, 22–48*. New York: Cambridge University Press.

Pinckaers, S. (1995), *The Sources of Christian Ethics* (translated from the third edition by Sr Mary Thomas Noble, O. P.) Washington DC: The Catholic University of America Press.

Pope, S. J. (ed.) (2002), *The Ethics of Aquinas.* Washington DC: Georgetown University Press.

Porter, J. (2010), *Ministers of the Law: A Natural Law Theory of Legal Authority.* Grand Rapids MI: William B. Eerdmans Publishing Co.

5

Hume

Peter Millican

Hume's theory of morals is widely misunderstood and often
unwittingly caricatured, partly because it is subtle and fits
uneasily into popular taxonomies and partly owing to Hume's talent
for the eloquent aphorism, which is easily remembered while the
subtleties are overlooked. Most notorious is the famous statement in
his youthful *Treatise of Human Nature* that

> [r]eason is, and ought only to be the slave of the passions, and can
> never pretend to any other office than to serve and obey them.
> (*T* 2.3.3.4, 415)

This is commonly read as an insistence on the total impotence of
human reason, apparently implying its lack of any jurisdiction over
the principles of action and a consequent moral scepticism or at least
irrationalism:

> I have prov'd,[1] that reason is perfectly inert, and can never either
> prevent or produce any action or affection. . . . Moral distinctions,
> therefore, are not the offspring of reason. Reason is wholly inactive,
> and can never be the source of so active a principle as conscience,
> or a sense of morals. (*T* 3.1.1.9–10, 458)

But Hume is no moral sceptic or irrationalist, and there is plenty else in the *Treatise* to indicate that he sees reason as playing a major role in determining moral principles. To remove any doubt, both of these points were emphasized very clearly when he later composed *An Enquiry Concerning the Principles of Morals*, his favourite work and one that he explicitly insisted should be taken as his authoritative voice[2]:

> Those who have denied the reality of moral distinctions, may be ranked among the disingenuous disputants; nor is it conceivable, that any human creature could ever seriously believe, that all characters and actions were alike entitled to the affection and regard of every one. (*M* 1.2, 169–70)
>
> One principal foundation of moral praise being supposed to lie in the usefulness of any quality or action; it is evident, that *reason* must enter for a considerable share in all decisions of this kind. (*M* App. 1.2, 285)

The overall moral theory of the two works is the same, but their approach and presentation is very different. Book 3 of the *Treatise*, entitled 'Of Morals', aims to place morality within a general theory of the human mind, starting from an analysis of the mind's faculties and contents – notably the passions that drive us – and strongly highlighting theoretical arguments about human motivation. The *Enquiry*, by contrast, starts from an analysis of the moral judgements that Hume observes to be generally accepted, aiming to identify what is common to them. Only then does it turn to morality's place within the human mind, and accordingly the famous theoretical arguments that had appeared in the first section of *Treatise* Book 3 – having been significantly edited and shortened – are relegated to the first 'Appendix' of the later work. Since these arguments are very famous and controversial, giving plenty of scope for interesting critical examination, Hume's moral theory has tended to be discussed overwhelmingly with reference to the *Treatise*. The *Enquiry* has been largely neglected until recently, an unfortunate irony given that Hume's relegation of the famous arguments may well reflect a recognition that some of those arguments, at least as presented in the *Treatise*, are fundamentally defective. To get a faithful overall picture of Hume's moral theory, therefore, we must take account of both works, embellishing the broad and clear strokes of the mature *Enquiry* with the theoretical detail supplied by the *Treatise*, but with a keen eye for differences between the two that apparently indicate changes of mind rather than of approach or emphasis.

Hume's utilitarian virtue ethics

Hume approaches morality not only as a *scientist of human nature*, aiming to understand its 'springs and principles' (*E* 1.15, 14), but also – inevitably – as himself a human being who partakes of that nature. As a human scientist, Hume observes our ubiquitous tendency to praise and censure actions and personal 'characters', and he seeks for the principles that underlie this behaviour. He finds the common thread to be that we generally judge actions according to the character they reveal, and that we judge characters according to their general tendency to be 'useful or agreeable' to the possessor or to others:

> If any *action* be either virtuous or vicious, 'tis only as a sign of some quality or character. It must depend upon durable principles of the mind, which extend over the whole conduct, and enter into the personal character. Actions themselves, not proceeding from any constant principle, have no influence on love or hatred, pride or humility; and consequently are never consider'd in morality. . . . We are never to consider any single action in our enquiries concerning the origin of morals; but only the quality or character from which the action proceeded. (*T* 3.3.1.4–5, 575)
>
> PERSONAL MERIT consists altogether in the possession of mental qualities, *useful* or *agreeable* to the *person himself* or to *others*. (*M* 9.1, 268)

That moral judgement applies primarily to *characters* or mental qualities rather than to *actions* makes this a form of *virtue ethics*. That the distinction between virtues and vices is drawn according to *usefulness* and *agreeableness* (rather than any appeal to divine or ultimate human purposes) makes it a form of *utilitarian virtue ethics*.[3]

There is of course plenty of scope for debate about both of these principles. An act-utilitarian, for instance, would insist that moral judgement applies primarily to individual acts rather than to characters, while a rule-utilitarian or Kantian would judge acts according to their guiding rule or maxim. Likewise, there is scope for disagreement over which mental qualities are appropriately to be classed as 'virtues' or 'vices' – *pride*, for example, has traditionally been viewed by Christians as the primary 'deadly sin', and *humility* as a cardinal virtue, whereas Hume sees 'pride or self-esteem' and 'vanity or the desire of reputation' (*T* 2.2.1.9, 332) as crucial spurs to moral behaviour, a point he emphasizes in the very last paragraph of the *Treatise*:

> [W]ho can think any advantages of fortune a sufficient compensa-
> tion for the least breach of the social virtues, when he considers,
> that not only his character with regard to others, but also his peace
> and inward satisfaction entirely depend upon his strict observance
> of them; and that a mind will never be able to bear its own sur-
> vey, that has been wanting in its part to mankind and society?
> (*T* 3.3.6.6, 620)

He also expresses very similar thoughts at the end of the final section of the *Enquiry* (*M* 9.21–5), where he famously confronts the challenge of the 'sensible knave' who hopes to benefit by appearing moral while secretly taking advantage of opportunities for immoral gain. It is debatable whether Hume has a fully satisfactory answer; indeed, he acknowledges (at *M* 9.23) that someone who is completely unmoved by the desire to view himself as virtuous might well be beyond persuasion. No doubt this is disappointing for anyone who seeks a universally persuasive answer to the question 'Why be moral?' But it does not present any objection to Hume's theory, for it is a sad fact of life that someone who is overwhelmingly self-interested is indeed unlikely to appreciate the richer happiness that typically comes from the 'social virtues' – from genuinely caring about others – and from the shared affection and companionship they make possible. As many philosophers have recognized, at least since Aristotle, an appreciation of the virtues is best achieved by parental example, training and habituation, not by self-interested calculation. It is very plausible to argue that parents, wishing the best for their children, have excellent reason to inculcate *sincere* virtuous desires and affections, since the greatest satisfactions in life are thus made possible. But a person who has already grown up with a purely selfish disposition may well find it impossible to understand how this could be the case, as indeed Hume infers from his famous Copy Principle: 'A man of mild manners can form no idea of inveterate revenge or cruelty; nor can a selfish heart easily conceive the heights of friendship and generosity' (*M* 2.7, 20).[4] Perhaps the best hope for such a person is that habituation of *simulated* concern for others will open the way in time to feelings of *genuine* concern, so that even the 'sensible knave', despite himself, can ultimately develop the empathetic Humean virtues. All this should give pause for thought to those who, under the spell of crude economic theory (and often an even cruder theory of psychology),[5] have been all too ready to pronounce that 'greed is good', without regard either for the psychological health of those brought up with this message or for the social health of a society in which so little encouragement is given even to *present an appearance* of selfless virtue.

The language of morals

It might seem that disputes about the identification of the virtues and vices would be hopelessly intractable, with philosophers simply disagreeing in ways that reflect their differing theories. But Hume begins his *Enquiry* by proposing an ingenious method of resolution, by appeal to the nature of *common language*:

> [W]e shall endeavour to follow a very simple method: We shall analyse that complication of mental qualities, which form what, in common life, we call PERSONAL MERIT: We shall consider every attribute of the mind, which renders a man an object either of esteem and affection, or of hatred and contempt; every habit or sentiment or faculty, which, if ascribed to any person, implies either praise or blame, and may enter into any panegyric or satire of his

character and manners. . . . a philosopher . . . needs only enter into his own breast for a moment, and consider whether or not he should desire to have this or that quality ascribed to him, and whether such or such an imputation would proceed from a friend or an enemy. The very nature of language guides us almost infallibly in forming a judgment of this nature; and as every tongue possesses one set of words which are taken in a good sense, and another in the opposite, the least acquaintance with the idiom suffices, without any reasoning, to direct us in collecting and arranging the estimable or blameable qualities of men. (*M* 1.10, 173–4)

He then begins to build his catalogue of virtues accordingly, starting with 'the benevolent or softer affections', which, 'wherever they appear, engage the approbation and good-will of mankind', as shown by the positive colouring of the words through which they are expressed:

The epithets *sociable*, *good-natured*, *humane*, *merciful*, *grateful*, *friendly*, *generous*, *beneficent*, or their equivalents, are known in all languages, and universally express the highest merit . . . (*M* 2.1, 176)

Hume seems to be on fairly solid ground in his assertion that these words are universally taken as expressions of virtue, though clearly not all would agree that they reach 'the highest merit', Kant being the most conspicuous opponent of this view.[6]

Even if Hume's catalogue of terms is agreed, however, there is a risk that his method of appeal to language might sometimes fail to deliver substantial results. For as Aristotle famously taught, many virtues are associated with complementary vices, lying on a scale with the ideal character placed at a 'mean' between the two extremes. Thus, *courage* is a virtue, *cowardice* and *rashness* both complementary vices, and we can all agree on the colouring of these words, but this does not imply that we will agree on the substantial question of where the ideal 'mean' lies nor where each boundary is crossed between virtue and vice. Aristotle has often been criticized for the vacuity of his 'doctrine of the mean' for precisely this reason, and Hume at least provides a relatively determinate answer:

No quality, it is allowed, is absolutely either blameable or praise-worthy. It is all according to its degree. A due medium, say the PERIPATETICS,[7] is the characteristic of virtue. But this medium is chiefly determined by utility. A proper celerity, for instance, and dispatch in business, is commendable. When defective, no progress is ever made in the execution of any purpose: When excessive, it engages us in precipitate and ill-concerted measures and enterprises: By such reasonings, we fix the proper and commendable mediocrity in all moral and prudential disquisitions; and never lose view of the advantages, which result from any character or habit. (*M* 6.2, 233)

Questions remain about how the various utilities involved are to be assessed, predicted and compared, but Hume's example convincingly illustrates how the appropriate balance – for example, between speed and caution in performing some industrial process – might be judged in particular cases. However, his particular solution in terms of utility, though certainly plausible, is not implied by the agreement in language on which he hopes to base his theory. Someone could agree that *courage* is a virtue, and *rashness* a vice, without agreeing that the boundary between them is to be determined by considerations of utility.

A similar point can be made by returning to *pride*, which Hume again considers as involving something like an Aristotelian mean between extremes[8]:

We shall begin with examining the passions of *pride* and *humility*, and shall consider the vice or virtue that lies in their excesses or just proportion. An excessive pride or over-weaning conceit of ourselves is always esteem'd vicious, and is universally hated . . . (*T* 3.3.2.1, 592)

But tho' an over-weaning conceit of our own merit be vicious and disagreeable, nothing can be more laudable, than to have a value for ourselves, where we really have qualities that are valuable. . . . nothing is more useful to us in the conduct of life, than a due degree of pride, which makes us sensible of our own merit, and gives us a confidence and assurance . . . (*T* 3.3.2.8, 596–7)

Hume is well aware that Christian philosophers such as Aquinas take a far more negative view of pride, and he emphasizes, in a conciliatory tone, the universal consensus that an *appropriate* degree of the passion is entirely acceptable: 'The most rigid morality allows us to receive a pleasure from reflecting on a generous action . . .' (*T* 2.1.7.8, 298–9). Aquinas would indeed agree, since he considers the sin of pride to involve 'an *excessive* desire for one's own excellence which rejects subjection to God'.[9] But this just serves to illustrate how easily agreement *in words* can mask *substantial* disagreement between widely diverging moral systems. If we restrict the words 'pride' and 'vanity' to what we consider to be cases of *excessive* self-regard, then of course we can agree that they denominate vices rather than virtues, but we might still disagree radically about the degree of self-regard that is appropriate.[10] And thus Hume's appeal to the agreed positive (or negative) moral tone of our words for virtues (or vices) gives far less solid evidence of a genuine moral consensus than he sometimes appears to suggest.

The corruptions of religion

All this does not entirely undermine Hume's method, and of course he is well aware that there is plenty of disagreement about moral issues, notwithstanding the established moral tone of much of our language. But the crucial result that he takes from his survey of virtues and vices is that they all plausibly depend on considerations of *agreeableness* and *usefulness*, either to the person who has them or to others. He then appeals to this implicit common standard to provide a criterion for judging alleged virtues and vices, sometimes in a way that rejects the view of them taken by orthodox moralists, especially those inspired by religion:

And as every quality, which is useful or agreeable to ourselves or others, is, in common life, allowed to be a part of personal merit; so no other will ever be received, where men judge of things by their natural, unprejudiced reason, without the delusive glosses of superstition and false religion. Celibacy, fasting, penance, mortification, self-denial, humility, silence, solitude, and the whole train of monkish virtues; for what reason are they every where rejected by men of sense, but because they serve to no manner of purpose; neither advance a man's fortune in the world, nor render him a more valuable member of society; neither qualify him for the entertainment of company, nor encrease his power of self-enjoyment?[11] We observe, on the contrary, that they cross all these desirable ends; stupify the understanding and harden the heart, obscure the fancy and sour the temper. We justly, therefore, transfer them to the opposite column, and place them in the catalogue of vices; nor has any superstition force sufficient among men of the world, to pervert entirely these natural sentiments. A gloomy, hair-brained enthusiast, after his death, may have a place in the calendar;[12] but will scarcely ever be admitted, when alive, into intimacy and society, except by those who are as delirious and dismal as himself. (*M* 9.3, 270)

Section 14 of Hume's *Natural History of Religion*, entitled 'Bad Influence of Popular Religions on Morality', sets out to explain – with examples – why religious people, even when supposedly devoted to the service of a morally perfect God, will typically attempt to win His favour 'either by frivolous observances, by intemperate zeal, by rapturous extasies, or by the belief of mysterious and absurd opinions' (*N* 14.1).[13] Hume's ingenious explanation is that the very qualities which make genuinely virtuous actions desirable in themselves – their agreeableness and usefulness – make them less attractive to the superstitious believer, who wants to find some *distinctive* way of showing devotion to God. Such a believer will therefore be more attracted towards a devotional practice which is either pointless or painful, such as fasting in Lent or Ramadan, or self-flagellation: 'It seems the more purely religious, because it proceeds from no mixture of any other motive or consideration' (*N* 14.6). And for similar reasons, such corrupted morality is likely to be encouraged by priests who see an opportunity for consolidating their influence: 'the more unaccountable the measures of acceptance required by [the divinity], the more necessary does it become to abandon our natural reason, and yield to their ghostly guidance and direction' (*N* 14.8).

Hence Hume accounts for the common observation that religious fervour is often associated not with devotion to genuine morality but rather with appalling crimes and barbarity. And he quotes historians to confirm that in the ancient world, as often in modern times (such as the religious wars of the seventeenth century, or recent terrorist atrocities), '*Those who undertake the most criminal and most dangerous enterprizes are commonly the most superstitious*' (*N* 14.7).[14] Hume points out that monotheism, in particular, is prone to zealous intolerance, enforcing religious conformity to reflect the unity of the deity (*N* 9.3). And his anti-religious animus becomes especially evident in a long footnote to the essay 'Of National Characters' (*Essays* 199–201 n. 3), where he explains how the character and position of clergymen is especially liable to lead them into hypocrisy, ritualism, promotion of superstition and fraud, conceit, intolerance of disagreement and vengeful vindictiveness. He takes it as a commonplace 'that all prudent men are on their guard, when they meet with any extraordinary appearance of religion', while acknowledging that 'probity and superstition, or even probity and fanaticism, are not altogether incompatible'.[15]

A naturalistic account of morality

Hume's moral philosophy has become particularly influential in recent years, inspiring a wide range of thinkers, from emotivists (e.g. A. J. Ayer) and error-theorists (e.g. J. L. Mackie) to 'quasi-realists' (e.g. Simon Blackburn and Allan Gibbard). Some of Hume's appeal derives from the specific detail of his meta-ethics, which we have yet to consider. But much is also due to his position as the greatest pioneer of the project to develop a positive moral theory within a fully naturalistic framework, explaining morality as part of a 'science of human nature' that makes no appeal to religious doctrine and which fits comfortably into the post-Darwinian worldview. Crucial to this is Hume's forthright rejection of religion as the ground of morality, a rejection made all the more emphatic by his insistence that religion – so far from providing even a valuable inducement towards moral behaviour (as then universally taken for granted by Christian apologists) – is frequently a corrupting influence. Similar themes would later be emphasized by Nietzsche, though with the very different aim of *undermining* morality, at least as it is generally understood. But Hume, as we saw earlier, is no moral sceptic, and he seeks a naturalistic explanation of morality which ultimately *vindicates* it as a crucial aspect of the good life, rather than a debunking explanation which dismisses it as a superstitious illusion or conspiracy of the weak.

Nietzsche was writing in the wake of Darwin's *Origin of Species* (1859) and *Descent of Man* (1871), but nevertheless Hume's philosophy – dating from over a century earlier – fits even more comfortably with the modern evolutionary outlook that sees humankind as just one species of animals, set within a natural order that operates according to all-embracing causal laws and without intrinsic purpose.[16] No fewer than three of the six parts of the 1739 *Treatise*,[17] respectively, giving accounts of human *reason, pride and humility*, and *love and hatred*, end with sections devoted to the corresponding features of animals (*T* 1.3.16, 2.1.12 and 2.2.12), while a fourth part, on *the will and direct passions*, omits such a discussion only for the sake 'of avoiding prolixity . . . since nothing is more evident, than that . . . the will and direct passions, as they appear in animals . . . are of the same nature, and excited by the same causes as in human creatures' (*T* 2.3.9.32, 448). As animals among others, we cannot expect nature to make our lives easy, a thought vividly expressed by the character Philo in Hume's posthumous *Dialogues Concerning Natural Religion*:

Look round this universe. What an immense profusion of beings, animated and organized, sensible and active! You admire this prodigious variety and fecundity. But inspect a little more narrowly these living existences, the only beings worth regarding. How hostile and destructive to each other! How insufficient all of them for their own happiness! How contemptible or odious to the spectator! The whole presents nothing but the idea of a blind Nature, impregnated by a great vivifying principle, and pouring forth from her lap, without discernment or parental care, her maimed and abortive children. (*D* 11.13)

Hume sees morality as an adaptation to the situation in which we find ourselves, starting off from the affection and benevolence that we naturally feel towards those close to us. He takes this natural benevolence as an obvious fact and does not present an evolutionary account of its origin. But a great deal of what he says in building the rest of his moral theory on this foundation is extremely congenial to an evolutionary viewpoint.

In the *Treatise*, Hume draws a distinction between *natural* and *artificial* virtues (of which there are echoes in Appendix 3 of the *Enquiry*). Natural virtues, on this account,[18] are qualities of mind that we possess by a natural instinct (e.g. kindness to children, pity for the unfortunate, gratitude to benefactors) and which we also naturally approve of, because they tend to bring immediate good on each occasion of their exercise. Artificial virtues, by contrast, are those 'that produce pleasure and approbation by means of an artifice or contrivance, which arises from the circumstances and necessities of mankind' (*T* 3.2.1.1). Hume's paradigm example of such an artificial virtue is *justice* – by which he means mainly property rights – while others involve promises, government, international law and chastity. It is characteristic of these that they can fail to bring good on specific occasions, and can even cause harm, because their value comes from the overall system of which they are a part:

> A single act of justice is frequently contrary to *public interest*; and were it to stand alone, without being follow'd by other acts, may, in itself, be very prejudicial to society. When a man of merit, of a beneficent disposition, restores a great fortune to a miser, or a seditious bigot, he has acted justly and laudably, but the public is a real sufferer. . . . But however single acts of justice may be contrary, either to public or private interest, 'tis certain, that the whole plan or scheme is highly conducive, or indeed absolutely requisite, both to the support of society, and the well-being of every individual. 'Tis impossible to separate the good from the ill. Property must be stable, and must be fix'd by general rules. Tho' in one instance the public be a sufferer, this momentary ill is amply compensated by the steady prosecution of the rule, and by the peace and order, which it establishes in society. And even every individual person must find himself a gainer, on balancing the account; since, without justice, society must immediately dissolve . . . (*T* 3.2.2.22, 497)

The artificiality of justice is also revealed by the complex rules that property relations typically involve, regarding 'possession acquired by occupation, by industry, by prescription, by inheritance, by contract, &c. Can we think, that nature, by an original instinct, instructs us in all these methods of acquisition?' (*M* 3.41, 201–2). Hume is keen to insist, however, that the artificiality of such rules does not undermine either their moral significance or their essential place in human society:

Mankind is an inventive species; and where an invention [such as justice] is obvious and absolutely necessary, it may as properly be said to be natural as any thing that proceeds immediately from original principles, without the intervention of thought or reflection. (*T* 3.2.1.19, 484)

Thus, Hume believes that morality – though an essential part of human life – is, to a significant extent, *invented* rather than *discovered* (and as we shall see, this even applies somewhat to his 'natural virtues'). Morality starts from our natural instincts but is then refined by thought and reflection into a system whose features – though *actually* dependent on human nature – can easily give the *illusion* of being an independent aspect of reality such as might be divinely created and discoverable through reason. Let us now look a bit more closely at this Humean account of the genealogy of morals.

The genealogy of morals

The *Treatise* discusses the artificial virtues before the natural,[19] whereas the *Enquiry* follows a more logical sequence, starting with Section 2 on benevolence. We have already seen (in § 2 above) how Hume draws attention to the positive colouring of the words '*sociable, good-natured, humane, merciful, grateful, friendly, generous, beneficent*' (*M* 2.1, 176). In pursuit of his general (quasi-)utilitarian strategy,[20] he then goes on to argue – by appeal to common human experience of, and judgement about, these 'softer affections' – that 'the UTILITY, resulting from the social virtues, forms, at least, a *part* of their merit, and is one source of that approbation . . . so universally paid to them' (*M* 2.8, 179).

In Section 3 of the *Enquiry*, Hume moves on to justice, and it is here that we see the germs of an evolutionary account of morality which explains it as starting from family affection and tribal allegiance, then moving out to society more generally. Justice is necessitated by the human situation in which we need to cooperate with other people but are greatly partial to our own interests in preference to theirs. If we had never had a need of others for any of our wants – because nature 'bestowed . . . such profuse *abundance* . . . that . . . without . . . care or industry', we could obtain whatever we wanted, then 'the cautious, jealous virtue of justice would never once have been dreamed of' (*M* 3.3, 184). Likewise, 'the divisions and barriers of property and obligation' would never have been thought of if everyone felt 'no more concern for his own interest than for that of his fellows' (*M* 3.6, 185). Families can exhibit such 'enlarged affections', mutually benevolent to such an extent that – corroborating Hume's theory – 'all distinction of property [is], in a great measure, lost and confounded among them' (*M* 3.7, 185). Another condition for the development of justice is that through cooperation, we can indeed mutually achieve the necessities of life. Thus, in dire emergencies such as 'a city besieged . . . perishing with hunger' or a shipwreck, 'the strict laws of justice are suspended . . . and give place to the stronger motives of necessity and self-preservation' (*M* 3.8, 186). Hume sums up these points by emphasizing again his key theme of utility:

> Thus, the rules of equity or justice depend entirely on the particular state and condition, in which men are placed, and owe their origin and existence to that UTILITY, which results to the public from their strict and regular observance. Reverse, in any considerable circumstance, the condition of men: Produce extreme abundance or extreme necessity: Implant in the human breast perfect moderation and humanity, or perfect rapaciousness and malice: By rendering justice totally useless, you thereby totally destroy its essence, and suspend its obligation upon mankind. (*M* 3.12, 188)

Utility explains our need for cooperation, and the need is sufficiently obvious that it is relatively straightforward to explain, in general terms, how morality – including the artificialities of justice and its rules – is likely to have arisen.

Again Hume starts from the nature of humanity, this time 'that natural appetite betwixt the sexes, which unites them together, and preserves their union, till a new tye takes place in their concern for their common offspring' (*T* 3.2.2.4, 486).[21] From this minimal foundation,

> a family immediately arises; and particular rules being found requisite for its subsistence, these are immediately embraced; though without comprehending the rest of mankind within their prescriptions. Suppose, that several families unite together into one society, which is totally disjoined from all others, the rules, which preserve peace and order, enlarge themselves to the utmost extent of that society; but becoming then entirely useless, lose their force when carried one step farther. But again suppose, that several distinct societies maintain a kind of intercourse for mutual convenience and advantage, the boundaries of justice still grow larger, in proportion to the largeness of men's views, and the force of their mutual connexions. History, experience, reason sufficiently instruct us in this natural progress of human sentiments, and in the gradual enlargement of our regards to justice, in proportion as we become acquainted with the extensive utility of that virtue. (*M* 3.21, 192)

What needs to be explained, in this story, is how people who have already learnt 'some rule of conduct and behaviour' within their immediate family (*M* 3.16, 190), in which their affection and benevolence towards each other is instinctive and strong,[22] can then be induced to extend this rule-respecting behaviour to a progressively wider circle where such natural bonds are far weaker (or even entirely absent). The benefits of cooperation with others are indeed obvious even in a primitive society, whether to combine in dealing with external threats, hunting animals and harvesting crops, or simply recognizing that 'it will be for my interest to leave another in the possession of his goods, *provided* he will act in the same manner with regard to me' (*T* 3.2.2.10, 490). Appealing to promises as the original basis of such cooperation is hopeless, because the 'observance of promises is itself one of the most considerable parts of justice; and we are not surely bound to keep our word, because we have given our word to keep it' (*M* 3.7, 306).[23] Besides, society obviously pre-dates language, and Hume's far more plausible account is in terms of the development of a tacit *convention* whereby we help each other conditionally on observing the other's cooperation: 'Thus two men pull the oars of a boat by common convention, for common interest, without any promise or contract' (*M* App. 3.9, 306, cf. *T* 3.2.2.10, 490). Each knows that the other will stop cooperating if he attempts to 'free ride' by taking advantage without reciprocating, and this mechanism can also extend to instances of cooperation that are not simultaneous, as long as the interactions are foreseen as repeating[24]:

> I learn to do a service to another, without bearing him any real kindness; because I forsee, that he will return my service, in expectation of another of the same kind, and in order to maintain the same correspondence of good offices with me or with others. And accordingly, after I have serv'd him, and he is in possession of the advantage arising from my action, he is induc'd to perform his part, as foreseeing the consequences of his refusal. (*T* 3.2.5.9, 521)

This overall Humean account is far more plausible than stories about rational intuition of moral forms or intrinsic purposes, identification of morality with knowledge of the divine or Kantian respect for law as such, while at the same time being supportive of morality as a valuable institution. Hence, it is not surprising that a variety of contemporary thinkers have seen it as the core of a correct and fruitful account, with potential for enrichment from the insights of evolution, game theory, psychology and the philosophy of language.[25]

Reason, passion and systematization

We saw in Section 2 that, in the *Enquiry*, Hume begins his investigation with a study of the *language* of virtues and vices, looking at our already established institution of moral ascription with the aim of identifying its central unifying feature, namely, the endorsement of *character traits* that are *useful* or *agreeable*.[26] He then goes on to build on this theoretical unity by inviting his readers to adjust their view of those exceptional *supposed* virtues that fail to fit the framework (notably the 'monkish virtues' of celibacy, fasting, penance, mortification, etc.) He thus appeals to systematization as a means of shifting moral perception: when we see the true shape of our overall moral framework, we can be motivated to adjust our outlying judgements to conform to it. This is a clever strategy in a contentious field, using the established consensus enshrined in our very language as a lever of persuasion (though we also saw that this verbal consensus may be less than it initially appears). The order of discussion also ultimately gives Hume a neat way of answering the 'controversy started of late . . . concerning the general foundation of MORALS; whether they be derived from reason or from SENTIMENT' (*M* 1.3, 170):

> One principal foundation of moral praise being supposed to lie in the usefulness of any quality or action; it is evident, that *reason* must enter for a considerable share in all decisions of this kind; since nothing but that faculty can instruct us in the tendency of qualities and actions, and point out their beneficial consequences to society and to their possessor. . . . But though reason . . . be sufficient to instruct us in the pernicious or useful tendency of qualities and actions; it is not alone sufficient to produce any moral blame or approbation. Utility is only a tendency to a certain end; and were the end totally indifferent to us, we should feel the same indifference towards the means. It is requisite a sentiment should here display itself, in order to give a preference to the useful above the pernicious tendencies. This sentiment can be no other than a feeling for the happiness of mankind, and a resentment of their misery; since these are the different ends which virtue and vice have a tendency to promote. Here, therefore, reason instructs us in the several tendencies of actions, and humanity makes a distinction in favour of those which are useful and beneficial. (*M* App. 1.2–3, 285–6)

By *reason* in these contexts, Hume means simply our *cognitive* faculties, by which we discover what is true and what is false.[27] And his argument for saying that reason so understood is insufficient for morality is very straightforward and commonsensical: belief or knowledge of what is the case cannot motivate us unless we *care* about the relevant facts.

In the earlier *Treatise*, Hume follows a very different path, starting from an account of our passions (in Book 2) and then immediately setting out to prove that 'Moral Distinctions [are] not deriv'd from Reason' (title of *T* 3.1.1). Here, he most famously appeals to an argument drawn from Section 2.3.3, 'Of the Influencing Motives of the Will', to the effect that reason *cannot* motivate:

> REASON is the discovery of truth or falshood. Truth or falshood consists in an agreement or disagreement either to the *real* relations of ideas, or to *real* existence and matter of fact. Whatever, therefore, is not susceptible of this agreement or disagreement, is incapable of being true or false, and can never be an object of our reason. Now 'tis evident our passions, volitions, and actions, are not susceptible of any such agreement or disagreement; being original facts and realities, compleat in themselves, and implying no reference to other passions, volitions, and actions. 'Tis impossible, therefore, they can be pronounced either true or false, and be either contrary or conformable to reason. (*T* 3.1.1.9, 458)

Though this argument has been extremely influential, its logic is unclear and its upshot obscure. In particular, although it has commonly been taken to imply that the *products* of reason – namely beliefs – cannot *cause* actions, this is not something that Hume believes.[28] Passions (e.g. desires, hopes and fears) certainly motivate us, but beliefs can do likewise: 'The effect then of belief, is to raise up a simple idea to an equality with our impressions, and bestow on it a like influence on the passions' (*T* 1.3.10.3, 119). And Hume begins his discussion of the 'direct' passions by making clear that the prospect of pleasure and pain, and the belief that these will be the consequences of certain behaviour, are the chief driver of our actions (*T* 2.3.9.1, 7).[29] The famous argument is therefore probably best seen instead as merely expressing a logical taxonomy, dividing the role of *reason* – that is, the discovery of truth or falsehood – from that of *will* – that is, intentional action.[30] It is probably no coincidence that Hume dropped this misleading argument from his recasting both of Book 2 of the *Treatise* (i.e. the *Dissertation on the Passions*) and of Book 3 (i.e. the *Enquiry*).[31]

Another major difference between the *Treatise* and the *Enquiry* is that in the former, Hume provides a sophisticated explanation of our concern for others based on the mechanism of *sympathy*, whereby we literally come to share the feelings of those we encounter by responding to their manifestation of those feelings (T 2.1.11.2–3, 316–17). In the *Enquiry*, he more straightforwardly identifies 'humanity' or 'a fellow-feeling with others' as a clearly observable 'principle in human nature' and implies that his previous attempt to 'resolve it into principles more simple and universal' had been mistaken (M 5.17 n. 19, 219–20).

Nevertheless the themes we have already explored – involving moral language, systematization and the benefits of cooperation – combine powerfully (especially within an evolutionary perspective) to provide such an explanation of our 'moral sentiments'. First, the establishment of morality leads naturally to our judging things from 'a general point of view', since only thus can we consistently converse with (and thus influence and negotiate with) others. Language itself provides a powerful facilitator of such impartiality:

> General language, . . . being formed for general use, must be moulded on some more general views, and must affix the epithets of praise or blame, in conformity to sentiments, which arise from the general interests of the community. . . . Sympathy, we shall allow, is much fainter than our concern for ourselves, and sympathy with persons remote from us, much fainter than that with persons near and contiguous; but for this very reason, it is necessary for us, in our calm judgments and discourse concerning the characters of men, to neglect all these differences, and render our sentiments more public and social. Besides, that we ourselves often change our situation in this particular, we every day meet with persons, who are in a situation different from us, and who could never converse with us, were we to remain constantly in that position and point of view, which is peculiar to ourselves. The intercourse of sentiments, therefore, in society and conversation, makes us form some general unalterable standard, by which we may approve or disapprove of characters and manners. And though the heart takes not part entirely with those general notions, . . . yet have [they] a considerable influence, and being sufficient, at least, for discourse, serve all our purposes in company, in the pulpit, on the theatre, and in the schools. (M 5.42, 228–9)

Since language is our medium of thought, moreover, we shall inevitably find ourselves considering matters in the same terms that we use to converse with others: as Hume points out against the 'sensible knave', it is simply not possible (at least for most of us) to maintain an outward pose that is radically different from our inner orientation. Partly for this reason, the moral outlook – whereby we attempt to take account of others' interests from a general point of view – is usually *in our own interest*. The benefits of mutual cooperation in society are so great that anything which tends to fit us better into such cooperative relationships will – most of the time – be to our advantage: useful to ourselves, as well as to others. Hence evolution, both biological and societal, will naturally lead us genuinely to *care* about others and also about moral considerations such as fairness. So we should not be at all surprised to find that nature has 'hardwired' us to do so to a significant extent.[32] Such hardwiring, together with the evident importance of morality and its enshrinement in our language, helps to explain our common tendency to *objectify* our moral judgements and to see them as part of external reality even though they are not. Hume observes that this tendency towards objectification applies even in aesthetics, where critical discussion and consideration – identification of, and agreement on, desirable and undesirable features, etc. – naturally leads us in the direction of systematization of our language and thought.[33] But in morals, practical utility provides a far stronger force in the same direction. So although morality is not part of the world – the province of objective truth and falsehood – our moral judgement makes it appear to us as though it were:

> Thus the distinct boundaries and offices of reason and of taste are easily ascertained. The former conveys the knowledge of truth and falsehood: The latter gives the sentiment of beauty and deformity, vice and virtue. The one discovers objects as they really stand in nature, without addition or diminution: The other has a productive faculty, and gilding or staining all natural objects with the colours, borrowed from internal sentiment, raises, in a manner, a new creation. (*M* App. 1.21)

This 'new creation' of morality is one of which Hume fully approves, and his 'anti-realism' here is constructive and not part of any debunking exercise.[34] His account of morality fits very plausibly within a scientific framework that shuns postulation of any fanciful extra-sensory realities of divine purposes, moral forms or *a priori* duties. And it shows how morality, in a thoroughly benign form, can make *good* sense without such dubious encumbrances, as an institution of which we likewise can fully approve, as worthy of cultivation both in our own lives and those of our children.

Notes

1 Here, Hume provides a footnote reference back to *T* 2.3.3. See Section 6 below for more on this argument.

2 In his short autobiography 'My Own Life', Hume describes the *Enquiry* as 'in my own opinion . . . of all my writings, historical, philosophical, or literary, incomparably the best' (*MOL* 10). In 1775, he asked his printer William Strahan to affix an 'Advertisement' to the volume of his works containing his two *Enquiries*, *Dissertation on the Passions* and *Natural History of Religion*. In this, he renounces the *Treatise* and ends: 'Henceforth, the Author desires, that the following Pieces may alone be regarded as containing his philosophical sentiments and principles' (*E* Adv, 2).

3 The word 'utilitarian' as applied to moral theories was coined by Jeremy Bentham, but Hume frequently speaks of 'utility', as for example in the title of Section 5 of the *Enquiry*: 'Why Utility Pleases'.

4 What is widely known as Hume's Copy Principle states that 'all our ideas are nothing but copies of our impressions, or, in other words, that it is impossible for us to *think* of any thing, which we have not antecedently *felt*, either by our external or internal senses' (*E* 7.4, cf. *E* 2.5). At *T* 1.1.1.12, Hume describes this as the 'first principle I establish in the science of human nature'.

5 Hume is completely opposed to the psychological egoism that is so frequently presumed by those who praise him – together with his younger friend Adam Smith – as heroes of 'free-market' economics (see note 29 below).

6 Indeed, one of Kant's most implausible suggestions is that an action done from pure benevolence, rather than out of respect for moral duty, lacks any moral worth. The humanity and warmth of Humean morality here seems far more attractive than the relatively puritanical legalism of Kant. Consider whether you would prefer to inhabit a world where everyone treats you with genuine benevolence, naturally empathizing with your pleasures and pains and spontaneously acting accordingly, or a world where people feel no personal concern for you, but all act morally out of undiluted respect for the Moral Law.

7 'Peripatetics' are followers of Aristotle, for example, the mediaeval schoolmen.

8 Shortly after these passages, Hume echoes the Aristotelian thought that proper pride or 'greatness of mind' is an especially central virtue, since 'Courage, intrepidity, ambition, love of glory, magnanimity, and all the other shining virtues of that kind, have plainly a strong mixture of self-esteem in them' (*T* 3.3.2.13, 599–600). Likewise in the *Enquiry*, 'A desire of fame, reputation, or a character with others, is so far from being blameable, that it seems inseparable from virtue . . . and a generous or noble disposition' (*M* 8.11, 265). He later remarks that pride 'may be either good or bad, according as it is well or ill founded, and according to the other circumstances which accompany it' (*M* App. 4.3 n. 66, 314).

9 Quoted (with my emphasis) from Eileen Sweeney, 'Vice and sin', in Pope 2002, 162: 'Pride . . . has a central place in Aquinas's account. Pride is the first sin, the source of all other sins, and the worst sin. He defines pride as an excessive desire for one's own excellence which rejects subjection to God (Ia IIae, q. 162, aa. 1, 5). . . . every sin begins in turning from God and hence all sins begin in pride. . . . the motive for acquiring all the lesser goods one prefers to God is pride, that through them one 'may have some perfection and excellence' . . . (Ia IIae, q. 84, a. 2). . . . In the *Secunda secundae*, Aquinas depicts pride as the original sin'.

10 Note that Hume's own usage of these words also varies, sometimes designating general characteristics and sometimes *excessive* levels of these characteristics (thus risking the false impression that he is contradicting himself). Compare 'self-satisfaction and vanity may not only be allowable, but requisite in a character' (*T* 3.3.2.10, 597) with 'VANITY . . . is so justly regarded as a fault or imperfection' (*M* 8.11, 266). At the beginning of his essay 'Of the Standard of Taste', Hume himself observes that the use of terms that carry a positive or negative flavour can mask substantial differences of judgement, both in aesthetics and morals.

11 Notice that the last four clauses state in turn that the 'monkish virtues' are not useful to the man himself, nor useful to others, nor agreeable to others, nor agreeable to himself.

12 That is, he might be made a saint.

13 Indeed Hume even jokes that 'if . . . a popular religion were found, in which it was expressly declared, that nothing but morality could gain the divine favour; if an order of priests were instituted to inculcate this opinion, in daily sermons, and with all the arts of persuasion; yet so inveterate are the people's prejudices, that . . . they would make the very attendance on these sermons the essentials of religion, rather than place them in virtue and good morals' (*N* 14.3).

14 Compare the comment in the *Dialogues* that 'If the religious spirit be ever mentioned in any historical narration, we are sure to meet afterwards with a detail of the miseries, which attend it' (*D* 12.11).

15 James Boswell reports Hume as saying on his deathbed 'that the Morality of every Religion was bad . . . that when he heard a man was religious, be concluded he was a rascal, though he had known some instances of very good men being religious'. Boswell suggests that Hume may here have been deliberately reversing the then widely accepted principle that unbelievers, lacking fear of divine punishment, are generally immoral.

16 Hume is a *determinist*, believing that everything happens in accordance with universal causal laws; for the relevant texts, see Millican 2010. He is also a *compatibilist*, taking determinism to be entirely consistent with moral responsibility, though his view is distinctive and commonly misunderstood. For excellent discussions, see Russell 1995 and Botterill 2002. Determinism fits very comfortably with Hume's virtue ethics, which judges actions according to the *character* from which they flow. Accordingly, he sees moral judgement as requiring that actions be thus determined by character (*E* 8.28–30, 97–9). Note also that Hume's *sentimentalism* – by basing moral judgements on natural emotions – neatly sidetracks any metaphysical claim to the effect that determinism makes moral judgement inappropriate (*E* 8.34–5, 101–3).

17 Only Books 1 and 2 of the *Treatise* were published in late January 1739, whereas Book 3 did not appear until 21 months later.

18 Hume points out at that the word 'natural' can be understood differently depending on whether it is contrasted with the miraculous, the unusual or the artificial (*T* 3.1.2.7–9, 473–5; *M* App. 3.9 n. 64, 307–8).

19 Justice is discussed in *T* 3.2.1–2 and 6, property rights in *T* 3.2.3–4, promises in *T* 3.2.5, government in *T* 3.2.7–10, international law in *T* 3.2.11 and chastity and modesty in *T* 3.2.12. The natural virtues are considered – far more briefly – in Part 3, specifically 'greatness of mind' in *T* 3.3.2, goodness and benevolence in *T* 3.3.3 and natural abilities in *T* 3.3.4. Note that Hume's analysis of the virtues makes it hard to draw a clear line between so-called *natural abilities* and *moral virtues*, since both are typically useful or agreeable. In Appendix 4 of the *Enquiry*, he develops the argument of *T* 3.3.4 to maintain that this supposed distinction is 'merely verbal'.

20 Recall that Hume is not a classical utilitarian, but a virtue theorist who takes utility to be a criterion of virtue.

21 Such appetites are, of course – though Hume understandably does not say this – very easy to explain from an evolutionary perspective.

22 And, one might add, very easily explicable from a genetic viewpoint, in terms of 'inclusive fitness', whereby one would expect creatures that are capable of discriminating behaviour to evolve to favour those that share their genes. See Dawkins 1989, Chapter 6.

23 Hume expands on this point in *T* 3.2.5, explaining why 'the obligation of promises' must be considered as artificial rather than natural, depending as it does on the existence of society. Once respect for property is established, the value of an institution of promising becomes clear, as in Hume's example of bargaining about mutual help in harvesting crops that ripen at different times (*T* 3.2.5.8, 520–21). But attempting to explain the historical origin of society in terms of some form of promise or social contract is hopeless, as Hume makes clear also in his classic essay 'Of the Original Contract'.

24 This point was famously illustrated by Robert Axelrod's computer experiments on the Iterated Prisoner's Dilemma, in which repetition proves to be the key factor that favours cooperative strategies over the selfish behaviour that dominates the 'one-shot' case. See Dawkins 1989, Chapter 12.

25 See, for example, the books by Binmore, Blackburn, Mackie and Ridley in the 'References' section.

26 Or, of course, both. Hume's fourfold classification of the virtues does not require that a virtue be *exclusively* useful or agreeable, *exclusively* to oneself or others. Virtues can be useful *and* agreeable, to oneself *and* others.

27 See, for example, *T* 3.1.1.9, 458; *M* App. 1.21, 294 and *P* 5.1.

28 It is a central principle of Hume's philosophy that causal relations can be known only through experience and not by any such aprioristic reasoning.

29 However, not all our behaviour is driven by the prospect of personal pleasure and pain, and Hume is no psychological egoist. Various direct passions 'frequently arise from a natural impulse or instinct, which is perfectly unaccountable. Of this kind is the desire of punishment to our enemies, and of happiness to our friends; hunger, lust, and a few other bodily appetites. These passions, properly speaking, produce good and evil . . . or in other words, pain and pleasure . . . and proceed not from them, like the other affections' (*T* 2.3.9.8, 439). This last point hints that the psychological egoist puts the cart before the horse in considering all behaviour to be selfish, since it is typically through the satisfaction of *antecedent* desires (for something other than pleasure) that we derive pleasure. Hume refutes the 'selfish hypothesis' most forcefully in Appendix 2 of the *Enquiry*, and also attacks it in his essay 'Of the Dignity or Meanness of Human Nature'.

30 This distinction is now commonly expressed in terms of 'direction of fit': what Hume calls our *reason* – our *cognitive* faculty – aims to conform our mind (i.e. our beliefs) to the world, whereas the *will* – our *conative* faculty – aims to conform the world to our mind (i.e. our desires).

31 The contrast is especially marked given how conspicuously he presented it *twice* in the *Treatise*. Hume was an acute detector of sophistry, and it seems most likely that he became well aware of the argument's problems.

32 See, for example, Prinz 2006, who usefully surveys recent evidence for a close link between emotion and moral judgement (thus undermining the Kantian claim that rationality – rather than emotion – provides the key). For more details on these issues, see the book by Churchland in the 'References' section. The books by Binmore and Blackburn also stress how natural moral sentiments – by enhancing the sanctions associated with non-cooperation – can play a valuable role in helping to establish the reciprocal altruism that lies at the basis of much moral behaviour.

33 Hume seems rather complacent about the extent to which our judgements can be expected to converge under the pressure of this sort of systematization (especially in his essay 'Of the Standard of Taste', where he deals with aesthetic judgement). He confronts the issue of moral relativism in 'A Dialogue' (effectively a fifth appendix to the *Enquiry*), arguing that the variation in moral attitudes between different cultures can be accounted for in a uniform manner, by appeal to the variability of utility with context.

34 There has been considerable discussion in the scholarly and philosophical literature of the extent to which Hume should be considered a 'projectivist' about morality, and in what sense(s). Such discussions have provoked much interesting philosophy, though they seem unlikely to result in any determinate conclusion given the scarcity of the relevant textual evidence, and the unlikelihood that Hume himself thought through the issues with anything like the same sophistication that we are able to bring to the issue after another 250 years of philosophical development. If Hume were alive today, I think he would be more interested in the scientific exploration of morality than in such subtle philosophical explication of ways of thinking about it.

References

References to Hume's *Treatise* (*T*), *Enquiry concerning Human Understanding* (*E*) and *Enquiry concerning the Principles of Morals* (*M*) provide section and paragraph numbers, followed by page references to the standard Oxford Selby-Bigge editions. Several recent printed editions include both means of reference, and they can also be found on the web editions at *www.davidhume. org*, from which the quotations are taken. These web editions were also used for his *Dialogues concerning Natural Religion* (*D*), in which the page references are to the standard Kemp-Smith edition (Macmillan, 1947). In the case of Hume's *Natural History of Religion* (*N*), *Dissertation on the Passions* (*P*) and various essays (always referenced by name), only paragraph numbers are given: these also are available at *www.davidhume.org*.

Botterill, G. (2002), 'Hume on Liberty and Necessity', in P. Millican (ed.), *Reading Hume on Human Understanding*. Oxford: Clarendon Press, 277–300.

Dawkins, R. (1989), *The Selfish Gene* (new edition). Oxford: Oxford University Press.

Millican, P. (2010), 'Hume's Determinism', *Canadian Journal of Philosophy* 40: 611–42.

Prinz, J. (2006), 'The Emotional Basis of Moral Judgments', *Philosophical Explorations* 9: 29–43.

Russell, P. (1995), *Freedom and Moral Sentiment*. Oxford: Oxford University Press.

Sweeney, E. (2002), 'Vice and sin', in Stephen J. Pope (ed.), *The Ethics of Aquinas*. Georgetown: Georgetown University Press, 51–68.

Recommended reading

Baillie, James, *Hume on Morality* (London: Routledge, 2000) gives a systematic account of Hume's theories of the passions and morality, in both the *Treatise* and the *Enquiry*, in a form that is likely to be especially useful to students working through these texts.

Binmore, Ken, *Natural Justice* (Oxford: Oxford University Press, 2005), written by a prominent economist, explains morality as the solution to a game-theoretic coordination problem, with Hume given credit for finding the solution more than two centuries before others (pp. 8–9).

Blackburn, Simon, *Ruling Passions* (Oxford: Clarendon Press, 1998) is a sophisticated but accessible treatment of morality by one of the foremost moral philosophers in the world today. It covers a wide range of issues, developing a Humean theory towards Blackburn's favoured 'quasi-realist' account of morality.

Churchland, Patricia, *Braintrust: What Neuroscience Teaches Us about Morality* (Princeton: Princeton University Press, 2011) gives a biological explanation of morality in a similar spirit to the Humean account sketched in Sections 5–6.

Leslie Mackie, John, *Hume's Moral Theory* (London: Routledge & Kegan Paul, 1980) provides an excellent philosophical discussion of Hume's theory of morals (as presented in the *Treatise*), placing it within its historical context and stressing the 'error theory' for which Mackie is well-known through his book *Ethics: Inventing Right and Wrong* (London: Penguin, 1977).

Ridley, Matt, *The Origins of Virtue* (London: Penguin, 1997) gives a lively popular discussion of the evolution of morality, with Hume's insight from *T* 3.2.5.9 given prominence in the discussion of the Prisoner's Dilemma.

6

Kant

Ralph Walker

Kant's moral philosophy has sometimes been summarized as 'Duty for Duty's Sake'. Its central requirement is that we should act from a sense of duty: only an act done out of a sense of duty can have genuine moral worth. That is not to say that acts done out of a mistaken idea of duty have moral worth: for Kant, to act out of a sense of duty is to act out of respect for the Moral Law, and the Moral Law is a standard that is objective and independent of us. Adolf Eichmann, at his trial in Jerusalem for Nazi genocide, maintained that he had always lived in accordance with Kantian principles. He meant that he had always tried to do what he believed to be his duty. He took his duty to involve the killing of many innocent people. Kant would have said that he was guided not by duty but by a set of highly inappropriate feelings, themselves no doubt the product of his background. People often fail to see what duty requires and confuse it with what they want to do anyway. Kant considers this only highlights the need to reflect carefully and honestly to see what duty really does require.

The Moral Law is a fundamental principle of reason: of pure practical reason. It binds all human beings, but not because of any contingent facts about human nature. It binds human beings because they are rational, and it equally binds whatever other rational beings there may be. Its status is similar to that of logical laws, which are basic laws of pure theoretical reason; and it is known in the same way, *a priori* – independently of experience. 'We can become aware of pure practical laws just as we are aware of pure theoretical principles, by attending to the necessity with which reason prescribes them to us and to the setting aside of all empirical conditions to which reason directs us' (Kant (1788) V:30).[1] Like the principle of non-contradiction, it is a basic rational principle, one that cannot be derived from anything else. The Moral Law is 'given, as it were, as a fact of pure reason of which we are a priori conscious and which is apodictically certain' (Kant (1788) V:47).

Being a law of practical reason, the Moral Law can motivate us to moral action. That has a further important consequence in Kant's eyes. It means that moral action and moral responsibility require freedom of choice in a very strong sense: the freedom to be moved to action by a purely rational law. Such free choice must be entirely independent of the mechanism of cause and effect that governs the world as it is known to science.

In saying that morality is a matter of practical reason Kant is in agreement with Plato, but in disagreement with Hume. For Hume, reason can only be the slave of the passions, showing us the most effective ways of achieving our ends, our ends themselves being always set by our feelings. The person who for Plato is most blind to the Good uses reason only as the slave of his passions, to work out how best to satisfy his lusts and not to learn what morality requires. Hume denies that reason can tell us about morality at all, and many modern thinkers would agree with him. Kant on the other hand, like Plato, holds that it is through practical reason that we can discern what we ought to do: not just what we should do if we are to achieve a particular aim that we happen to have, but what we morally ought to do – and what aims we morally ought to have. In fact, he distinguishes two kinds of 'imperative' that practical reason lays down for us. There are hypothetical imperatives, the kind that Hume allows, and there are categorical imperatives. Both tell us that we ought to do something, but with hypothetical imperatives the 'ought' is non-moral: it tells us what we ought to do if we are to achieve a given end. Categorical imperatives, on the other hand, command us absolutely, by telling us what morality requires, and morality may very well require that we should override our non-moral aims and inclinations.

Kant says that strictly speaking there is only one categorical imperative. What he means is that there is one basic principle of pure practical reason from which we can derive concrete obligations, themselves categorical imperatives in particular kinds of circumstances. I shall give this basic principle capital letters, and call it the Categorical Imperative in what follows, to distinguish it from the particular specific categorical imperatives that may be derived from it. He formulates this Categorical Imperative in several different ways, but I think the differences are only apparent (though admittedly commentators disagree about this). His initial version of it is 'act only in accordance with that maxim through which you can at the same time will that it become a universal law' (Kant (1785) IV: 421). By a 'maxim' he means a principle of action, roughly what we should call an intention – though this will need refinement in due course. By its 'becoming a universal law', what he means is that it be a universal practice for everyone. So the thought is that if what you are intending to do is all right for you, it must be all right for everyone, and if you can see it would be unacceptable for everyone to do it, it must be unacceptable for you to do it. You should not act on that maxim.

It is because he sees the Moral Law as a requirement of reason that he gives the central place in his moral philosophy to duty, much as Plato, in the *Republic*, gives the central place to having one's actions controlled by the rational part of one's soul. For Kant, to act out of duty is to act in response to what reason demands. He distinguishes, in fact, between acts which have *moral worth* and acts which are merely *right*. Acts which are right are acts that conform to what duty requires, regardless of motive; to be right they do not need to be done *because* they conform to what duty requires. But acts which have moral worth, or which Kant will count as *virtuous*, are those that not only conform to what duty requires, but are also done out of respect for duty: out of respect for the Moral Law. What matters is to be a virtuous person, a person with a good will: one whose controlling will is to act out of respect for the Moral Law, doing what the Moral Law requires *because* that is what it requires. 'Duty is the necessity of an action from respect for law' (Kant (1785) IV:400).

In the *Groundwork of the Metaphysics of Morals*, Kant's most influential work in moral philosophy, he comes close to saying that an action can have no moral worth unless it is done out of respect for the Law and with *no other supporting motive*. He takes the example of someone who at first performs kindly acts because he enjoys it, but who through some catastrophe comes to feel quite differently, and to hate acting kindly. If despite this he still performs a kindly act, 'without any inclination, simply from duty', Kant says, 'then the action first has its genuine moral worth' (Kant (1785) IV:398). This seems to impose a very demanding standard on us: our acts can have moral worth only if we have absolutely no inclination to perform them, and do them from duty alone. In recent years, however, Barbara Herman and others have argued persuasively that Kant cannot mean this.[2] His requirement must be that the motive of duty must be active in determining what one does, but not that it be the sole motivation. Elsewhere, indeed, he stresses the value of cultivating sympathetic feelings, and in the *Groundwork* itself he says that states of character like moderation and self-control are advantageous to the good will, and 'make its work very much easier' (Kant (1785) IV:393). That leaves open the question how *much* influence the motive of duty must have if an action is to have moral worth, and how large a role inclinations and feelings can play. But Kant's view about this may well be very similar to Aristotle's view about practical wisdom (*phronēsis*). It seems to me that practical wisdom – which for Aristotle too provides a *rational* motivation – frequently operates as a second-order motive. The agent has other first-order motives, often supplied by those non-rational dispositions that Aristotle calls 'virtues of character', but the role of practical wisdom is to tell her which of these first-order motives she should act on in a particular circumstance, and to motivate her accordingly. Practical wisdom can act as a first-order motive as well, but it usually works in this second-order way.

People sometimes contrast Kant and Aristotle on the grounds that someone who has Aristotle's 'virtues of character' may act simply from inclinations that she has acquired through habituation or through her natural disposition. This seems sharply different from Kant's saying that an act can count as virtuous only if it is done out of a sense of duty. But if there is a difference here, it is terminological at most; indeed, it is barely even that. For Aristotle makes it clear that someone who acts only from inclinations that are grounded in habit, without practical wisdom in control, lacks 'complete virtue'. One is not fully virtuous if one lacks practical wisdom and acts on feeling alone. In the properly virtuous person, practical wisdom is in control, and practical wisdom is inherently rational.[3]

In a similar way, Plato holds in the *Republic* that the truly virtuous person must have a just soul, one which is controlled by reason. But Kant is firmer than either Plato or Aristotle in assigning primacy to agents' motives for actions and not to the actual consequences of actions. He has no great interest in consequences, and says they can do nothing to affect the value of the good will: the value, that is, of the good intentions of the good agent. 'A good will is not good because of what it effects or accomplishes', rather 'it is good in itself'.

Even if, by some special disfavour of fortune or by the niggardly provision of a stepmotherly nature, this will should wholly lack the capacity to carry out its purpose – if with its greatest efforts it should yet achieve nothing but only the good will were left (not, of course, as a mere wish but as the summoning of all means insofar as they are in our control) – then, like a jewel, it would still shine by itself, as something that has its full worth in itself. Usefulness or fruitlessness can neither add anything to this worth nor take anything away from it. (Kant (1785) IV:394)

As this implies, he is opposed to utilitarians and other consequentialists who regard the value of an action, or of an intention, as deriving from its beneficial consequences or from the likelihood of its having beneficial consequences. Consequences are not what matters. The good will does not derive its value from them. It does not derive it from anything. Kant begins the *Groundwork* with the words 'It is impossible to think of anything at all in the world, or indeed even beyond it, that could be considered good without limitation except a *good will*' (Kant (1785) IV:393).

Consequentialists reply to Kant that they do not see how the good will can have intrinsic value in this way. The value of any kind of will, or any kind of propensity to make one sort of choice rather than another, must ultimately derive from something else – what is achieved. Mill and Bentham take this something else to be pleasure or happiness; Aristotle and many other Greek philosophers take it to be the *eudaimōn* life, the happy or worthwhile life, and find the value of moral action in its contribution to that end. Kant's response is to ask where the value of that something else, that end to be achieved, is itself supposed to come from. One cannot discover the value of things by means of experience: by experience one can find out that certain things are enjoyable or painful, but that is not the same as finding that they are valuable or worthwhile. Painful things can be good, and pleasures can easily be bad and wrong. One can discover value only through reason, and here 'reason by itself and independently of all appearances commands what *ought* to happen' (Kant (1785) IV:408, my italics). In the moral sphere, reason does not reveal to us straightforward facts, as it does in mathematics when it tells us that $2 + 3 = 5$. It tells us what we *ought* to do – in other words, it issues commands. In the terminology used by moral philosophers nowadays, it is prescriptive. Its commands inevitably motivate us, at least to some degree, once we recognize them as such. They do not motivate us so strongly that we automatically act on them: unlike Socrates, Kant thinks moral weakness is common. We know what we ought to do, but we do not do it, choosing rather to follow our own desires. But the commands of reason are a motivating force nonetheless, and because of this prescriptive quality, reason's 'ought'-statements cannot be derived from statements about what is the case.

Hume had also held that one cannot derive an 'ought' from an 'is'. But Hume maintained that conclusions about what we morally ought to do must be based on human sentiments, not on reason. Kant believes that we cannot take that idea seriously, any more than we can take seriously the idea that the laws of logic and mathematics are just human habits of thought. We take these laws to be genuinely objective, and moral obligation likewise. Moreover, Kant argues that Hume and those who think like him cannot account for the *universality* of the Moral Law. The Moral Law applies not just to one or another group of human beings that happen to have similar tastes and interests. It applies so extensively that 'it must hold not only for human beings but for all *rational beings as such*' (Kant (1785) IV:408). Hume, who tries to derive morality from human feelings, gets into real difficulty when he attempts to reconcile the fact that our feelings are strongest for those closest to us, with the fact that we apply our moral judgements equally to everyone, however remote.

For Kant, universality is at the heart of morality. We saw that his initial formulation of the Categorical Imperative effectively says that it cannot be morally acceptable for me to act on a maxim that it would be unacceptable for everyone to act on. My own maxim need not involve any internal contradiction, if I frame my intention as applying just to myself: there is nothing inherently self-contradictory about planning to borrow money on the basis of a lying promise that I never intend to honour (to take Kant's favourite example). But Kant says a contradiction arises as soon as I consider the maxim as if it held universally, as applying not just to me but to everyone, so that everyone acts on it – so that acting on it becomes, as Kant puts it, a 'universal law of nature'. The Categorical Imperative requires me to act only in a way that I can will to be a universal law for everyone. Of course, I can ignore the Categorical Imperative; that would not be the proper course to take, but I can and often do choose to act selfishly, disregarding my duty. If I do, I am not contradicting myself, but I am contradicting what morality requires of me.

His account of how this works is not entirely satisfactory. He suggests the problem is that in making the lying promise I would be doing something that would destroy the practice of promising if everyone were to do the same. But (as has often been pointed out) the same objection would apply to refusing bribes, since if everyone refused bribes the practice of bribery would also be destroyed. The important point seems to be not that a practice would be destroyed but that in the one case a good practice would be destroyed and in the other a bad practice would.

Has Kant overlooked this? Another of his examples suggests his thinking is more complex than has so far appeared. This example concerns the duty to develop one's talents. No practice, like the practice of making and keeping promises, is involved here. There could perfectly well be a world in which people universally neglected their talents and devoted themselves to pleasure instead. Kant recognizes this and even wistfully suggests that life is like this in the South Sea Islands where people let their talents rust and devote themselves 'merely to idleness, amusement, procreation – in a word to enjoyment' (Kant (1785) IV:423). But the problem here, he says, is that nobody can 'possibly *will* that this become a universal law or be put in us as such by means of natural instinct. For, as a rational being, he necessarily wills that all the capacities in him be developed, since they serve him and are given to him for all sorts of possible purposes' (ibid.).

This looks odd. Why should one not want to live in such a state of affairs? A similar problem appears to arise with another of his examples – the duty to help others in need. Again, he says that a world could exist in which people never helped others but that it is impossible to *will* that it should. 'For, a will that decided this would conflict with itself, since many cases could occur in which one would need the love and sympathy of others and in which, by such a law of nature arisen from his own will, he would rob himself of all hope of the assistance he wishes for himself' (Kant (1785) IV:423). Still, might one just not care about that? It may be unusual, or even eccentric, but surely there *are* people who do not care either about helping others or about needing help themselves.

The clue to what is going on here lies in the word 'will'. It is very natural to read it as though it meant 'want'; and indeed Kant, who is never very consistent in his terminology, does sometimes use it in that way. But these passages make sense only if one looks at what he has said about 'will', without drawing much attention to it, a few pages earlier. 'Only a rational being has the capacity to act … in accordance with principles, or has a will. Since *reason* is required for the derivation of actions from laws, the will is nothing other than practical reason' (Kant (1785) IV:412). So to will is not just to want: it is to want *rationally*. The person who wants to neglect her talents, or who does not care about helping or being helped, is not wanting rationally: her wants are not rational wants. So there is indeed a conflict between what a rational being must *will* and these non-rational wants. Similarly, it is rational to want that there be a practice of making and keeping promises, and irrational to want anything that destroys that practice. It is not rational to want that there be a practice of bribery, and not irrational to want its destruction.

But Kant has not yet given us a proper account of what makes a want rational or non-rational. All we have been told is that the Categorical Imperative (and therefore practical reason) requires us to act only on maxims which we could also will to be universal laws, acted on by everyone. It does not just say we should act only on maxims which we could also *want* to be acted on by everyone, or which we should at least be happy to see acted on by everyone. That would be nothing like an adequate account of what morality requires. Not only might somebody be perfectly happy if everyone always neglected their talents or refused to help others but also they might equally welcome a lifestyle in which everyone had property and partners in common – something Kant would not have wished to countenance for a moment. But just for this reason we do not yet know exactly what Kant's initial statement of the Categorical Imperative really amounts to, for the crucial word 'will' requires more to be said about practical rationality if it is to be elucidated.

Many people do interpret him as meaning simply 'want' by the word 'will', but they have difficulty in making sense of the examples as a result; and they have also to admit that the initial formulation of the Categorical Imperative is far from satisfactory on their reading. On the other hand, they would ask why, if Kant is using 'will' as a technical term, he is not more explicit about it. I think any reading of Kant has to recognize that he is not good at setting out his case; his presentation can be distinctly misleading at times. This is particularly true of works designed for a wide readership, as the *Groundwork* was. He was aware that readers found his writings difficult to understand, and he responded by oversimplifying, trying to present his points one by one, without explaining clearly enough what he was doing. He can be careless too. In consequence he has often been misunderstood and has certainly been understood in many different ways. One needs to try to understand him as sympathetically as one can.

Although he never says there is a need to say more about what practical rationality consists in, he goes on to reformulate the Categorical Imperative in ways which appear to be rather different, although he also says that they all amount to the same thing (Kant (1785) IV:436). He does not make it clear how the versions fit together, and this has puzzled people, but it seems reasonable to look to them for some further light on what he has in mind. The formulation that seems most clearly to be adding something substantial (or at least making it explicit) says, 'So act that you use humanity, whether in your own person or in the person of any other, always at the same time as an end, never merely as a means' (Kant (1785) IV:429).

What is it to 'use humanity as an end, never merely as a means'? Kant says little to spell it out. He applies this formulation to his examples, saying that making a lying promise involves treating others as means to one's own ends, and that by failing to develop one's talents one fails to promote humanity as an end in oneself (Kant

(1785) IV:430). However, in a much later (and unfinished) work, *The Metaphysics of Morals*, he says that there are two 'ends which are also duties', and they are '*one's own perfection* and *the happiness of others*' (Kant (1797a) VI:385). In other works he emphasizes that moral action must be directed towards an end which he calls 'the highest good': it must be directed towards producing a state of affairs in which virtue and happiness are jointly maximized in such a way that people are happy in direct proportion to their virtue. This suggests that promoting the perfection of others might be a duty as well as promoting one's own, and that it could be a duty to promote one's own happiness as well. Indeed, Kant does say that it is a duty to promote one's own happiness in those rare conditions under which one is not already sufficiently inclined towards it anyway (Kant (1785) IV:399), and his writings on anthropology and education are full of advice designed to help promote the moral development of children. So one should conclude that 'treating humanity as an end in itself' involves aiming to promote human perfection and happiness together in such a way as to help bring about the highest good. That is what it is *rational* to want.

It may seem puzzling that Kant talks of 'ends' at all or of 'promoting' perfection and happiness. For we saw that he repudiated the view of utilitarians and other consequentialists, that moral value lies in producing some worthwhile result, like the greatest happiness of the greatest number. He insisted that an act's value is unaffected by whether it is successful in producing some outcome: 'Usefulness or fruitlessness can neither add anything to this worth nor take anything away from it' (Kant (1785) IV:394). This was because he saw the source of value to lie *not* in the achieving of an objective but in the good will itself and in the Moral Law which determines its choices. He has not changed position on that. But what the Moral Law requires is that we should *try* to promote perfection and happiness and thereby the highest good. What is of ultimate value is not that we should achieve that or any other aim but that we should strive for it. It is *trying* to achieve that end that has intrinsic worth.

These ideas about the highest good give us some guidance as to what it may be rational for us to want or not to want, but they do not take us as far as we should like. 'Perfection' must primarily be moral perfection, but it must include the perfection of those aspects of humanity – such as our talents and our intellectual capacities – that are conducive to moral perfection. 'Happiness', Kant says, is 'complete well-being and satisfaction with one's condition' (Kant (1785) IV:393), a condition in which one's desires are satisfied as fully as they legitimately can be – which is to say, resolving inconsistencies between one's own desires and discounting desires that would infringe the happiness of other people. Much more detail is needed here, and Kant does little to supply it. We should want to know how conflicts between different people's desires are to be handled, and we should want to know more about what constitutes perfection. Kant's writings on applied moral philosophy are distinctly unhelpful here, for the practical moral advice he gives is very largely that which was standard in his own time, and he fails to relate it satisfactorily to the rational principles of his philosophy.[4] Still, setting that aside, his requirement to treat people as ends in themselves at least points us in a promising direction, even if much work remains to be done.

Some of the specific moral claims he makes seem to be quite inconsistent with the rational requirements of the Categorical Imperative. Late in life he published a paper 'On a Supposed Right to Lie from Philanthropy', in which he argues that it is always wrong to tell a lie. He considers a case in which a murderer asks whether a friend of yours, whom he is trying to kill, is concealed in your house. Is it right to say that the friend is not there – assuming that the murderer will trust you and go away if you do? Kant says it is not right: 'Truthfulness in statements that one cannot avoid is a human being's duty to everyone, however great the disadvantage to him or to another that may result from it' (Kant (1797b) VIII:426). It is this, above all, that has given Kant the reputation of being unduly, even absurdly, rigoristic in his adherence to rigid rules. And this rigorism may seem to be the inevitable consequence of adherence to the Categorical Imperative. To lie to the murderer, Kant appears to think, is to treat him as a mere means – though one might of course argue that not to lie to him is to treat one's friend as a mere means. More plausibly perhaps, going back to the initial formulation of the Categorical Imperative, he may think that the maxim 'I shall tell a lie whenever it suits me' would be no more tenable in universal form than 'I shall make a deceitful promise whenever it suits me' – the practice of truth-telling, and so the practice of communication between people, would disappear if everybody told lies whenever it suited them. Indeed, there is evidence that this is exactly what he does think. But to put it that way is to forget the subtlety of his own original account: a subtlety that the simplistic character of his examples (like the example of the deceitful promise) does much to obscure. For what one has to put into universal form is not just *any* description under which the proposed action may be considered, but the description under which the agent intends it including *all its morally relevant features.* A maxim is '[A] rule that the agent himself makes his principle on subjective grounds' (Kant (1797a) VI:225) – 'the subjective principle of volition' (Kant (1785) IV:401n). So in lying to the murderer your maxim is *not* 'I shall tell a lie whenever it suits me', but 'I shall tell a lie to a murderer if it will save the life of a friend'. And one could be quite rational in willing that everyone should tell lies to murderers under circumstances like these.

Despite writing that unfortunate paper, Kant is sometimes clear about this. In *The Metaphysics of Morals* he includes a place for what he calls 'Casuistical Questions', by which he means questions in which the specific character of the circumstances may make it difficult to know how to assess what one should do. In the *Groundwork*, he argued that the Categorical Imperative ruled out suicide, but in *The Metaphysics of Morals* he raises a Casuistical Question about whether 'a great king who died recently' was wrong to take a fast-acting poison into battle with him to kill himself rather than bring harm to the state (Kant (1797a) VI:423). He leaves it as a question. But the king was Frederick the Great whom he admired immensely. It is at least plain he does not think all cases of suicide are automatically wrong. It is essential to consider the circumstances – to take account of just *what* the agent's maxim is. That is incompatible with adhering rigoristically to simplistic rules.

There is another version of the Categorical Imperative that seems to introduce something new. It says 'every rational being must act as if he were by his maxims at all times a lawgiving member of the universal kingdom of ends' (Kant (1785) IV:438). 'Universal kingdom of ends' may sound strange, but it is just a picturesque way of thinking of a state of affairs in which all rational beings are treated as ends in themselves and are governed by universal laws – the laws of reason by which what is all right for you is all right for everyone. More important here is the conception of every rational being as a *lawmaker*. A will that makes law in this way is, Kant says, 'autonomous'. 'Autonomy of the will is the property of the will by which it is a law to itself' (Kant (1785) IV:440). The concepts of autonomy, and of the will as a lawmaker, can be confusing. It is important to recognize that the autonomous will is the rational will, 'will' in Kant's technical sense, and it is autonomous only insofar as it legislates the Moral Law for itself. To choose anything different would not be autonomy; for Kant, it would be the reverse – heteronomy: allowing oneself to be governed by one's desires and inclinations and not by the objective Moral Law. And the will is a law*maker* only in the sense that it 'legislates for itself' that same objective Moral Law. One might ask: in what sense can it 'legislate', if there is only one Law that can be 'legislated'? The answer is that the rational will adopts the Moral Law and makes it its own, being motivated by that respect for the Law which constitutes the sense of duty, and acting accordingly. So here too Kant is finding a dramatic way to express something we have already met: the prescriptive character of the Moral Law.

By saying people are 'autonomous' only when they rule themselves by the Moral Law, Kant comes to need two different senses in which human agents can be called 'free'. In one sense, we are free only when we are autonomous: in other words, only when we are acting out of respect for the objective Moral Law. In the other sense, we are free when we choose between doing right and doing wrong, or when we choose between alternatives that are morally indifferent.[5] Unfortunately he does not always distinguish clearly between these two senses, at any rate in the *Groundwork*, though he does better later.[6] The first of them may seem strange, but it has a long history. St Paul says that to serve God is perfect freedom; Marxists talk of forcing people to be free, when they don't much want to be. In his later works Kant calls this freedom of *Wille*, freedom of *will* in his technical sense of will. Freedom, in the second and more familiar sense, he calls freedom of *Willkür*, freedom of *choice*. In human beings, who (unlike God) are only imperfectly rational, freedom of *Wille* presupposes freedom of *Willkür*, and it is always up to us to decide whether we shall choose to do what morality requires. All of us, he says, always recognize the Moral Law as providing an incentive for us, and all of us find a different, frequently conflicting incentive in our own desires and inclinations. The question is which of these incentives one subordinates to the other (Kant (1793) VI:36), and this is a matter for our free choice.

Kant maintains that this freedom of choice is quite incompatible with the choice being determined by causal laws. Many people say that to choose freely is simply to choose as one wants to, and that one's wants are determined by physical or psychological factors – determined and in principle predictable. Such people are often called compatibilists, since they claim that freedom of choice is compatible with determinism. Kant holds that a causally determined choice could not be genuinely free. He calls compatibilist free choice 'the freedom of the turnspit', a 'wretched subterfuge' (Kant (1788) V:97, 96). At the same time, however, it creates a serious difficulty for him. For his theoretical philosophy in *The Critique of Pure Reason* commits him to holding that the world as we can know it through science and sense-experience is deterministically governed by causal law, so that every event that occurs is in principle predictable.

His attempts to resolve the apparent contradiction do not appear to get him very far. He says that causal determinism is entirely right at one level, the level of scientific explanation, but that there is another and deeper level at which human choice is always genuinely free and undetermined. This other and deeper level is the level of things as they are in themselves. Here Kant's general metaphysical position impinges directly on his moral philosophy. His 'transcendental idealism' holds that the world of ordinary empirically discoverable things, governed by causal law, is 'empirically real' in that it satisfies all our ordinary criteria for objectivity and reality. It is all that we can properly know about. Yet this familiar world is a world of 'appearances', because it is simply the world as our human cognitive capacities present it to us. It represents our way of seeing an underlying reality, the reality of things as they are in themselves. What things are like in themselves, Kant says, we can never know. The ordinary things that we see, feel and hear around us are empirically real (because they belong to that picture of the world that we ordinarily think of as reality), but ultimately – 'transcendentally' – they are not real but ideal. His solution to the apparent contradiction between freedom and determinism is to say that from an empirical point of view we are indeed determined in all our choices, but from the underlying, transcendental point of view we are nevertheless entirely undetermined and free.

This will not work. If freedom of choice matters for morality, it must be the freedom that allows me to choose to act one way rather than another in a particular, knowable, real-life circumstance that presents itself to me. Either that choice is determined and in principle predictable on the basis of causal law, or it is not. Kant might be suggesting that somehow my unknowable free self – together with all the other unknowable free selves – is in some way responsible for the whole causal series that constitutes the knowable world, and therefore responsible for all the choices that are made. But even if we could make good sense of this it would not place freedom where morality wants it, and where Kant needs it: in the making of specific choices at particular times in particular circumstances.

Since this seems obvious, why does Kant not abandon either the freedom or the determinism? Perhaps he did not know quite what to say. In theoretical philosophy, he found himself intellectually compelled to causal determinism within the world as we can know it; in moral philosophy, he found himself intellectually compelled to the freedom of choice he insists on. He may not have been able to resolve the matter. Alternatively he may have thought that we really do have genuinely free and undetermined choice: that this is the truth about how things are in themselves, specifically the truth about how we are in ourselves. In that case, the everyday world as we ordinarily take it to be must indeed be no more than appearance, and its causal determinism cannot be a genuine reality. I am inclined to think this was his real view, but many passages in his work are hard to reconcile with it.

What matters most is that he should have felt so powerfully compelled to his conclusion that morality requires free choice, as he understands it. It is a consequence of his main theses about morality: that the Moral Law is a rational law and that an action has moral worth only if it is done out of respect for the Law. Moral action must therefore be *motivated* by reason, for 'respect' is not something distinct from the recognition of what the Law requires (Kant (1788) V 75–6). In a deterministic world there can certainly be acts that are in accordance with the law and not motivated by reason: such acts are right, but they do not have moral worth. There is no room in a deterministic world for *reason itself* to act as a motive, and it is only where reason itself is a motive that an act can have moral worth. There is a parallel here with theoretical reasoning, as Kant points out: 'one cannot possibly think of a reason that would consciously receive direction from any other quarter with respect to its judgements, since the subject would then attribute the determination of his judgements not to his reason but to an impulse' (Kant (1785) IV:448). If we are to be influenced by reason – to draw a conclusion or to perform an action *because* it is the rational thing to do – what we do cannot be causally determined, because *reason* is not an element in the world of causes and effects. A computer can be programmed so that it draws the conclusions that reason would approve, but then it is influenced not by reason but by its programme. It acts in accordance with reason, but it is not motivated by reason. When reason convinces us, or when we act out of respect for the Law, we do what we do *because* reason requires it. That 'because' is not the 'because' of causal explanation. Reason itself cannot be a cause in the way that one billiard ball may cause another's motion by hitting it or in the way somebody's remark may cause feelings of anger or panic.

Kant must be right about this. That being so, the view that morality is a matter of reason carries with it a commitment to freedom of choice, as Kant understands it. This might be thought to be an objection to the view that morality is a matter of reason. But then it would equally be an objection to the idea that we (at least sometimes) draw the conclusions we do because reason requires them, given the premises we have. Free choice in this radical sense is a difficult and a controversial idea, as is that of morality as a matter of reason. But despite the shortcomings of his exposition, Kant mounts an impressive case for the two of them together. Where he leaves things unfinished, he leaves an important task for his successors to complete.

Hegel was much influenced by Kant's conception of autonomy. But he criticized his Categorical Imperative as 'empty formalism', abstract and lacking in content. We have seen that this charge is unfair, for it does have content, even in its initial formulation: content that has often been missed because it is built into Kant's conception of what it is to 'will', though it is brought out by the later formulation in terms of promoting rational nature as an end in itself, never merely as a means. This in turn is further explicated in Kant's later writings through the idea of the highest good, the synthesis of perfection and happiness, which it is our duty to promote. Still, it remains true that Kant does not tell us nearly enough about what this involves. So he leaves us with a task here too; a task which has been taken up by many, for the idea of treating rational beings as ends in themselves has become common in ethical thought. But no one, so far, has found an entirely satisfactory way of elucidating it.

Notes

1 References in the text are to the standard edition of Kant's works published by the German Academy of Sciences. Its volume and page numbers are given in the margins of most translations, including *The Cambridge Edition of the Works of Immanuel Kant*, from which the quotations are taken. The relevant volumes are those edited by Gregor (1996) and Wood and di Giovanni (1996).

2 See, especially, Herman (1981).

3 Aristotle, *Nicomachean Ethics* VI, especially Chapter 13.

4 On this, see Louden (2000).

5 Kant is sometimes thought to have denied that there are morally indifferent choices, but he insists that there are, using the choice between beer and wine as an example: Kant (1797a) VI:409.

6 Cf. Kant (1797a) VI:226, and see further Beck (1960), pp.176–81.

References

Beck, L. W. (1960), *A Commentary on Kant's Critique of Practical Reason*. Chicago: University of Chicago Press.

Gregor, M. J. (trans. and ed.) (1996), *Cambridge Edition of the Works of Immanuel Kant: Practical Philosophy*. Cambridge: Cambridge University Press.

Herman, B. (1981), 'On the value of acting from the motive of duty', *Philosophical Review* 90 (1981), 359–82.

Kant, I. (1785), *Groundwork of the Metaphysics of Morals*. Trans. in Gregor (1996). Cambridge: Cambridge University Press.

—(1788), *Critique of Practical Reason*. Tr. in Gregor (1996). Cambridge: Cambridge University Press.
—(1793), *Religion within the Boundaries of Mere Reason*. Tr. in Wood and di Giovanni (1996). Cambridge: Cambridge University Press.
—(1797a), *The Metaphysics of Morals*. Tr. in Gregor (1996). Cambridge: Cambridge University Press.
—(1797b), *On a Supposed Right to Lie from Philanthropy*. Tr. in Gregor (1996). Cambridge: Cambridge University Press.
Louden, R. B. (2000), *Kant's Impure Ethics: from Rational Beings to Human Beings*. Oxford: Oxford University Press.
Wood, A. W. and di Giovanni, G. (1996), *Cambridge Edition of the Works of Immanuel Kant: Religion and Rational Theology*. Cambridge: Cambridge University Press.

Recommended reading

Guyer, P. (2007), *Kant's Groundwork for the Metaphysics of Morals*. London: Continuum.
— an excellent introduction to the *Groundwork* by a leading Kant scholar.
Guyer, P. (ed.) (1998), *Kant's Groundwork of the Metaphysics of Morals: Critical Essays*. Lanham: Rowman & Littlefield.
— a very useful collection of essays.
Herman, B. (1993), *The Practice of Moral Judgment*. Cambridge, MA: Harvard University Press.
— a careful and sensitive interpretation of Kant, frequently very illuminating; includes Herman (1981).
Hill, T. E. (ed.) (2009), *The Blackwell Guide to Kant's Ethics*. Oxford: Wiley-Blackwell.
— a valuable and wide-ranging collection of papers.
Korsgaard, C. M. (1996), *Creating the Kingdom of Ends*. Cambridge: Cambridge University Press.
— Korsgaard is a Kantian Constructivist, which is to say that her interpretation differs from that given here in that she sees it as up to us to construct our values in accordance with certain requirements of rationality.
O'Neill, O. (1989), *Constructions of Reason*. Cambridge: Cambridge University Press.
— O'Neill also provides a Constructivist reading of Kant, along rather different lines from Korsgaard.
Timmermann, J. (2007), *Kant's Groundwork of the Metaphysics of Morals – a Commentary*. Cambridge: Cambridge University Press.

— this is a detailed commentary on the *Groundwork*, clear and helpful but less introductory than Guyer's book or Wood's.

Wood, A. W. (2008), *Kantian Ethics*. Cambridge: Cambridge University Press.

— a clear, readable overview of Kant's ethics in general, not Constructivist but differing from the account above on a number of matters, notably on freedom.

7

Hegel

Kenneth Westphal

Much like Aristotle, Hegel analyses what we commonly distinguish as 'ethics' and 'theory of justice' as integrated aspects of his social philosophy of morals. The title of his main work, *Grundlinen der Philosophie des Rechts, oder Naturrecht und Staatswissenschaft im Grundrisse* (1821; '*Rph*'), requires comment. Hegel's main title is rendered in English as the *Elements of the Philosophy of Right*. Using 'right' to render '*Recht*', however, doesn't translate Hegel's term, which is the German counterpart to the Latin *ius*, 'justice' in its broadest and most basic normative sense, which might be glossed as normative theory of right action. This accords with Hegel's mention of natural law (*Naturrecht*) in his subtitle; traditional natural law theories embraced both ethics and justice. (Hegel confirms his comprehensive use of the term '*Recht*' in his *Encyclopaedia*, § 486.) 'Right action' includes both acting as morality requires and so doing because it is right. Hegel's moral philosophy covers both individual character and criteria of right behaviour. As for Hegel's mention of 'political science' (*Staatswissenschaft*) in his subtitle, he stresses that the 'science' he presents is a rational, normative systematic theory of social life, again construed broadly as life within the modern counterpart to a Greek *polis*, a nation. In sum, Hegel works with the traditional concept of morals (uncommon only to twentieth-century Anglophone ethicists), which embraces both ethics and theory of justice as proper coordinate parts.

Philosophers and political theorists have long been baffled about Hegel's standards, or apparent lack of standards, of political legitimacy. This is one aspect of the broader question, whether, how or how well Hegel justifies normatively his social theory of morals. Hegel claims to explicate and to justify the rational order of a modern Nation State. What, then, would constitute the 'rationality' of such a nation, and how does this purported rationality justify such a nation normatively? The best substantive answer to these questions is Frederick Neuhouser's (2000), who shows that the challenges of deciphering Hegel's views are rewarded 'by the discovery of a social theory that is unsurpassed in its richness, its philosophical rigour, and its insights into the nature of good social institutions' (1).[1] This chapter summarizes some central aspects of Neuhouser's illuminating analysis.[2]

Neuhouser identifies six basic reasons for the contemporary importance of Hegel's social theory:

1   Conceiving freedom only negatively, as lack of restraint, is limited and fails to recognize the rich kinds of freedom now available to us moderns.

2   Only an account of social freedom can respond effectively to the characteristic anomie, alienation and rootlessness many people feel in the face of the powerful forces of the free market.

3   A proper account of the ends of the State requires an understanding of functions and potentials of extant institutions, in particular, their potentials for enabling individuals to develop and lead excellent human lives.

4   Social institutions condition fundamentally the subjectivity of their members, and so must be assessed in terms of how and how well they foster rational individual freedom.

5   The values of individuality and social membership are mutually supporting.

6   Hegel's conception of social freedom helps identify and reconcile many of the apparent differences dividing liberals and communitarians, although Hegel does not side squarely with either view. (14–15)

These are considerable reasons which indicate both how distinctive Hegel's moral philosophy is and how it may address some common deadlocks in modern and contemporary moral philosophy. Hegel's account of the 'rationality' of modern social institutions includes their normative justification and is largely independent of his metaphysics and philosophy of history. Hegel justifies the social institutions of the family, civil society (the realm of industry, commerce and public services) and government by arguing that they are essential to realizing human freedom (4). Hegel's account of freedom involves personal freedom, moral freedom and social freedom. Social freedom is Hegel's most distinctive innovation (5). Hegel's account of social freedom involves an objective aspect: rational laws and institutions must provide social conditions required to realize the freedoms of all citizens, together with a subjective aspect: rational laws and institutions must allow citizens to affirm them as good, because they realize their individual freedom, so that citizens can regard the principles which structure and inform their social involvements as coming from their own wills (6). Hegel ascribes 'freedom' to rational social institutions themselves, though their freedom is achieved only insofar as they realize *individual* freedom.

The general problem addressed by Hegel's account of social freedom is to determine whether or how particular (self-regarding) and universal (other-regarding) wills can harmonize within the individuals who belong to and sustain the social order's three main institutions. To integrate these two aspects of willing, Hegel contends that each of these institutions fosters a distinctive and valuable kind of particular identity, as a family member, as a professional and as a citizen. Individuals can and will work freely for the collective goods of the social groups to which they belong because so doing also expresses particular kinds of identity which they rationally take to be central to who they each are, where these activities generate substantial (not merely instrumental) attachments to others (13). Practical freedom involves acting successfully upon one's self-conception as having a self-determining will as an individual person, as a moral subject and as a member of a rational social order (23). In this regard, Hegel's concept of freedom is much closer to familiar notions of freedom than is often recognized (24).

One basic problem addressed by Hegel's account of freedom is that, though none of us is *sui generis*, freedom requires thorough-going *self*-determination. As human beings, we are ineluctably dependent beings, dependent on both our natural and our social environments. One key to reconciling individual autonomy and human dependence is to show how those upon whom, or that upon which, we depend are not radically foreign; if they are rationally ordered, they contribute to our own individual autonomy (19) and to our self-actualization as free rational beings (22). In view of our natural *in*capacity to act freely (149), Hegel's social theory is designed to show how social institutions develop individuals' capacities for, and facilitate their inherent aspiration to freedom. A second key to reconciling those two aspects of our agency is to recognize how societies transform our basic biological needs into specific needs and desires for the socially available means for fulfilling those needs (168).

Personal freedom is the freedom to pursue one's elective ends. Such pursuit is a form of self-determination simply because one chooses one's own ends to pursue, and how to pursue them. Freedom to choose and pursue one's ends requires social and legal protection to restrict any unjust interference by others. The principles of 'Abstract Right' (Part 1, *Rph* §§34–104), which govern production, exchange and ownership within civil society, serve to define and to protect personal freedom (24). However, exercising personal freedom legitimately also requires not interfering unjustly with others. Understanding what counts as 'unjust interference' and why it ought to be both proscribed and avoided requires richer reflection, and a richer form of self-determination, than is afforded by the pursuit of elective ends. It also requires moral reflection on practical norms and principles of action. Hence, personal freedom must be augmented by moral freedom, which Hegel examines in Part 2, 'Morality' (*Rph* §§105–41).

Moral freedom involves a richer conception of subjectivity, the moral subjectivity involved in evaluating and affirming moral principles which inform one's behaviour, both in respecting others as moral agents and in pursuit of the moral good. A social order which supports moral freedom both encourages and withstands rational scrutiny (26–7). Such a social order must establish, publicize and as needed enforce restrictions on personal freedom required for avoiding unjust mutual interference. Pursuing one's elective ends while recognizing the necessity and legitimacy of such restrictions is a richer and more adequate form of free self-determination than is the simple pursuit of elective ends. Hegel contends, however, that moral subjectivity cannot, by itself, generate a legitimate, non-arbitrary conception of the good. Generating a tenable conception of the good is a collective undertaking.

Hegel's account of morality is fundamentally Kantian. He extols Kant's profound insight into the autonomy of the will (*Rph* §135, Remark), which he adopts at the outset (*Rph* §§5–7). His claim that the Categorical Imperative as such is 'empty' (*Rph* §135, Remark) has been widely misunderstood. Hegel's claim points to a very basic feature of Kant's metaphysical system of practical principles, namely, that their application to human beings requires 'practical anthropology', which Kant mentioned throughout his ethical writings, but relegated to an unwritten 'appendix' to his *Metaphysics of Morals*. Hegel's account of *Sittlichkeit* or 'ethical life' (Part 3, *Rph* §§142–360) provides the required social and practical anthropology to use Kant's principles to assess and, to the extent possible, to justify the institutions of a modern nation, and how they are properly integrated into a rational, normatively justified social order (Westphal 2005).

Social freedom involves consciously participating in social institutions which expressly promote and protect personal and moral freedom, where such participation is itself an act of freedom: once rationally understood, such institutions can be rationally endorsed in a way that allows and encourages participants to affirm the aims, procedures and principles of their social order. In this way, these social institutions contribute to constituting and to specifying individuals' identities as free rational agents. Moreover, social institutions capable of performing these functions are self-sustaining and self-determining in a way that itself counts as free and provides an objective form of social freedom in which individuals participate and through which they recognize each other as free, rational, contributing members (24–35).

Hegel's account of social freedom must show that social freedom is a form of self-determination of the will and that it is properly ascribed to individual members of society (37). Achieving the good of individual members of society is indispensable to society's achieving its primary good, and social institutions are crucial to individuals' developing their individuality (46). Hegel's account of our social life (*Sittlichkeit*) includes a distinctive kind of *social* freedom, a species of practical freedom or freedom of the will which supplements individual and moral freedom (47). This is an additional requirement in Hegel's moral philosophy for the adequacy of social institutions. Fulfilling it entails that individuals are not merely cogs in a social machine (47, 52). Social freedom is an essential human good for individuals independently of any account of them as some sort of vehicle of cosmic spirit (51).

Hegel's account of social freedom develops complementary accounts of 'objective' and of 'subjective' freedom: these are the institutional and individual requirements for full freedom; taken together, they satisfy the requirement that in a rationally ordered society, within which individuals must obey legitimate law, individuals are autonomous (48).[3] The objective components of freedom concern the laws and institutions of a rational social order; the subjective components concern the attitudes and dispositions that individuals have towards those institutions. To be rational, and to be rationally justifiable, social institutions must facilitate and embody individual freedom; to fully realize both objective and subjective freedom, individuals must recognize and affirm the rationality of their social institutions (82–3).[4] Only if these demanding requirements are satisfied can dependent, mutually interdependent individual agents be fully autonomous (84). Consequently, individuals can 'regularly and willingly take the collective ends of social institutions as their own', not merely instrumentally, but as intrinsically valuable forms of social participation. In this way, the 'practical identities' (see below) of individual members of society are 'constituted by and expressed through their social membership' (86–7). These requirements for subjective freedom directly generate a host of requirements for the normative adequacy of social institutions (87).

One aspect of the identity between particular and universal wills is the coincidence, so far as possible, between particular goods and the common good, a coincidence Hegel learnt from Adam Smith (87). However, this coincidence is generally implicit; it is not the explicit aim of individual participants in a market economy (88), at least not until our economic activity is reconsidered as part of our individual and collective social freedom (92). Achieving the common good can often require constraining one's private interests. This can be done freely and voluntarily only if individuals recognize that their activities on behalf of the common good are also intrinsic and fundamental to their own individual good (92). This holds as well of our involvements in the other basic social institutions, the family and the government.

To explicate Hegel's understanding of both the personal and the institutional dimensions of our social involvements, Neuhouser uses the phrase, 'practical identity' (93 f.). On Hegel's view, in our practical activities, we identify first and foremost with our particular roles within various social institutions, as particular members of particular families, as professionals within specific commercial enterprises or as members of other social institutions (e.g. schools, hospitals, public agencies) and as citizens of a specific nation. Our practical identities are thus particular to each of us and serve to individuate and distinguish us from one another; these roles and activities are central to who each of us takes him- or herself to be. Such particular identities are not mere self-conceptions; because they are rooted in our social involvements, our self-conceptions are genuinely instantiated in our lives (95). We can be fully and rationally free only if we can reflect on, examine and (rightly) endorse our social involvements (95). Only in this way can we be fully self-determining or autonomous.

Hegel thus contends that social roles constitute the practical identities of free individual members of society. Social roles, with their attendant involvements with others, furnish us with projects and ends which are fundamental to our engagement with the world, which give meaning and value to our lives and which specify a host of the most fundamental positive obligations we undertake because we define ourselves as having undertaken them. Our very sense of ourselves lies in undertaking and fulfilling these fundamental engagements. Likewise, undertaking and fulfilling these engagements provides each of us with a specific and significant identity as a member of society, as someone of social value and standing; our engagements provide for both social esteem and self-esteem (97–8). Unlike our formal equality before the law, our positive social engagements provide bases for our social recognition as particular individuals. These important particular engagements are not idiosyncratic. They have deep and important social dimensions: they specify our memberships within society, they provide us grounds (when need be) for subordinating our individual interests to the common good and they are integral (not extraneous) to who we as individuals are (99–100). Hence our practical identities as members of a rational social order differ in kind from our abstractly universal identities as persons (rights holders) or even as moral subjects. Nevertheless, our social involvements are of recognizable *kinds*; otherwise, they could not appear in or as social institutions, as members of families, professions or a nation. Hence, they provide rich *shared* identities and substantive interests with other members of society (101). Finally, Hegel argues that these institutions and our institutional engagements are 'universal' in the sense that they admit of full rational justification on the basis of thorough philosophical scrutiny (see below).

A third subjective component of social freedom is that individuals are aware that social institutions exist and are sustained only through the voluntary activities of their members. This is true even though individuals are born into many of the institutions to which they belong, and our elective memberships are conditioned by our social upbringing (102–3). (According to Hegel, individuals and their society are mutually interdependent for their existence and characteristics; neither is primary, neither is more basic than the other; 42, 237.)[5] By recognizing that social institutions exist, are sustained or are reformed only due to our ongoing engagements, individuals can recognize these institutions as their own and as their own product right here and now (103). Social members can thus take pride and satisfaction in seeing their ends and their activities realized presently in the world. This is crucial to genuine self-determination and hence to freedom (104). To the extent that the content of the general institutional will, its aims and requirements, coincides with the content of the wills of individuals, participation in social institutions harmonizes with free individual activity. In this way, individuals can act freely and autonomously within their institutionalized activities (106). Moreover, social members find confirmation of who they are by participating in such institutions because those institutions realize the concrete personal identities of individual members (107).

Social roles are never fully determinate; in participating in them, individuals must interpret those roles and act within them in ways they think best instantiate those roles (108). Hence, working for the 'universal' ends of an institution is also working for one's particular ends as a member of that institution (109). Executing our roles is not self-less; it is self-expressive and self-constitutive. Executing our social roles is thus self-determining in three ways: it is guided by our self-conceptions, it realizes our self-conceptions, and in these ways we constitute ourselves as beings with value (110). Hegel contends that this form of social freedom is a substantial good, which is consistent with and enriches our conceptions of personal and moral freedom.

Hegel's view of our trust or confidence in rationally ordered social institutions has both a cognitive content and a subjective form. The cognitive content of trust is the (justifiable, true) belief that one's fundamental interests are integrated harmoniously with, and facilitated by, the basic institutions of society. This is an aspect of freedom; its absence would jeopardize one's sense of being free (111). The subjective form of trust can range from immediate faith in social institutions to fully grounded comprehension of their rational structure and justification. This latter is a crucial condition for realizing the moral subjectivity of individual autonomy, which requires being obligated only by principles whose rationality one recognizes (112). This requires social institutions to be rationally transparent, not only to philosophers, but also to common citizens (113). (This is a key function of Hegel's account of political representation; see below.)

This strong justificatory requirement stems directly from the demands of rational scrutiny from a universal, moral perspective. The social freedom of ethical life is 'objective' in three senses: it is genuine freedom, it exists in the spatio-temporal world and it exists and is free independently of anyone's consciousness of it. An objectively free social world secures a kind of individual freedom even if individuals fail to recognize it, because rational laws and institutions are objectively free if they are necessary conditions of individual freedom (118). Such institutions are also objectively free if they form a self-regulating, self-reproducing integrated set of institutions that conform to Hegel's philosophical account of a 'self-determining' structure. These two aspects of objective freedom may appear to differ greatly. However, this second aspect of objective freedom is a distinctively Hegelian way of formulating and analysing the first aspect, because this 'objective freedom' of rational social institutions lies in their grounding and facilitating personal and moral freedom (120).

Central to Hegel's claim about the self-regulating and self-reproducing character of rational institutions is that a self-determining social order is a teleologically organized and self-reproducing whole, articulated into specialized, semi-autonomous functional components, whose characteristics and interrelations derive from the single concept of the rational will (122). One aspect of the self-reproduction of social institutions is material: the next generation is raised in the family (*Rph* §§158–81), the supplies for current and future generations are produced and distributed within civil society (*Rph* §§182–256), while these two institutional spheres are coordinated and facilitated by government and legislation (*Rph* §§257–340). However, Neuhouser notes, 'the social world functions only in and through the conscious wills, attitudes, and beliefs of its constituent . . . human beings' (128–9). This fact requires, in part, that individuals be raised in order to fulfil their social roles on the basis of their own understanding and motivation. This requirement can be met only if individual activity directed towards social ends affords more substantial satisfaction than mere self-seeking. This is why social institutions must be so structured that in acting on their behalf, individuals act on their own, not a foreign will. Hence the concern with individual freedom is fundamental to Hegel's conception of the proper ends of society as a whole, and to each of its functional components, that is, specific social institutions (130–31). Indeed, it is essential to a rational social order to reproduce itself in ways that maximize individual freedom. Hence, the systematic and the individual views of society converge in Hegel's account of the rational structure of the modern social order (131).

Hegel's main concern about the three basic institutions of ethical life – namely, the family, civil society and government – is how they function individually and conjointly in order that the social order can reproduce itself. The aim in each case is to determine how, and how effectively, each of these social institutions ineliminably contributes to the material reproduction of society and to the reproduction of the rational autonomy of society's members. Only by fulfilling these aims and functions are social institutions *constitutive* of freedom, are they necessary for the social whole to realize its proper end and are they rationally justifiable (132–3).

Neuhouser shows how the family, civil society and government can be meaningfully aligned with the three aspects of Hegel's account of an intrinsically rational, fully integrated subject, namely: immediate unity, differentiation and mediated unity. Each of these three social institutions involves a kind of social unity, each involves a collective end or relevant kind of general will and each displays a distinctive kind of unity and also distinctive relations among its members (135).

The family (*Rph* §§158–81) exhibits an 'immediate' unity, and its members exhibit 'immediate' interrelations, because the family is based upon and bonded by strong natural feelings of love. This love allows each family member to regard the good of other family members and the good of the family itself as intrinsic to his or her own good. Familial love fosters substantial mutual attachments; these are substantial because they are part, and are recognized to be part of who one *is*; they are partially constitutive of one's identity as a particular individual. Family membership is a profound source of socially shared final ends (135).

Civil Society (*Rph* §§182–256) displays differentiation to the point of 'atomism' (Hegel's term) because people participate in the economy as independent agents who cooperate only in order to satisfy their individual needs. Their relations are merely 'formal' (rather than substantial) because they are guided only by rules of the market. Market rules provide for coordination among individual agents, thus serving the social end of efficiently producing and increasing social wealth, but these features of market activity are not conscious aims or motives of individual agents. In the market, social institutions and other economic agents appear to have merely instrumental value (136). This kind of socially atomized economic activity is partially meliorated by professional corporations (137; *Rph* §§250–56).

The government (*Rph* §§257–340) provides a 'mediated unity' for the social whole, by codifying and enforcing laws designed to coordinate and to further the aims and activities both of the family and of civil society, and by informing citizens through their political representatives about their roles within the social whole and about how legislation aims to facilitate the common good. This enables individuals to experience and embrace their roles as citizens as an important component of their individual, practical identities. In turn, this enables citizens, when needed, to subordinate some of their individual interests to the common good (137). The mediated, substantial unity among the members of the social whole ultimately takes the form of rational legislation – legislation that is rational because it serves, and is recognized to serve the common good (138).

Legislation and the legislative process (*Rph* §§260–320) must be transparent to the public, and legitimate legislation must take into account all basic interest groups, the various associations, communities and corporations within the nation. Only by manifesting this universal (nationwide) scope of legislation and the fundamental aim of serving the common good can the rationale for any piece of legislation – and indeed for the constitution as a whole – be made manifest to citizens at large, who are able to see their own interests represented by their representatives in the legislature. Only in this way can the individual wills of citizens coincide with the universal will of society as a whole, and only in this way can individual citizens recognize this coincidence (139).

Hegel was acutely aware that unregulated markets do not and cannot guarantee comprehensive distribution of social wealth. Though he allows for great disparities of wealth, he insists that all members of society need and deserve a socially relative (not an absolute) minimum level of material well-being in order to act and to be recognized as free rational agents, as full participants within society. One key task Hegel assigns to professional and trade 'corporations' (*Rph* §§250–56) is to tend to the welfare of their individual members during periods of unemployment. However, corporations alone cannot resolve problems of poverty. Hegel's 'public authority' (*Rph* §§230–49) is charged, in part, with ensuring that basic commodities are available to all and with ministering to public health, safety and public works. Hegel was deeply troubled by poverty (*Rph* §241–5) and was unsatisfied with any scheme he considered for its alleviation. Though this is a major setback for Hegel's attempt to demonstrate the rationality of the modern social world, it does not reflect adversely on his basic requirements for a rational social order. Indeed, it highlights one important way in which Hegel's normative social theory provides a basis for rational criticism of extant institutions (172–4).

Hegel's account of the subjective and objective conditions of social freedom has important implications for the relations between individual and collective goods. These relations pertain to the relations between Hegel's social philosophy and familiar forms of liberal individualism. Like liberal individualism, Hegel contends that collective goods of a (rationally organized) group are goods to and for participating individual members. In contrast to liberal individualism, Hegel denies that the good of the social group can contain ends which can be derived only from the interests of their individual members, considered *as individuals* (175–6). One reason Hegel denies such reducibility is that, at least under favourable conditions, individuals can and do find that contributing to attaining collective goods is intrinsically valuable (182). Hegel's position is intricate because he defends three linked theses: (1) social freedom requires that social institutions be self-determining (because they are self-sustaining and rational), (2) individuals within a rational social order enjoy a distinctive kind of *social* freedom, along with personal and moral freedom, and (3) they do this only because a rational social order provides both the subjective and objective social conditions required to foster and achieve these three kinds of individual freedom, each of which is free because it is autonomous, subject to no foreign will (177–9).

In this regard, Hegel's views strike a chord which resonates with communitarianism. However, contrary to communitarianism, Hegel insists that societies are subject to stringent, non-parochial standards of rational acceptability. They must withstand the scrutiny of 'universal' reason, which requires *inter alia* that no collective ends be achieved at the expense of the fundamental interests of individual members in freedom and welfare. Modern individual freedom requires both rich and effective social membership *and* the capacity to reflect and assess as a rational agent in general. This is essential for Hegel's view that collective, ethical life can be fully rational only if it can be rightly affirmed by *moral* subjects.

Hegel's social philosophy does not rest on an account of the basic interests of mutually independent agents nor does it construct from this or any other basis an ideal set of social institutions. Hegel contends that a basically rational social order has already been developed historically. The main point of his social philosophy is to explicate the rationality of the modern social order, so that it can be recognized and affirmed by us. Hence, Hegel addresses his social philosophy to us as individuals capable of exercising rational scrutiny, assessment and, where appropriate, endorsement. To this extent, and in this way, Hegel's social philosophy does and is designed to minister to some of the most important aims of modern political theory, including the social contract tradition. The 'foundations' of Hegel's social philosophy are thoroughly normative (198–201).

Hegel plainly contends that modern freedom is possible only through the host of social involvements reviewed above; freedom can be fully realized only within a rational social order. However, Hegel contends equally that this freedom resides in the wills of individual social members, not merely in the structure of the social whole. Achieving freedom requires that individuals can and do affirm the laws and norms which govern the social participation of all. By choosing, pursuing and identifying with their social roles, individuals develop and achieve their particular self-conceptions and win social standing and recognition. In these ways, individuals find and fulfil themselves through being with others. These forms of self-determination are constitutive of freedom; they are not merely means to it (202). For this reason, too, Hegel denies that the interests of individuals *qua* individuals suffice to account for the rationality of a well-ordered society, because a rationally ordered society achieves goods which are irreducibly collective (203).

Unlike any social contract theory, Hegel's social philosophy holds that the specialization characteristic of civil society justifies distinctive political rights and duties of citizens, depending on their class and roles within civil society (*Rph* §§287–320). All citizens are equally and fundamentally committed to freedom, though their distinctive economic roles distinguish the specific ways in which they achieve specifically political freedom. Civil servants in the government formulate and execute legislation, in consultation with representatives of commercial corporations (in the lower house) and with unelected gentry (in the upper house) who represent the agricultural interests of both landowners and peasants.[6] Because the economic structure of modern society generates these distinctive kinds of group interest, the structure of government must ensure that they are all accounted for in the legislative process. Because of their distinct kinds of social role, members of these various groups require suitable, though distinctive access to the ways in which legitimate law ministers to the common good (206–8). Neuhouser contends that this is the only tenet of Hegel's social philosophy that distinguishes his views from liberalism and that it is a dispensable aspect of his philosophy (205–6).

In contrast to social contract theory, Hegel contends that the government, 'the State' or nation in its political aspect (*Rph* §§273, 276) is fundamentally integral to all other non-political institutions, all of which taken together constitute the whole social order. Hence, the proper ends of political institutions can be defined and understood only in conjunction with these other institutions, and how they jointly serve to realize practical freedom in all its forms (209–10). Hegel's claim that a well-ordered social whole is rational and is an 'absolute end of reason' encapsulates his contention that ethical life realizes freedom by exhibiting the rational structure of the concept, in part by being self-sustaining, by securing the necessary conditions of personal and moral freedom, by enabling individual members to develop their particular identities through their social participation and by enabling individuals to be subject only to their own wills through embracing the general will as their own (210). Furthermore, this internal end of the rational social order is made expressly conscious to all members of society through the publicity of law, the self-prescribed participation of individual members and the full transparency of the ways in which legitimate law serves the common good (211–13).

Appearances to the contrary notwithstanding, the 'absolute authority' that Hegel ascribes to a well-ordered State in fact concerns narrowly circumscribed conditions in which a government can obligate citizens to serve the State as a whole, namely, to respond to military threats (or to natural disasters) that threaten to undermine or to seriously compromise the social whole. Obligations to support the military come first in the form of material support, either in taxes or goods; induction is justified only in extreme exigency. In these matters, Hegel's views accord with standard liberal doctrine. Moreover, Hegel's central thesis that individual freedom can be realized only through rich forms of social participation suffices to justify these obligations without appeal to the alleged 'absolute authority' of the State. Here, too, Hegel advocates an attitude on the part of citizens towards such duties which differs from liberalism, an attitude based on their awe for and pride in their self-sufficient social order. This attitude is based on recognizing the systematic rationality of a well-ordered society, which lies in its coordinated achievement of the various components of the individual and common good specified earlier (218–21).

A common objection to Hegel's social philosophy is that the kind of identification with the social order it requires precludes rational criticism of society. Typically this objection presumes a rigid distinction between 'is' and 'ought', which occludes Hegel's contrary view that it is possible to grasp what something is only by also grasping what it ought to be (and *vice versa*). This jointly factual and normative comprehension is commonplace when assessing individual actions morally; Hegel shows that it also holds for understanding and assessing social institutions. Hegel contends that the social institutions his theory identifies contribute to the development, and facilitate the exercise of moral subjectivity through the varieties of character formation discussed earlier, through securing the basic material and social resources required for reflective rational agency and through structuring and conducting itself only on the basis of principles and laws that moral subjects can recognize as good (225–7). Although his social philosophy safeguards individuals against unjust incursions by others or by the government, Hegel places primary stress on ensuring the transparency to its members of the basic rationality and goodness of the modern social order, to ensure that individual action within that social order can be undertaken on the basis of what individuals understand to be right and good (228–9).

As indicated, Hegel holds that moral autonomy can be achieved and exercised only within a rationally ordered society. The criteria of rational acceptability embedded in Hegel's socially grounded form of moral autonomy involve both formal universalizability and also a substantive conception of the good (237). Hence, the inviolable rights of conscience are respected only on condition that individuals obey principles and laws that they consciously endorse as good, that this endorsement results from their own rational reflection and assessment of these laws from a universal moral perspective, that the principles individuals thus affirm accurately represent the just and the good and that the goodness of these principles or laws derives from how these latter serve the fundamental value intrinsic to human beings, rational self-determination of the will (240).

The kind of self-effacing 'identification' with political society feared by liberals entirely fails to fulfil Hegel's express requirements for genuine moral subjectivity. The kind of 'conscience' Hegel repudiates is an alleged kind of moral intuitionism, which purports to be a *sui generis* source and criterion of norms, while failing to guard against idiosyncrasy or wilful arbitrariness (246–8). In contrast, the kind of 'conscience' Hegel advocates requires rational insight into, and rational justification of, basic norms and principles. Hegel holds, that is, that individuals are to be bound only by laws and norms they themselves endorse, where their endorsement is based in rational reflection and reasoning; the norms they endorse truly represent the right and the good, and the relevant goodness lies in promoting rational self-determination (freedom and autonomy), a good intrinsic to the human will. In turn, these subjective requirements can be fulfilled only in a social order which promotes rational self-determination, which can be rationally justified and which is widely perceived to be justified.

That Hegel's political philosophy allows for, even requires a critique of extant institutions, is reflected in the fact that the social order he advocates is an *idealized* account of what he contends is the rational core of modern political society, an ideal that did not fully exist in his day. Hegel advocates reform based on an internal critique of social institutions, in part because he contends that we are incapable of effective or even a rational critique based on *a priori* schemes for an ideal society. The object of political affirmation, 'identification' or 'reconciliation', in Hegel's view, is not extant institutions as such, but rather the rational core of extant institutions. Hegel's stance regarding dissenting communities (his examples are Jews, Quakers and Mennonites) is a consistent, characteristically liberal position. Hegel holds, namely, that conscientious dissenters are entitled to public criticism of society and to non-compliance with laws which violate their understanding of the right and the good. This right is based on their dignity as moral subjects and can be overridden only by compelling State interests in protecting freedom, or protecting the very existence of the social order. (Hegel insists on equal human and civil rights, in which connection he insists on these rights for Jews, to whom they had been only recently granted in Prussia.)

Unlike some recent communitarians, Hegel denies that the social roles of individuals exhaust their practical identities (244). Hegel recognizes that differing levels of intelligence, differing degrees of exigency on various occasions, together with the basic soundness of well-ordered institutions, permit individuals to act typically as a matter of course, without full-blown moral reflection. There are a variety of appropriate affirmative attitudes towards society and one's social engagements. (Deliberating about whether to feed one's children – in contrast to when or how to feed them – is not rationally commendable, it is morally vicious.) Nowhere does Hegel advocate mindless compliance with social norms; the only forms of conscience he banishes are defective forms in which individual conviction cannot distinguish insight from caprice (246–8). Because reason-giving is a social practice, the rational aspirations of conscientious reflection must take public considerations into account (249).

Instead of beginning with circumstances in which individual reflection might diverge from accepted principles and practices, Hegel's project first articulates the requirements of fully developed moral subjectivity and then considers how the social order can be constituted in order to facilitate individuals' satisfaction of these requirements (251). The first condition a well-ordered society must meet, then, is that it be good, and thus merit reflective acceptability (252). This requires a social order to satisfy the conditions outlined above. Second, the rational well-orderedness of society must be made apparent to its members. Hegel's moral philosophy is his philosophical contribution to such transparency. Hegel's emphasis on reconciliation with social institutions concerns their rational core. This is compatible with social criticism aimed at the reform of extant institutions rather than their radical overhaul (257–8). There is no conflict between reconciliation or identification with the rational core of extant institutions and conscientious criticism directed towards improving them. Indeed, these may be mutually supporting attitudes, so long as extant institutions at least approximate their rational core (259). Hegel opposes radical criticism because he is convinced that modern institutions sufficiently approximate their rational requirements (260–61). If this may no longer seem plausible, it is worth considering the ways in which or the extent to which contemporary social institutions satisfy, fail to satisfy or perhaps work against the roles Hegel assigns to them in contributing to our individual and collective goods, freedoms and autonomy.

Historical events quickly raised, however, the question of radical critique. Two reasons for this may be mentioned briefly. First, following the German defeat by Napoleon at Jena in 1806, Prussian political conservatism was in retreat as liberal reformers gained control of the government. Hegel was called to Berlin in 1818 to aid these reforms. Political conservatism began to recover in 1815 and accelerated as the liberal cabinet ministers aged and as the even more reactionary Friedrich Wilhelm IV succeeded Friedrich Wilhelm III. Hegel saw the worrying political storm gathering, but the Prussian Restoration broke open only after his death, as the prince called the embittered elder Schelling and Schopenhauer to Berlin to 'stamp out Hegelianism root and branch'. (The 'received wisdom' about Hegel's philosophy was promulgated by his bitterest critics, who never bothered much about accuracy.) Second, the Industrial Revolution reached the Continent in the 1840s, causing vast problems of poverty and unemployment, far beyond anything Hegel anticipated. In this context, Hegel's claims that 'the actual is rational' and that political and social reality were converging with their normative actuality appeared as sheer wishful thinking. The class interests driving both the Prussian Restoration and the Industrial Revolution were palpable and exposed the political impotence of normative political theory. In this milieu, Marx began to seek the roots of both political theory and political systems in political economy and the history of economic development.

Notes

1 Otherwise unattributed parenthetical page references in the text are to Neuhouser (2000).

2 For a comprehensive synopsis, from which this one draws, see Westphal (2002).

3 Hegel adopts Kant's account of autonomy, but argues that it does not require Kant's Transcendental Idealism. Hegel's critique of Kant's Categorical Imperative has been widely misunderstood; see Westphal (2005).

4 'Recognize' is a success term; recognizing something requires that something is there to be recognized as being what it is. In the case of normative phenomena (moral actions, justified or justifiable social institutions), this requires that these be as they ought to be, or very nearly so.

5 The mutual interdependence of individuals and society is a basic component of Marx's notion of 'species-being' (*Gattungswesen*).

For a discussion of Hegel's view, see Westphal (2003), Chapter 10.

6 Hegel's model here is England, which at the time was decidedly more liberal than Prussia under Friedrich Wilhelm III.

References

Hegel, G. W. F. (1991), *Elements of the Philosophy of Right*. A. Wood, ed., H. B. Nisbet, trans., Cambridge: Cambridge University Press; abbreviated '*Rph*', cited by main sections (§) or by Hegel's published Remarks (§*n*, Remark).

Neuhouser, Frederick (2000), *The Foundations of Hegel's Social Theory: Actualizing Freedom*. Cambridge, MA: Harvard University Press.

Westphal, Kenneth R. (2002), 'Hegel's Standards of Political Legitimacy'. *Jahrbuch für Recht und Ethik/Annual Review of Law and Ethics* 10: 307–20.

—, (2003), *Hegel's Epistemology: A Philosophical Introduction to the Phenomenology of Spirit*. Cambridge, MA: Hackett Publishing Co.

—, (2005), 'Kant, Hegel, and Determining Our Duties'. In: S. Byrd & J. Joerden eds, *Philosophia Practica Universalis. Festschrift für Joachim Hruschka. Jahrbuch für Recht & Ethik/Annual Review of Law & Ethics* 13: 335–54; rpt. in: D. Knowles, ed., *G. W. F. Hegel* (Aldershot: Ashgate, 2009), 337–56.

Recommended reading

Brooks, Thom, (2007), *Hegel's Political Philosophy: A Systematic Reading of the Philosophy of Right*. Edinburgh: Edinburgh University Press.

Chitty, Andrew, (1996), 'On Hegel, the Subject and Political Justification'. *Res Publica* 2.2: 181–203.

D'Hondt, Jacques, (1988), *Hegel in his Time: Berlin 1818–1831*. Peterborough (Ontario): Broadview Press.

Hardimon, Michael, (1992), 'The Project of Reconciliation: Hegel's Social Philosophy'. *Philosophy and Public Affairs* 21.2: 165–95.

—, (1994a), *Hegel's Social Philosophy: The Project of Reconciliation*. Cambridge: Cambridge University Press.

—, (1994b), 'Role Obligations'. *Journal of Philosophy* 91.7: 333–63.

Knowles, Dudley, (2002), *Hegel and the Philosophy of Right*. London: Routledge.

—, ed., (2009), *G. W. F. Hegel*. International Library of Essays in the History of Social and Political Thought; Aldershot: Ashgate.

Neuhouser, Frederick, (2008), 'Hegel's Social Philosophy'. In: F. C. Beiser, ed., *The Cambridge Companion to Hegel and Nineteenth Century Philosophy* (Cambridge: Cambridge University Press), 204–29.

—, (2011), 'The Idea of a Hegelian "Science" of Society'. In: S. Houlgate and M. Baur, eds, *A Companion to Hegel* (Oxford: Blackwell), 281–96.

Westphal, Kenneth R., (1991), 'Hegel's Critique of Kant's Moral World View'. *Philosophical Topics* 19.2: 133–76.

—, (1993), 'The Basic Context and Structure of Hegel's *Philosophy of Right*'. In: F. C. Beiser, ed., *The Cambridge Companion to Hegel* (Cambridge: Cambridge University Press), 234–69.

—, (1995), 'How "Full" is Kant's Categorical Imperative?' *Jahrbuch für Recht und Ethik/Annual Review of Law and Ethics* 3: 465–509.

—, (2007), 'Normative Constructivism: Hegel's Radical Social Philosophy'. *SATS—Nordic Journal of Philosophy* 8.2: 7–41.

—, (2010), 'Hegel'. In: J. Skorupski, ed., *The Routledge Companion to Ethics* (London: Routledge), 168–80.

Wood, Allen, (1999), *Hegel's Ethical Thought*. Cambridge: Cambridge University Press.

8

Marx

Sean Sayers

Marx was primarily a social theorist, and he wrote very little specifically about ethics, yet he has been responsible for some of the most influential ideas about ethics in the modern world. His criticisms of capitalism and of the human impact of capitalism are widely shared even by those who would reject many aspects of his thought; and the social and historical account of ethics which, I shall argue, is fundamental to his thought, raises issues of relativism that are central to the current discussion of ethics.

These claims are controversial. Indeed, almost everything about Marx's thought is controversial, particularly in the field of ethics. There is disagreement even about whether it involves ethical values at all, and, if it does, about what sort of values these are. Marx himself is to blame for much of this confusion. What he says about the place of ethics in his thought is puzzling and apparently contradictory. On the one hand, he maintains that his approach is that of a social scientist. The primary purpose of his work, he insists, is to understand and explain the nature of the social world (and particularly its present – capitalist – form) and the 'natural laws of its movement' (Marx 1961, 10), rather than to judge it in moral terms or put forward ideal conceptions of how a future society ought to be. Indeed, he applies this approach even to ethical ideas and values themselves, treating them as social and historical products – as forms of 'ideology' – and analysing them accordingly. He explicitly denies that his account of capitalism and his conception of communism rely on an appeal to ethical principles (Marx 1978a, 635–6; Lukes 1985, Chapter 2). On the other hand, it is evident that Marx's writings do not constitute a 'value free' or ethically neutral sort of social theory. They quite explicitly espouse a political outlook and involve a practical commitment to the overcoming of capitalism and creation of an alternative form of society.[1]

It is sometimes argued that Marx adopted an ethical perspective only in his youth, and particularly in his writings on alienation, when he was still strongly influenced by Hegel, but that he breaks with this decisively in his later work. That view was influentially advocated by the French philosopher Louis Althusser (1969). However, the idea that there is a radical discontinuity of this kind in Marx's philosophy has been widely criticized and now has little support. Even Althusser himself came to question it in his final writings, and acknowledged that moral ideas are present throughout Marx's work (Althusser 2006). In short, Marxism involves both a social theory and an ethical outlook, and it seeks to combine these two aspects within a unified whole.[2]

These claims are frequently criticized for being confused and contradictory, particularly by the 'analytical Marxists'[3] who have dominated recent discussion of Marxism in the English-speaking world. Marx's work does involve a critical perspective, they argue, but this cannot derive from a social account of ethics of the kind that Marx claims to hold. If ideas and values are the products of existing conditions, they can only reflect and endorse those conditions. Social criticism must involve appeal to values that transcend them. The social and historical account of values must be abandoned if Marx's social critique is to be upheld. Insofar as Marx is critical of present society – as he clearly is – he must be appealing to transhistorical values, even though he himself explicitly denies this. Various accounts are then given of what these values are supposed to be. For the most part, these repeat the familiar positions of liberal moral philosophy. Either Marxism is interpreted as a form of ethical naturalism that relies on a concept of universal human nature or it is said to appeal to universal standards of justice and right. Both of these approaches reject the social and historical approach that is fundamental to Marxism and attribute to it transhistorical ethical foundations in the manner of Enlightenment liberalism.

Marx's approach is quite different. It involves a historical and immanent form of critique. Marx's philosophy is not drawn from Enlightenment liberal sources, nor does it drop from the skies, it has its origins in Hegel's philosophy, as Marx himself explicitly acknowledges. But this is beyond the deliberately restricted horizons of 'analytical' Marxism, which has had the programme of trying to reinterpret ('reconstruct') Marx without reference to Hegel. Such self-chosen ignorance is not a satisfactory basis upon which to interpret Marx's approach. For Marx follows Hegel (1991) in maintaining that ethical values are social and historical products. They should not be interpreted as abstract principles (*Moralität*) in the manner of Enlightenment philosophy, but rather as forms of 'ethical life' (*Sittlichkeit*), as norms embodied in social institutions and practices. And yet Hegel is also committed to specific ethical values, though of course these are very different to those of Marxism.

The historical approach

According to Marxism, then, ethical values are social and historical products, they do not have a transhistorical source. It is wrong to think that if values are social phenomena, they cannot be critical but must simply endorse the current social order. Actual societies are not monolithic unities, they contain conflicting forces within them. Some of these support the established order, others oppose it. Social reality is contradictory. Negative and critical tendencies exist within it, they do not need to be brought from outside in the form of transcendent values: they are rooted in forces that are present within existing conditions themselves. In this way, Marx's social theory, so far from undermining his critical perspective, provides the basis on which it is developed and justified.

Moreover, as Marx is well aware, this account must also apply to his own values. For Marxism, like any other outlook, is a product of particular social and historical circumstances. Insofar as Marxism is a political outlook, Marx maintains that it expresses the aspirations and interests of the critical forces, the working class of modern industrial society (Marx and Engels 1978b, part 3).

A social account of this sort must answer the charge of relativism, for it appears to imply that Marxism is just one among a number of conflicting outlooks with no better claim to validity than any of the others. How does Marxism respond to this sort of objection?

According to Marx, the social world is not static. The conflicts it contains lead to change. The present order is not fixed and final. Ultimately, it will be superseded by a new and different form of society. Moreover, historical change is not a mere succession of different social systems. It takes the form of a development through stages and involves progress. These Hegelian notions are crucial to the Marxist theory of history and essential to its response to ethical relativism. Historical development is made up of a succession of distinct stages or 'modes of production'. In the West, ancient slave societies were followed by feudalism and then by capitalism. And this is not the end of the story. The conflicts that are an ineliminable feature of the capitalist system will eventually give rise to further historical stages. Marx maintains that capitalism will eventually be succeeded by communism, which itself will go through a process of development.

These different historical stages do not simply replace each other in an arbitrary succession. Each new stage arises on the basis of the previous stage. It provides a resolution of the conflicts of the previous stage and constitutes a progressive change, but the new stage then gives rise to new conflicts and the development continues. Each stage is a necessary part of the overall process, justified for its time and relative to the conditions which it supersedes.[4] But each constitutes only a particular and ultimately transitory stage, destined eventually to perish and to be replaced by a higher and more developed one. In the process of development, the conditions for the emergence of the next stage gradually take shape within the 'womb' of the present. To the extent to which this occurs, present conditions cease to be progressive and become, instead, a fetter and a hindrance to the process of development.

This historical theory provides the basis on which Marx criticizes capitalism and advocates a communist alternative. He regards both in historical terms. He does not attempt to criticize the present system on the basis of universal principles or to spell out a transhistorical ethical ideal of how a future society ought to be. His critique does not appeal to transcendent standards; it is immanent and relative. Relative to the feudal conditions that it replaces, capitalism constitutes a progressive development. From the perspective of capitalist society and the values associated with it, feudal society – with its fixed hierarchy of ranks and privileges, its restrictions on commerce and trade and on personal beliefs and practices – appears oppressive and unjust. However, as the conditions for a higher, communist form of society take shape within it, capitalism in turn becomes a fetter to further development. From the standpoint of this emerging form of society, capitalist social relations in their turn increasingly act as hindrances to human development, and the inequalities they generate appear to be unjust. This standpoint – which comes into being only with the development of capitalist society, and is immanent in it and relative to it – provides the basis for Marx's ethical perspective.

Marx's conception of communism is similarly historical and relative. It does not attempt to envisage an ideal future society on the basis of transcendent ethical notions, either of human flourishing or of justice. For it does not regard communism as the realization of a transhistorical moral ideal, but rather as a concrete historical stage which will eventually supersede capitalism, and which will be the outcome of forces which are at work within present capitalist society.[5] 'Communism is for us not a *state of affairs* which is to be established, an *ideal* to which reality [will] have to adjust itself. We call communism the *real* movement which abolishes the present state of things' (Marx and Engels 1978a, 162).[6]

The concept of progress

The historical account of ethics that I have just sketched relies crucially on the concept of progress. It is often argued that this concept cannot provide a valid basis for ethics. The use of the concept in this way, it is said, violates the fact/value distinction. If the term 'progress' is being used purely factually to mean 'whatever comes next', then it provides no basis for the value that is put on progress. Alternatively, the concept of progress tacitly embodies values, and these values must be justified, but this cannot be done simply on the basis of a factual account of history. Marx is thus accused of confusing facts and values and committing a version of the 'naturalistic fallacy' (Geras 1992).

Marxism is, indeed, a form of naturalism. This is a well-established approach in ethics. As naturalistic moral philosophers from Aristotle on have argued, some facts have evaluative implications – namely, facts about the necessary conditions for human flourishing. More specifically, Marxism is a form of historicism which rejects the dualistic distinction of facts and values which this criticism presupposes.

Marxism is primarily a historical theory, but that is not to say that it is a purely descriptive and explanatory theory on the model of physics or chemistry. It also involves a political commitment to communism; practical ends are integral to it. This is not necessarily fallacious. It is quite possible to combine both a descriptive and an evaluative aspect validly within a single outlook. Medicine provides a familiar example. Medical practice attempts to base itself on a scientific understanding of facts about the working of the body, and yet it is also committed to a practical end: the promotion of health and well-being. This end is not an optional or arbitrary one in medicine; it is not a mere preference on the part of the doctor. Not only is it integral to the practice of medicine (it is enshrined in the Hippocratic Oath ('The Hippocratic Oath' 2003)) but also the end of health is given for medicine objectively, by the human body itself, as *its* end.

Similarly, if Marx is correct in his analysis of capitalism, communism is not merely a subjective preference of communists; it is the objective tendency of history itself; and in adopting it as an end, Marxists are aligning themselves with the movement of history. This involves both a historical judgement and a choice of values. The concept of progress in Marx has *both* a descriptive and an evaluative meaning. Capitalism is not only the stage after feudalism but also a 'higher' and 'more developed' stage than feudalism.

Happiness and the human good

'Higher', in what sense? So far, I have focused on the historical and immanent *form* of Marx's ethical outlook. But to answer this question, we must consider its *content*, we must look at the specific values to which Marx appeals when he criticizes capitalism and advocates communism.

Two opposed approaches have dominated accounts of these values. On the one hand, some locate them in the naturalistic, utilitarian and economic tradition. They maintain that Marx criticizes capitalism on the basis of a notion of universal human nature and that he argues that communism will better promote human flourishing and the human good.[7] Others insist that Marx criticizes capitalism for its exploitation and inequality by appealing to universal standards of justice and right.[8] The same two approaches dominate liberal Enlightenment moral thought. They are often treated as exclusive alternatives, but they need not be. As we shall see, Marx's philosophy involves elements of both, and in this again there are similarities with Hegel.

Marx clearly has a conception of human happiness and the human good. He criticizes capitalism for the way it systematically impoverishes the lives of working people, even while it leads to a massive increase in social productive power. In general, material and economic values quite clearly play a fundamental role in Marx's thought. 'Machinery, gifted with the wonderful power of shortening and fructifying human labour, we behold starving and overworking it. The newfangled sources of wealth, by some strange weird spell, are turned into sources of want' (Marx 1978c). He sees in communism a form of society which will enable people of all classes to develop and flourish more fully.

Development of the productive forces is, for Marx, the main index of historical development. He does not romanticize the simple life. In this respect, he agrees with the outlook of classical political economists and utilitarian thinkers such as Adam Smith, Hume and Bentham. However, Marx's conception of human flourishing is much wider than the narrow economic and utilitarian hedonism of these thinkers. He does not see economic development solely as a means to satisfy the material needs of *homo economicus*. He has a much broader and fuller notion of human nature.

This is developed most explicitly in connection with the concept of alienation and its overcoming in his early writings. Humans are not only creatures of material needs, mere individual consumers, but also active, productive and social beings. Sometimes it is suggested that these ideas are derived from Aristotle (Meikle 1985; Pike 1999), but there is little evidence for that view. Marx seldom refers to Aristotle. Moreover, Aristotle regards material labour as a lowly and despicable activity, whereas for Marx it is, potentially at least, a primary form of satisfaction and fulfilment. Hegel is the most important source for these ideas, as Marx himself acknowledges. Hegel's 'outstanding achievement', he says, is that he 'conceives the self-creation of man as a process . . . he therefore grasps the nature of *labour* and comprehends objective man – true, because real man – as the result of his own labour' (Marx 1975, 386).

These ideas are embodied in Marx's claim that the human being is a 'species being' (*Gattungswesen*). The immediate roots of this notion are in Feuerbach's philosophy, where the term condenses a variety of ideas about human nature in a rather cloudy way. The ideas of conscious, free, universal (i.e. rational), social and productive being are all contained in it (Feuerbach 1957, 1–4). The notion is a direct descendant of the Hegelian idea of 'spirit' (*Geist*) which also combines these elements. Our species being is our distinctively human being. According to Marx, this consists in the fact that we are conscious, active, universal, productive and social beings. Conscious social productive activity is our 'species activity', which distinguishes us from other animals.

> The practical creation of an *objective world*, *fashioning* of organic nature is proof that man is a conscious species-being . . . It is true that other animals also produce . . . But they produce . . . one-sidedly, while man produces universally, they produce only when immediate physical need compels them to do so, while man produces even when he is free from physical need and truly produces only in freedom from such need (Marx 1975, 328–9)

Although Marx used the term 'species being' for only a brief period in 1844, the ideas it embodies remain fundamental to his thought. It implies an account of human nature and of the role of work in human life very different to the utilitarian views of the classical economists. Productive activity need not be unpleasant toil, a mere means to the end of satisfying our material consumer needs. Human beings get satisfaction from actively shaping and forming the world and seeing their powers objectified and confirmed in the product. We gain satisfaction from exercising our powers and being productive (Sayers 2011, Chapter 2).

This thought, inherited from Hegel and Feuerbach, is taken up and developed by Marx as the basis for a moral critique of capitalist society. Our productive activity, instead of being a source of fulfilment, has been made into hated toil. Similarly, modern technology constitutes enormous developments of human social productive and creative capabilities. We should be able to recognize and affirm it as the expression of our power and find realization in and through it. But for the most part we do not do so. Rather, it often seems to be an independent and hostile force, out of our control and working against us. To describe this situation, Marx uses the graphic image of a Genie that we ourselves have summoned up but which, 'by some strange weird spell' (Marx 1978c), has now become an alien and malignant power. This need not, should not and, in future society, will not be the way in which we relate to our own products and powers, Marx argues. This is the critical force of the concept of alienation and a fundamental part of Marx's critique of capitalist society.

Human nature as historical

Through work we not only change the world, but in the process we also change ourselves. 'By . . . acting on the external world and changing it [man] at the same time changes his own nature' (Marx 1961, 177). The development of the productive forces goes together with the development of human nature, of needs and of capacities. Human nature is historical, needs are historical, they develop both quantitatively and qualitatively: 'our desires and pleasures spring from society . . . Because they are of a social nature, they are of a relative nature' (Marx 1958, 94).

This is not to deny that there are universal human needs. To say that a need such as hunger, for example, is historical is not to deny that all human beings – indeed all living organisms – require material sustenance, or that there is a core of basic needs the satisfaction of which is required simply for biological survival. However, the specific form that hunger takes – what food will satisfy it, even what constitutes food – goes beyond this and varies socially and historically. The need for food now, in this society, differs from what is needed in other societies and at other times.

Of course, Marx criticizes capitalism insofar as it fails to meet even minimum biological needs and results in malnutrition, hunger and even starvation. But his critique goes beyond this. He condemns capitalism, not just because it fails to satisfy basic and universal needs, but also because it fails to meet the more developed needs that it itself has created. His standard of assessment here is historical and relative, not absolute.

Why should the satisfaction of such historically created needs be valued? Only our basic and universal needs, it is sometimes argued, are 'true' needs. Modern society creates a host of 'unnecessary' desires and 'false' needs: desires whose satisfaction is not necessary for life and does not lead to genuine happiness. Marx, I am suggesting, does not share these views. Some, at least, of these new desires are 'true' needs relative to the social conditions in which they arise, in that their satisfaction is necessary for a minimum standard of social life and for happiness. This is not to reject the distinction between 'true' and 'false' needs altogether, but it is to insist that this distinction is a historical and relative one, and it is thus to abandon the attempt to use a universal core of 'true' needs as a standard by which all development beyond it is to be judged.

Similar points apply to the need for productive and creative activity. Although this, too, is a universal human need, the specific form that it takes has varied. For most of history, people have sought fulfilment mainly outside of economic work (work to satisfy material needs). The very idea that economic work can or should be a source of satisfaction is a relatively recent development in the main, as is the recognition that self-expression and self-realization are human needs.[9] These characteristically socialist values are not transhistorical; they have come onto the agenda only in the modern period, with the emergence of the real historical prospect of overcoming alienation.[10]

Marx's account of needs and human nature thus involves much more than the narrow utilitarian and economic conceptions of them, and so too his notions of wealth and, ultimately, of the human good. The familiar economic idea of wealth reduces it to the acquisition of property and to material consumption. Marx insists that it must be replaced by a much fuller notion based on the idea of the human being 'rich in needs' – the human being who has developed the needs and capacities inherent in his or her 'species being' in an all-round way, unrestricted by the effects of private property and the division of labour. 'The *rich* man and the wealth of human need take the place of the wealth and poverty of political economy. The rich man is simultaneously the man *in need* of a totality of vital human expression; he is the man in whom his own realization exists as inner necessity, as need' (Marx 1975, 356).[11] Human happiness is not restricted to the narrow satisfaction of our material desires. The true human good lies rather in the all-round development of our powers and capacities.

Justice and right

So far I have been focusing on Marx's ideas of human nature and the human good. Let us now turn to the role played in his philosophy by notions of justice and right. This gives rise to puzzles and problems similar to those raised by the role of naturalistic values. On the one hand, Marx denies that his account of capitalism or his conception of communism involve any reference to principles of 'eternal' justice. He associates such thinking particularly with utopian socialists like Proudhon and goes out of his way to repudiate it (Marx 1978b, 531). As I have stressed, he maintains that his aim is to understand capitalism and its 'laws of motion' rather than to criticize it, and he insists that principles of justice and right themselves must be comprehended as social and historical products.

On the other hand, at times he undoubtedly condemns capitalism for its injustice and envisages communism as a fairer and more equal form of society. For example, he says that the capitalist system is founded upon 'the theft of alien labour time' (Marx 1973, 705), and he attacks it for involving 'robbery', 'plunder', 'booty' and so on (Husami 1978; Geras 1985). These ways of talking cannot simply be discounted as rhetorical flourishes, they occur repeatedly. Furthermore, many Marxists share the view that capitalism is unjust – this is an important aspect of the Marxist outlook, even though Marxist theory has had problems in accommodating it into the socio-scientific stance that it claims for itself. In short, despite Marx's denials, it seems clear that criticism of capitalism as unjust, and a picture of a fairer society, do play a role in his thought.

Marx on justice

What standards does Marx appeal to in making these judgements? Many recent philosophers in the analytic tradition assert that Marx must be relying on transhistorical standards of justice, whatever he himself may claim to the contrary. As I have argued above, this assumption is unwarranted. Marx's approach is historical; his critical values are immanent and relative. He condemns capitalism and advocates communism on the basis of values that are rooted in forces that are immanent in the present.

What are these values? Various answers to this question have been proposed in the recent literature. According to Geras, Marx maintains that it is a universal principle of justice that those who labour are entitled to the product of their labour, on the grounds that 'it violates a principle of moral equality if the efforts of some people go unrewarded whilst others enjoy benefits without having to expend any effort' (Geras 1985, 160).

This is indeed a standard of justice that Marx uses to condemn capitalism, in which there is a class who can live off the work of others without themselves working, simply by owning capital. However, this is not a transhistorical standard of right, as Geras asserts. On the contrary, it is the standard that will apply in the initial stage of communism as Marx envisages it, when reward will be proportional to work done and no one will be able gain an income simply through ownership.

According to Marx, it will not be possible to create a fully communist society immediately after capitalism is overthrown, a transitional stage will be needed. In this, the capitalist State will be replaced by a communist one, which will take all private property in the means of production (i.e. capital) into common (State) ownership and use it for the common good rather than for private profit. After the State has withheld what is needed for reinvestment, for education and welfare provision and so on, the remaining social product will be distributed in the form of wages according to the amount of work performed. The more you work, the more you will receive. This is a principle of equal exchange similar to that governing economic exchange in capitalist society (Marx calls it the principle of 'bourgeois right') – except in one important respect: in communism, it will no longer be possible to gain an income simply by owning property (Marx 1978b, 530).

Geras is right that Marx criticizes capitalism for violating this principle and allowing the existence of a class whose ownership of capital allows them to gain a livelihood by exploiting the labour of others. In doing so, however, he is not appealing to a transhistorical or universal standard as Geras believes. Rather, he is adopting the ethical standpoint of a future communist society – a standpoint that is immanent in the present. This does not give rise to transhistorical values. For this future form of society and the norms it creates is in its turn destined eventually to be superseded by the further stage of full communism. In this, the idea that entitlement should be based on work done will be transcended altogether. It will be a society of abundance in which wages and the market will be completely eliminated. 'The narrow horizon of bourgeois right [will] be crossed in its entirety', as Marx puts it, 'and society inscribe on its banners: From each according to his abilities, to each according to his needs!' (Marx 1978b, 531).

Equality

Like Geras, Cohen also maintains that Marxism must invoke transhistorical principles of justice in order to criticize present society, but he gives a different account of what these are supposed to be. To explain them, Cohen gives the example of a camping trip by a group of friends in which equipment is shared and activities organized cooperatively and by mutual agreement. Claims to private ownership are suspended for the duration of the trip, and things are shared freely and help is given when it is needed, without any accounting of costs or expectation of payment.

Cohen argues that a camping trip of this sort – and full communism – is governed by a principle of distributive justice, a principle of what he calls 'radical equality of opportunity'. According to this, 'differences of outcome reflect nothing but differences of taste and choice, not differences in natural and social capacities and powers' (Cohen 2009, 18). This is questionable. Equality in various forms is the distributive principle that governs bourgeois society. With the abolition of private property and distribution according to need in full communism, the idea of an equal distribution is transcended. As Wood says, the principle of distribution according to need 'does not treat people alike or equally . . . but considers them simply as individuals with their own special needs and faculties' (Wood 1979, 292). Different people will have different needs and these will be satisfied in different ways. The National Health Service in Britain aspires to distribute health care in this way. Some individuals are seriously ill and need much in the way of resources, others are healthier and require less; each gets what they require to satisfy their needs. Equality is involved only insofar as each person's needs are fully and equally met, but there is no longer any concern to achieve a quantitatively equal distribution. In that sense, communism of this sort is 'beyond equality' (Sayers 2011, 118–30).

Is full communism also 'beyond justice'? It is sometimes said that Marx thinks so, and his philosophy is compared to Hume's in this respect. Hume argues that principles of justice serve to maintain social order in conditions of moderate scarcity. They are not needed when there is abundance and people can take as much as they want without preventing others from doing likewise. Rules of property and distribution have no useful purpose in these conditions (Hume 1894).

However, Marx's way of thinking about justice is quite different from this sort of consequentialism and utilitarianism. It should rather be located in the Hegelian tradition. Principles of justice and right are embodied in the norms governing social relations. All societies have such norms, all societies therefore have principles of justice. Communism means the abolition of private property and the individualist norms associated with it. It involves a communal form of property and communal notions of justice and right, not the elimination of property right altogether (Sayers 2011, Chapter 7).

Problems of relativism

For Marx, then, principles of justice are social and historical phenomena. They are the expressions of the norms governing social roles, institutions and practices. Like Hegel, he sees principles of right as arising out of particular forms of 'ethical life' or *Sittlichkeit* (literally, customariness). Different social relations and practices involve different principles of justice. These principles arise in specific conditions and are necessary and right for their time; but with time, as the conditions for a new social order develop, they lose their necessity and rightness. There is no single, universally right social order, no transhistorical and universally valid principles of justice. It is in these terms that Marx's critique of the injustices of capitalism must be understood.

As we have seen already, a social and historical account of values of this kind raises issues of relativism. Why should the communist conception of justice be valued in present conditions, even if it is immanent in them? The mere fact that the course of history is moving in this direction (assuming that it is) does not seem to be a sufficient justification: what will be is not necessarily what ought to be, historical might does not necessarily make right (Nietzsche 1983, 105). Marx maintains that the communist notion of justice expresses the interests and perspective of working people – but why should those in others classes support it? It seems that an historical theory cannot justify communist values.

Many philosophers see these as reasons to reject the historical account of values and insist that a critical perspective must rely on universal and transhistorical notions of justice. But these too face great problems of justification. The authors of the US 'Declaration of Independence' held their notions of justice and right to be 'self-evident'. That is not tenable. What appears self-evident in one period and to one group may not seem so to others. To the authors of the 'Declaration', it seemed self-evident that 'all men are created equal'; to Plato, Aristotle and many others in the ancient world, and indeed even to many of their contemporaries, it appeared just as self-evident that men (and women) are created unequal.

Others, like Rawls, follow Kant in arguing that the principles of justice are matters about which there can be a rational consensus. Marx gives good reason to question this. 'The history of all hitherto existing societies is the history of class struggle', say the well-known opening words of *The Communist Manifesto*. Conflicting classes have different and conflicting conceptions of justice. In these circumstances, rational consensus cannot be achieved. It seems clear that universal rational agreement about moral matters does not exist in present capitalist society (MacIntyre 1985); it is an imaginary ideological construct of liberal philosophers like Rawls. It cannot be achieved, Marx maintains, because the economic system of private ownership on which this society is based, and which is justified by its principles of justice, inevitably generates fundamental conflicts. This is the Marxist critique of liberal philosophies of justice and rights.

In present society, there is not and cannot be a universally agreed rational perspective on moral matters, and Marxism does not claim to provide such a perspective. It too is a product of these social and historical conditions. It is not the universal perspective of all rational beings, but rather the outlook of a particular class of modern industrial society. Why then should it have any wider appeal or rational authority? We are back with the issue of relativism.

Marxism does not attempt to answer this question by appealing to universal human nature or universal reason as do philosophers in the liberal tradition. Nor does it rely, in Nietzschean fashion, on a purely arbitrary commitment to the will and perspective of a particular class or kind of individual. However, insofar as the working class and its struggle for communism points towards the future course of history, Marx claims that it represents something more than the arbitrary will of a particular group.

How so? Various ways of answering this question have been suggested by philosophers in the Marxist tradition. The working class in Marx's sense are those who do not own the means of production and who must therefore sell their labour to earn a living. They are the great majority in modern capitalist society. By establishing a State that rules in their interests, communism claims to be more democratic than capitalist society ruled by a bourgeois liberal State. In the words of the *Manifesto*, it will 'win the battle of democracy' (Marx and Engels 1978b, 490). Its governing principles will thus, it is claimed, enjoy democratic legitimacy.

Another way of dealing with the problem of relativism is suggested by Sandra Harding, writing from a feminist position. She agrees with Marx that ethical values are social and hence inescapably embody a particular perspective. She argues, however, that not all perspectives are epistemologically equal, 'some . . . social locations are better than others' (Harding 1993, 56). The marginalized and oppressed have less stake in defending the established order than other more privileged groups. In the words of the *Communist Manifesto*, working people have 'nothing to lose but their chains'. Their outlook, it may be argued, is less deformed by their particular situation; they have less reason therefore to have a distorted outlook.

However, Marx claims not just that the working class constitutes the majority, nor that its outlook is less likely to be distorted than that of other groups, he also claims that the working class can claim for the first time to have a truly universal perspective. For the emancipation of the working class contains within it 'universal human emancipation' (Marx 1975, 333) and, more enigmatically, that communism will be the 'solution of the riddle of history' (Marx 1975, 348).

What he means by these phrases is explained by the Hegelian Marxist philosopher György Lukács. Previous revolutionary classes have claimed that they represented the universal social interest, but each soon found itself faced with opposing classes, and it transpired that it was in fact only a particular class struggling against others (Marx and Engels 1978a, 173–4). The modern working class, however, has the possibility of creating a classless society that is no longer characterized by fundamental class divisions and antagonisms. Its struggle is thus, according to Lukács, not simply for its own particular class interests, for these can be achieved only through the overcoming of all class divisions, and the abolition of itself as a particular class. Its aim is its own overcoming (*Aufhebung*). 'The proletariat only perfects itself by annihilating and transcending itself, by creating the classless society through the successful conclusion of its own class struggle' (Lukács 1971, 80). This society is one in which for the first time the notion of human universality will have a genuine basis. In that sense, the modern working class is what Lukács regards as the universal class, and an ethic based on its perspective can be genuinely universal in character.

The right and the good

I have been arguing that two sorts of moral values can be found in Marx's work: there are naturalistic values based on ideas of the human good (happiness, flourishing) and there are also values of justice or right. These two kinds of values are often treated as though they are incompatible and exclusive of each other.

Indeed, when such values are made into universal and abstract principles, they contradict each other and lead to familiar ethical dilemmas. Thus, the utilitarian and consequentialist approach when pushed to the extreme implies that actions should be judged solely according to their consequences and regardless of considerations of justice and right. Even great evil can then be justified if its consequence is to prevent greater evil: 'the ends justify the means'. This can lead to actions that seem quite evidently immoral, and this is often used as an argument against consequentialism and in favour of a morality of justice.

Conversely, principles of justice taken in abstraction imply that the demands of justice should be followed without regard to the consequences and even when these are disastrous: *fiat justitia, periat mundus* (let justice be done, though the world perish). This seems immoral to the point of madness, and this in turn is used as an argument against an ethic of justice and in favour of consequentialism. These arguments seem to be going around in circles.

As far as I am aware, Marx himself did not express a view on these issues. However, Hegel does, and his philosophy suggests a line that Marxism might well adopt. Hegel argues that standards both of goodness and justice have a valid place in moral thought, but only within limits, as long as they are not taken to extremes. For the most part, there need be no conflict between them and no need therefore to opt for one to the exclusion of the other. Both are to be found in Marx, as I have argued, and both have a role in his critique of capitalism and in his vision of a better society for the future.

However, these principles may and sometimes do conflict in real life. The issues that then arise have been well described and explored in the literature of Marxism. Particularly in the immediate post-war period, there was an extensive discussion of whether or not those on the Left should give their support to the Soviet regime during the cold war, when they were well aware of the terrible injustices that were being done by it, because it constituted the only effective opposition to the evil of US imperialism (Koestler 1946; de Beauvoir 1957; Sartre 1961; Lukes 1985, Chapter 6).

As this literature graphically shows, there is no straightforward way of resolving the dilemmas that result when fundamental moral principles of the good and justice are in conflict. It would be wrong to argue for either in an *a priori* philosophical way and insist that reliance should be placed solely *either* on naturalistic values *or* on principles of justice. Much of the recent disagreement among the analytical Marxists, who I have been criticizing, has been fuelled by insisting on just these positions. Such conflicts of principles reflect, rather, the fact that different aspects of actual social life are in fundamental conflict. The issue is practical not philosophical, it cannot be resolved purely theoretically.

Notes

1 See Lukes (1985, Chapter 2), for documentation of these apparently conflicting views in Marx and other Marxists.

2 For that reason Marxism used to be termed 'scientific socialism' by the Soviets. That phrase has now fallen into disuse.

3 That is, philosophers whose project has been to bring 'the techniques of analytical philosophy' to the interpretation of Marxism, for example, Cohen, Geras, Lukes, etc. For criticisms, see Sayers (1984; 1998, Chapters 7–8).

4 'Supersession' is the usual translation of the Hegelian term '*Aufhebung*'. Hegel (1969, 107) uses it to describe a dialectical process of development in which an earlier stage is both negated by a later one and at same time preserved in it.

5 The theory of history as a progressive process – on which these ideas depend – has been much discussed and criticized, but that is not my topic here.

6 See Sayers (1998, Chapters 7–8), for a fuller presentation of these arguments.

7 Lukes (1985), Wood (1980).

8 Geras (1985; 1992; 1995), Cohen (1988), Elster (1985).

9 It should be noted that there is also an earlier Christian tradition that values the dignity of labour.

10 Conversely, the utilitarian and economic view that we are mere consumers is itself a symptom and an expression of alienation. It portrays what is a specific historical condition as though it were the inevitable result of a supposedly universal human nature. Marx criticizes capitalism for reducing the pursuit of the human good to this narrow and limited form (Marx 1975c).

11 Marx is using the term 'man' in a generic sense, to include women.

References

Althusser, L. (1969), *For Marx*, London: Allen Lane.
— (2006), *Philosophy of the Encounter: Later Writings, 1978–1987*, London: Verso.
Cohen, G. A. (1988), 'Freedom, Justice, and Capitalism', in *History, Labour, and Freedom*, Oxford: Clarendon Press, pp. 286–304.
— (2009), *Why Not Socialism?*, Princeton NJ: Princeton University Press.
de Beauvoir, S. (1957), *The Mandarins*, trans. L. M. Friedman, London: Collins.
Elster, J. (1985), *Making Sense of Marx*, Cambridge: Cambridge University Press.
Feuerbach, L. (1957), *The Essence of Christianity*, trans. George Eliot, New York: Harper & Row.
Geras, N. (1985), 'The Controversy About Marx and Justice', *New Left Review*, (150): 47–85.
— (1992), 'Bringing Marx to Justice: An Addendum and a Rejoinder', *New Left Review*, (195): 37–69.
— (1995), 'Human Nature and Progress', *New Left Review*, (213): 151–60.
Harding, S. (1993), 'Rethinking Standpoint Epistemology: What Is "Strong Objectivity"?' in *Feminist Epistemologies*, edited by Linda Alcoff and Elizabeth Potter, New York; London: Routledge, pp. 49–82.
Hegel, G. W. F. (1969), *Science of Logic*, trans. A. V. Miller, London: Allen and Unwin.
— (1991), *Elements of the Philosophy of Right*, trans. H. B. Nisbet, Cambridge: Cambridge University Press.
'The Hippocratic Oath' (2003), http://www.bbc.co.uk/dna/h2g2/A1103798 (accessed: 19 July 2011).
Hume, D. (1894), 'An Enquiry Concerning the Principles of Morals', in *Enquiries*, 1st edn, edited by L. A. Selby-Bigge, Oxford: Clarendon Press.
Husami, Z. I. (1978), 'Marx on Distributive Justice', *Philosophy and Public Affairs*, 8, (1): 27–64.
Koestler, A. (1946), *Darkness at Noon*, Harmondsworth: Penguin.
Lukács, G. (1971), *History and Class Consciousness: Studies in Marxist Dialectics*, trans. R. Livingstone, London: Merlin Press.
Lukes, S. (1985), *Marxism and Morality*, Oxford: Oxford University Press.
MacIntyre, A. (1985), *After Virtue*, 2nd edn, London: Duckworth.
Marx, K. (1958), 'Wage, Labour and Capital', in *Marx-Engels Selected Works in Two Volumes*, I, Moscow: Foreign Languages Publishing House.
— (1961), *Capital*, I, trans. S. Moore and E. Aveling, Moscow: Foreign Languages Publishing House.

—(1973), *Grundrisse: Foundations of the Critique of Political Economy (Rough Draft)*, trans. Martin Nicolaus, Harmondsworth: Penguin.

—(1975), *Early Writings*, Harmondsworth: Penguin.

—(1978a), 'The Civil War in France', in *The Marx-Engels Reader*, 2nd edn, edited by Robert C. Tucker, New York: W.W. Norton, pp. 618–52.

—(1978b), 'Critique of the Gotha Program', in *The Marx-Engels Reader*, 2nd edn, edited by Robert C. Tucker, New York: W.W. Norton, pp. 525–41.

—(1978c), 'Speech at the Anniversary of the *People's Paper*', in *The Marx-Engels Reader*, 2nd edn, edited by Robert C. Tucker, New York: W.W. Norton, pp. 577–8.

Marx, K. and Engels, F. (1978a), 'The German Ideology: Part I', in *The Marx-Engels Reader*, 2nd edn, edited by Robert C. Tucker, New York: W.W. Norton, pp. 146–200.

—(1978b), 'Manifesto of the Communist Party', in *The Marx-Engels Reader*, 2nd edn, edited by Robert C. Tucker, New York: W.W. Norton, pp. 473–500.

Meikle, S. (1985), *Essentialism in the Thought of Karl Marx*, London: Duckworth.

Nietzsche, F. W. (1983), 'On the Uses and Disadvantages of History for Life', in *Untimely Meditations*, Cambridge: Cambridge University Press, pp. 57–124.

Pike, J. E. (1999), *From Aristotle to Marx: Aristotelianism in Marxist Social Ontology*, Aldershot: Ashgate.

Sartre, J.-P. (1961), *Les Mains Sales*, trans. K. Black, London: Methuen.

Sayers, S. (1984), 'Marxism and the Dialectical Method: A Critique of G. A. Cohen', *Radical Philosophy*, (36): 4–13.

—(1998), *Marxism and Human Nature*, London: Routledge.

—(2011), *Marx and Alienation: Essays on Hegelian Themes*, Basingstoke and New York: Palgrave Macmillan.

Wood, A. W. (1979), 'Marx on Right and Justice: A Reply to Husami', *Philosophy and Public Affairs*, 8, (3): 267–95.

—(1980), 'The Marxian Critique of Justice', in *Marx, Justice and History*, edited by M. Cohen, T. Nagel and T. Scanlon, Princeton: Princeton University Press, pp. 3–41.

Recommended reading

Cohen, G. A. (1988), *History, Labour, and Freedom*, Oxford: Clarendon Press.

Geras, N. (1985), 'The Controversy About Marx and Justice', *New Left Review*, (150): 47–85.

Hegel, G. W. F. (1991), *Elements of the Philosophy of Right*, trans. H. B. Nisbet, Cambridge: Cambridge University Press.

Lukes, S. (1985), *Marxism and Morality*, Oxford: Oxford University Press.

Marx, K. and Engels, F. (1978), 'The German Ideology: Part I', in *The Marx-Engels Reader*, 2nd edn, edited by Robert C. Tucker, New York: W. W. Norton, pp. 146–200.

Sayers, S. (1998), *Marxism and Human Nature*, London: Routledge.

—(2011), *Marx and Alienation: Essays on Hegelian Themes*, Basingstoke and New York: Palgrave Macmillan.

Wood, A. W. (1980), 'The Marxian Critique of Justice', in *Marx, Justice and History*, edited by M. Cohen, T. Nagel and T. Scanlon, Princeton: Princeton University Press, pp. 3–41.

9

Mill

Krister Bykvist

J ohn Stuart Mill was one of the most versatile intellectuals of the nineteenth century. As a liberal, he not only did groundbreaking work on the notion of liberty but also applied his liberalism in practice, for example, in his staunch support for the liberalization of women's position in society. As an empiricist, he defended the method of using the evidence of our senses to gain knowledge, heroically applying it to the most abstract sciences such as logic and mathematics. As a moral philosopher, he was steeped, at a very young age, in the utilitarianism his father inherited from Jeremy Bentham, but Mill went on to refine and modify the theory in many important ways. His commitment to utilitarianism was one of his most strongly felt intellectual commitments. In fact, it was so strongly felt that he described his conversion to utilitarianism in quasi-religious terms:

> It gave unity to my conceptions of things. I now had opinions; a creed, a doctrine, a philosophy; in one among the best senses of the word, a religion; the inculcation and diffusion of which could be made the principal outward purpose of a life. (Mill 1873, 'Last Stage of Education and First of Self-Education')

Mill's utilitarian doctrine is summed up and defended in his book *Utilitarianism*, which was first published as a series of three essays in 1861. This book will be our main tour-guide as we take a brief tour through Mill's utilitarian world, stopping at the major attractions. The main focus will be on the very definition of Mill's utilitarianism. Here, we follow Mill's own method, for he insists that '[t]he very imperfect notion ordinarily formed of its meaning, is the chief obstacle which impedes its reception; and that could it be cleared, even from only the grosser misconceptions, the question would be greatly simplified, and a large proportion of its difficulties removed' (Mill 1871, General Remarks, p. 208). Even though Mill cleared utilitarianism from many of the 'grosser misconceptions', there is still widespread disagreement about almost every aspect of Mill's utilitarianism. We will touch on the major disagreements and try to uncover the main strands of his theory.

First stop: Statement of the utilitarian principle

Most introductory books on ethics define classical utilitarianism as the theory that says that we ought to maximize the sum total of happiness (or well-being). More exactly, an action ought to be done just in case its outcome contains a greater sum total of happiness than that of any of its alternatives. The sum total of happiness in an outcome is calculated by assigning a positive value to each instance of pleasure in the outcome, a negative value to each instance of displeasure or pain and then summing up these values. Only the duration and the intensity matter for the value of an instance of pleasure or displeasure.

It is instructive to see that this definition is quite different from Mill's own statement of utilitarianism:

> [T]he Greatest Happiness Principle, holds that actions are right in proportion as they tend to promote happiness, wrong as they tend to produce the reverse of happiness. By happiness is intended pleasure, and the absence of pain; by unhappiness, pain, and the privation of pleasure. (Mill 1871, Chapter 1, p. 210)

First of all, Mill seems to be assuming that rightness and wrongness can come in *degrees*, since to say that actions are right in proportion as they tend to promote happiness seems to imply that if one action has a greater tendency to promote happiness than another, then the first action is 'more right' than the second.

Second, Mill's definition suggests that the rightness of an action depends on its *tendency* to produce overall happiness, rather than its actual effects on overall happiness.

Third, his definition does not explicitly tell us what we ought to do. Mill only suggests that an action that has a greater tendency to promote happiness than another is to that extent right, and an action that has a greater tendency to produce unhappiness is to that extent wrong. Mill does not explicitly say how these different tendencies should be weighed against each other so that we can say what we ought to do, all things considered.

Not all of these three differences in formulating utilitarianism run very deep, however. The expression 'in proportion as they tend to promote happiness', which suggests that rightness comes in degrees, is not used anywhere else in Mill's writings. Nor does Mill ever explicitly talk in comparative terms about rightness, for example, 'more right' or 'more wrong'. It is more plausible to interpret Mill as talking about the *strength of reason* for and against performing actions. In other words, the fact that an action has a tendency to produce some happiness is a reason *for* doing it. The greater the tendency to produce happiness, the stronger the reason is for performing the action. Similarly, the fact that an action has a tendency to produce some unhappiness is a reason *against* doing it. The greater the tendency to produce unhappiness, the stronger the reason is against performing the action.

It is a much more delicate issue how to understand Mill's use of 'tendency'. Indeed, some Mill scholars have understood Mill here as claiming that rightness depends on *probable* consequences of individual actions rather than actual ones. Others have taken him to be talking about the tendencies of act-*types*, so that an individual action is assessed not in terms of what would happen if it was performed, but in terms of what would happen if *everyone* were to perform actions of the same act-type. This is an issue we will come back to later.

The issue about weighing tendencies is also difficult, but it is not a coincidence that Mill did not simply say that we ought to maximize the *sum total* of overall happiness. For, as we will see in the next section, Mill rejected the idea that the value of a pleasure depends only on its duration and intensity.

Second stop: The distinction between higher and lower pleasures

Mill was well aware of the common complaints against utilitarianism. In particular, he was aware of the famous 'swine objection', which says that utilitarianism is a degrading doctrine worthy only of swine, because it says that the highest end for humans is to indulge in sensual animal pleasures. Mill's initial answer to this objection is to turn the tables and criticize the objector for degrading human nature. The swine objection assumes that humans are not capable of taking pleasure in anything but simple sensual experiences, but this is simply false. Most humans do take more intense pleasure in more intellectual endeavours, like literature, music and science. The swine, on the other hand, is incapable of enjoying these pleasures and is thus forced to get by with sensual pleasures. Furthermore, Mill claims that distinctively human pleasures will often have many pleasant side effects. As Bentham himself suggested, even though (quantity of pleasure being equal) pushpin – a child's game – is as good as poetry, in real life things are rarely equal because, unlike the simple-minded game of pushpin, poetry brings about many other pleasures, for example, fond memories, pleasant anticipations and the pleasures of improving one's abilities.

Mill acknowledges that this reply does not fully answer the objection, since if quantity of pleasure is the only thing that matters, a pig's life will be better than a human life, and a fool's life can be better than Socrates' life, whenever the pig's or the fool's pleasures are more intense or have a longer duration. Mill therefore claims that we need to 'take the higher ground' and distinguish between higher and lower pleasures on the basis of differences in their intrinsic natures.

To decide which pleasures are higher, Mill deferred to the preferences of competent judges:

> If I am asked, what I mean by difference of quality in pleasures, or what makes one pleasure more valuable than another, merely as a pleasure, except its being greater in amount, there is but one answer. Of two pleasures, if there be one to which all or almost all who have experienced both give a decided preference, irrespective of any feelings of moral obligation to prefer it, that is

the more desirable pleasure. If one of the two is, by those who are competently acquainted with both, placed so far above the other that they prefer it, even though knowing it to be attended with a greater amount of discontent, and would not resign it for any quantity of the other pleasure which their nature is capable of, we are justified in ascribing to the preferred enjoyment a superiority in quality, so far outweighing quantity as to render it, in comparison, of small account. (Mill 1871, Chapter 1, p. 211)

The passage is a bit puzzling. Mill starts off asking himself what he means by a difference of quality in pleasures, and then tells us that he will give *one* answer. But what follows seems to be *two* different answers. His first answer is that one pleasure is higher than another if all or almost all competent judges would prefer the first pleasure to the second, irrespective of any feelings of moral obligation to prefer the first. His second answer is that one pleasure is higher than another if all or almost all competent judges would prefer the first pleasure to the second, even if they knew that the first pleasure was attended by a greater amount of discontent, and would not resign it for any quantity of the second pleasure, which their nature is capable of.

Many Mill scholars have interpreted Mill as endorsing the second answer as the official criterion of a higher pleasure. Moreover, it is also common to interpret Mill as saying that whenever one pleasure has higher quality than another, then the higher pleasure is better than *any possible* quantity of the lower pleasure. This interpretation is not especially plausible, however.

First of all, note that the first answer then is false, strictly speaking. It is not true that a *mere* preference for one pleasure over another would be sufficient for the first pleasure to be greater in quality (when the two pleasures are of equal amount).

Second, note that Mill talks about competent judges not being willing to resign a pleasure for 'any quantity of the other pleasure *which their nature is capable of*' (my italics). This does not rule out that if the quantity of the lower pleasure were to be increased beyond the limits of what their nature is now capable of, the lower quality pleasure would outweigh the higher one. So it is, strictly speaking, false to say that Mill thinks that a higher pleasure is better than *any logically possible* amount of a lower pleasure.

An alternative interpretation is that the first answer gives us the criterion for a higher pleasure. The second answer is not a criterion but a *special case* of higher quality, in which the competent judge not only prefers one pleasure to another but is also unwilling to trade off quality against quantity (which their nature is capable of). This interpretation makes for a much more flexible theory.

First of all, if we go for the strict theory, according to which no amount of a lower pleasure can outweigh some amount of a higher pleasure, we run into difficulties when comparing intellectual pleasures. It does not seem plausible to assume that all intellectual pleasures have the same quality. Arguably, the pleasure of listening to Bach has a somewhat higher quality than the pleasure of listening to some slightly less talented composer (choose a suitable composer). On the strict interpretation, we would have to say that one minute of listening to Bach is better than *any* number of hours listening to the slightly less talented composer.

The flexible interpretation will still be able to say that in *some cases* the difference in quality is so great that no amount of the lower pleasure our nature is capable of can outweigh a sufficient amount of the higher pleasure. Think of a very long dull life in a coma interrupted now and then by short bursts of sensory pleasure (e.g. being stroked on the chin). The value of this life does not seem to outweigh the value of a life of normal length, full of artistic, athletic and intellectual pleasures.

Of course, on my interpretation, Mill has not ruled out the possibility that a dull life can be better than a normal life. We only need to imagine the dull life having a quantity that is greater than 'our nature is capable of', say, by being longer than any humanly possible life. But we might want to say that *no matter* how long the dull life is, it cannot be better than the normal life. It should be noted, however, that if Mill wants to go this far, he has to give up on the simple idea that the value of an outcome is the sum of the values of the pleasure and displeasures contained in the outcome. According to my interpretation, Mill can still claim to be summing the values of pleasure and displeasure. It is just that higher pleasures are weighted much higher (but not infinitely higher) than lower ones.

One major objection to Mill's distinction between higher and lower pleasures is that it is difficult to square with his hedonism. As a hedonist, Mill is committed to there being only one kind of value: pleasure. But how can he then claim that one pleasure can be better than another even when they are equally pleasant, that is, of exactly the same quantity? G. E. Moore made fun of Mill by likening him to someone who claims that colour is the only value, but then adds that green things are better than blue things, even when they are equally coloured.

In replying to this objection, it is important to note that Mill does not say that there are *other* values than pleasure. He insists that to pursue athletic, artistic and intellectual projects without feeling any pleasure would not be a higher pleasure, since it would not be a pleasure at all, and thus no value could be assigned to these projects, independently of the associated pleasure. On the other hand, when it comes to comparing the value of one pleasure to the value of another, Mill does think that not only duration and intensity matter; but also *quality* matters. So, if two pleasures have the same duration and intensity, the pleasure with higher quality will be better in itself. But this is not to say that quality has some value in itself; it is just to say that having quality *makes* the pleasure more valuable in itself. Quality is like duration in this respect. The fact that a pleasure has a longer duration makes it more valuable in itself, but that does not mean that duration has value in itself. The mere fact that one experience is longer than another does not make it better in itself.

Now, one could object that admitting quality as a further good-maker still betrays the true spirit of hedonism, for quality does not seem to be part of the *feel and flavour* of a pleasant experience. A true hedonist, the objection goes, must think that the value of a pleasure depends exclusively on how it feels to experience this pleasure.

It is difficult to answer this objection on Mill's behalf because he does not make it very clear what he means by 'quality'. In particular, he does not make it clear whether quality is a felt aspect of an experience or whether it is a feature of the object of experience, a feature of the intellectual activity you take pleasure in, for example. Indeed, when he invokes the competent judge's preferences he does not say what *makes* them prefer a higher pleasure to a lower pleasure. He only says that they do *not* prefer it because of its being greater in quantity or because of a feeling of obligation. I will come back to this issue later.

Third stop: The 'proof' of utilitarianism

Mill's proof of utilitarianism is one of the most ridiculed arguments in the history of moral philosophy. Indeed, some commentators have suggested that it would be a perfect example to use in an introductory book in logic, because it contains so many logical fallacies.

In his defence, it should first of all be said that Mill did not think that fundamental moral principles, such as utilitarianism's greatest happiness principle, admit of logical proof. Mill only wanted to give an argument that could rationally convince us to accept utilitarianism. Furthermore, as an empiricist, he did not rely on self-evident principles but only evidence provided by our senses.

It is common to interpret the proof as consisting of three stages. In the first stage, Mill argues that each person's happiness is desirable to that person. In the second stage, he argues that general happiness is desirable to the aggregate of persons, and in the final stage, he argues that nothing but general happiness is desirable.

The argument for the first claim, that each person's happiness is desirable to that person, is an analogy between being visible or audible and being desirable. Mill says: 'The only proof capable of being given that an object is visible, is that people actually see it. The only proof that a sound is audible, is that people hear it; and so of the other sources of our experience. In like manner, I apprehend, the sole evidence it is possible to produce that anything is desirable, is that people do actually desire it' (Mill 1871, Chapter 4, p. 234).

On the face of it, Mill makes an obvious mistake here. He seems to change the meaning of the term 'desirable' midway through the argument. It is true that we can prove that something is visible, in the sense of being something that *can* be seen, by showing that it is in fact seen, since what is in fact seen can be seen. The analogy with 'desirable' would then be that we prove that something is desirable, in the sense of being something that can be desired, by showing that it is in fact desired, since what is in fact desired can be desired. The conclusion of the argument, however, is that each person's happiness is desirable in a different sense, namely in the sense of being *good* for the person.

It is uncharitable to think that Mill made such a simple mistake. A better interpretation is that Mill is talking about *evidence* for what is desirable. In fact, 'evidence' is exactly the word Mill is using, not 'proof'. The idea is then that the fact that I desire something gives me evidence to think that it is good for me. This is not to say that my desire never goes wrong, only that it gives me reason to think that what I desire is good for me. This line of argument could be made more convincing if we think about what it means to desire something. Typically, when you desire something, it attracts you and it *appears* good to you. Mill would then be saying that if something appears to be good, this is evidence that it is good. The analogy with our other senses would then be more plausible and straightforward. Just as the fact that an object appears to be red is evidence that it is red, the fact that an object appears to be good is evidence that it is good.

The second stage of the argument is very short. Mill lays out the argument as follows: '[E]ach person's happiness is a good to that person, and the general happiness, therefore, a good to the aggregate of all persons' (Mill 1871, p. 234). Again, many commentators have thought that Mill is committing an obvious mistake here. He seems to be saying that if each person's happiness is a good to that person, the general happiness is a good to each person in the aggregate of people. But it is one thing to say that my happiness is good to me and your happiness is good to you, and a completely different thing to say that *our general happiness* is good to each of us.

Mill was in fact aware of this objection and gave a reply in a letter to Henry Jones: '[W]hen I said the general happiness is a good to the aggregate of all persons I did not mean that every human being's happiness is a good to every other human being, though I think, in a good state of society and education it would be so. I merely meant in this particular sentence to argue that since A's happiness is a good, B's a good, C's a good, &c., the sum of all these goods must be a good' (Mill 1868).

The general principle alluded to here seems simply to be that you get a good whole if you put good things together.

Now, some commentators have suggested that this reply does not help much since it now seems like Mill is committing the fallacy of composition, the fallacy of inferring that a complex whole has a certain feature just because every part of the whole has this feature. That this is indeed a fallacy is clear from examples such as a brick wall that consists of bricks, each weighing 3 kilograms. It obviously does not follow that the whole wall weighs only 3 kilograms.

Now, to attribute this fallacy to Mill seems itself to be a fallacy, for just because one thinks that *one particular* kind of feature is such that a whole has it, if each part of the whole has it, it does not follow that one must think that *any* feature is such that a whole has it, if every part has it. For example, if each brick in the wall weighs at least 3 kilograms, we can safely conclude that the whole wall weighs at least 3 kilograms. Mill can thus be understood as saying that goodness is in this respect like the property of weighing at least 3 kilograms.

It should be noted, however, that even if we grant Mill this principle, we don't seem to get the whole of utilitarianism, for remember that utilitarianism says more than that a situation in which everyone is happy is good. This part of utilitarianism seems quite uncontroversial and would be accepted by many non-utilitarians as well (at least if overall happiness is equally distributed). Mill's utilitarianism also says, much more controversially, that if a few people are very *unhappy* and a majority happy, this situation can still be good on the whole, if the duration, intensity or quality of happiness is sufficiently great.

The last stage of the proof is generally considered to be the most perplexing. Mill starts off by asking whether utilitarians deny that people desire virtue and that virtue is not to be desired. 'The very reverse', Mill answers, and continues, 'It maintains not only that virtue is to be desired, but that it is to be desired disinterestedly, for itself' (Mill 1871, Chapter 4, p. 235). Mill seems to be saying that virtue is also an intrinsic good, which is blatantly inconsistent with his claim that pleasure is the only intrinsic good. What is going on? Mill insists that this is not a departure from utilitarianism, for '[t]he ingredients of happiness are very various, and each of them is desirable in itself, and not merely when considered as swelling an aggregate. The principle of utility does not mean that any given pleasure, as music, for instance . . . [is] to be looked upon as means to a collective something termed happiness, and to be desired on that account. [Pleasures] are desired and desirable in and for themselves; besides being means, they are a part of the end' (Mill 1871, Chapter 4, p. 235). Now, this seems just to make things worse, for Mill is explicitly saying that virtue and music are intrinsic goods, but how can a hedonist who assigns value only to pleasant *experiences* admit that *activities* such as music and virtue are also good in themselves? Indeed, Mill seems to concede that activities are good in themselves when he says that 'Happiness is not an abstract idea, but a *concrete* whole; and these (music and virtue, for instance) are some of its parts' (my italics).

A lot of ink has been spilt on making sense of Mill's views here. Some argue that Mill slides between two senses of the term 'pleasure'. By 'pleasure' we can mean either a pleasant experience, the *pleasure* one takes in something, or the object of one's pleasure, the *thing* one takes pleasure in. One interpretation of Mill would have him assume the latter sense of pleasure and thus assign value to the objects of our pleasure, the things we take pleasure in. This interpretation would make it clear how happiness can be seen as a concrete whole, for my happiness can be seen as consisting of all the activities and objects I take pleasure in.

The alternative interpretation would understand Mill as using 'pleasure' to refer to the experience of feeling pleasure. So when Mill says that music and virtue are desired for their own sake and good in themselves, we should understand him as speaking loosely, and in fact implying that it is the *pleasant experiences* of music and virtue that are desired for their own sake and good in themselves. One problem with this interpretation is that it is then very difficult to make sense of Mill's talk about happiness being a concrete whole. In its favour, one could point out that Mill does say that '[t]hose who desire virtue for its own sake, desire it either because the consciousness of it is a pleasure, or because the consciousness of being without it is a pain, or for both reasons united'. One could read this as saying that we never really desire the activity of virtue for the sake of the activity itself; what we desire is the pleasant consciousness of the activity (or the absence of the pain we feel when the activity is not present).

On the other hand, it is also possible to read this in a way that makes it consistent with the first interpretation: when Mill says we desire virtue for its own sake because the consciousness of it is pleasant, this could be understood as saying that we would not desire the virtuous activity for its own sake, if we did not find the consciousness of virtuous activity pleasant. The 'because' is here signalling, not our reason for caring about virtue but an *explanation* of why we care about virtue. Moreover, it is an explanation of why we care about virtue *for its own sake*.

To make clear this distinction between reason and explanation, think about how evolutionary biology explains our altruistic desires towards our near and dear. The explanation is (very roughly) that humans who have this kind of desire will have certain evolutionary advantages. But this does not mean that our reason to desire the good of our near and dear mentions evolutionary advantages; we simply care about their good for their own sake.

This interpretation fits well with Mill's own *associationist* conception of psychological explanation, hinted at in his text. Mill claims there that a person's desires for virtue are *explained* by the person's association of virtue with pleasure. Initially, we desire virtue as a means to pleasure, later we come to associate virtue itself with pleasure and this *explains* why we then desire it for its own sake.

This interpretation would also help us decide the issue about the location of quality. What determines the quality of pleasures could be features of the activities the competent judges take pleasure in, not just features of the experienced pleasure.

It must be said, however, that if this interpretation is accepted, then Mill's hedonism turns out to be quite peculiar. It will now say that *what* is good may include concrete activities such as playing music or acting virtuously. At this level, his theory does not look especially hedonistic. The hedonistic element shows up when we ask *why* these things are good. They are good simply because they are things we take pleasure in, and they would not be good if we did not take pleasure in them.

Fourth stop: The utilitarian duty

So far we have been discussing the evaluative aspects of Mill's utilitarianism, how the values of pleasures are determined and how these values should be aggregated. We have not said much about exactly how these values are supposed to determine the *rightness* of actions.

Unfortunately, there is very little agreement on what Mill thought about this matter. What is clear is that Mill did not think that every agent should always be consciously trying to maximize overall value. Instead, we need to rely on 'secondary principles', rules that function as 'landmarks' and 'direction-posts' that help us find the way to the ultimate destination, general happiness. These secondary principles will include the rules of common-sense morality, such as 'Don't kill', 'Don't cheat' and 'Don't break promises'. The conformity to these rules will typically promote overall happiness. The utilitarian will therefore see them as rules of thumb.

It is also clear that Mill's utilitarianism does not require us always to act from a concern for the well-being of everyone in society. What is important for the rightness of an action is that the action promotes (foreseeable) overall happiness; it is not important that the action is done from a motive of promoting overall happiness. As Mill says, 'He who saves a fellow creature from drowning does what is morally right, whether his motive be duty, or the hope of being paid for the trouble' (Mill, 1871, Chapter 2, Section 19). Even if the motive of an action does not affect its rightness, Mill accepts that it can affect the *worth of the agent*, especially if the motive reflects a good or bad disposition, from which useful or harmful actions are likely to arise.

As pointed out in the first section, Mill's talk about the *tendency* of actions to produce happiness has led some commentators to think that Mill is a rule-utilitarian. So, for instance, some have claimed that only types of actions have tendencies to produce an outcome. An individual action either does or does not produce the outcome. The act-type of smoking cigarettes has the tendency to cause cancer. But *my* smoking cigarettes either does or does not lead to cancer. These commentators think that Mill wants to assess an individual action by looking at the consequences of *everyone* performing actions of the *same kind*. If 'same kind' is more precisely understood as 'falling under the same rule', this would make Mill a *rule-utilitarian*, according to which an action is right in a certain situation just in case it falls under the best rule applicable in the situation, and a rule is best just in case the consequences of everyone accepting it are better than the consequences of everyone accepting any alternative rule applicable in the situation. The difference between act- and rule-utilitarianism can be illustrated by a case in which it is clear that the best results would ensue if I evaded taxes. For the act-utilitarian, this would decide the issue: I ought to evade taxes. But for the rule-utilitarian, there is room to argue that in fact it is wrong, because the consequences of *everyone* feeling free to evade taxes would be very bad.

So is this good evidence that Mill is a rule-utilitarian? Again, there is a letter to John Venn in which Mill seems to come clean:

> I agree with you that the right way of testing actions by their consequences, is to test them by the natural consequences of the particular action, and not by those which would follow if every one did the same. But, for the most part, the consideration of what would happen if every one did the same, is the only means we have of discovering the tendency of the act in the particular case. (Mill 1872, Vol. 17, p. 1881)

This seems to be a clear statement of act-utilitarianism. It also undoubtedly shows that Mill is willing to ascribe a tendency to affect overall happiness to *individual* actions.

One obvious problem with this passage is that it is strange for an act-utilitarian to say that in order to know whether I am permitted to violate a certain general rule I need first to know what would happen 'if every one did the same'. For example, suppose I know that the consequences would be awful if everyone felt free to evade taxes. This does not seem to be relevant, since I know that it is extremely unlikely that my single act of tax evasion will cause everyone else to evade taxes.

It seems, however, that Mill simply assumed – very implausibly – that the harm produced by each individual violation of a rule is an equal share of the total harm produced by the general violation of the rule. More exactly, Mill assumed that:

> If a hundred infringements would produce all the mischief implied in the abrogation of the rule, a hundredth part of that mischief must be debited to each one of the infringements, though we may not be able to trace it home individually. And this hundredth part will generally far outweigh any good expected to arise from the individual act. (Mill 1852, p. 182)

To give an example, if the value of the consequences of everyone violating the rule against evading taxes would be –10000 and we are 100 people, the harm produced by my single act of tax evasion will be a hundredth of the total harm produced (i.e. –100).

Not everything Mill says fits so neatly with this interpretation, however. For example, Mill says that it is 'unworthy of an intelligent agent not to be consciously aware that the action is of a class which, if practised generally, would be generally injurious, and that this is the ground of obligation to abstain from it' (Mill 1871, Chapter 2, Section 19). This passage suggests that Mill thinks that the reason ('ground') why I ought not to evade taxes is that the consequences would be very harmful, if everyone evaded taxes.

To make this passage fit with an act-utilitarian interpretation, we need to assume that Mill is speaking loosely here. When Mill talks about the ground of obligation, we should understand him as talking about *evidence* for having an obligation, more specifically, evidence that tells us the harm caused by an individual violation of a general rule. On this interpretation, the fundamental reason why I ought not to violate a general rule is still the harm produced by my individual action, not the harm produced by everyone's violating the rule. It is just that I need to know the total amount of harm produced by the general violation of the rule in order to know the amount of harm produced by my individual violation of the rule.

Fifth stop: Utilitarianism, justice and liberty

Mill claimed that both justice and liberty can be squared with his version of utilitarianism. Mill's famous liberty principle, defended in his book *On Liberty*, says that the only reason society can interfere with the liberty of a person is to prevent harm to others. The reason can never be the good of the person herself. This, Mill thinks, would amount to an unwarranted form of paternalism. On the face of it, Mill seems to be contradicting his own utilitarian doctrine here, since it is easy to imagine situations in which preventing a person's harming *herself* (without violating any general rules) would maximize overall happiness, because no one else would be affected. Some commentators have argued that Mill in fact abandoned utilitarianism when working on *On Liberty* and was just paying lip-service to it. This is hard to reconcile with the fact that he worked on *On Liberty* and *Utilitarianism* during roughly the *same* period. He also explicitly claimed early on in *On Liberty* that 'It is proper to state that I forego any advantage to my argument from the idea of abstract right, as a thing independent of utility. I regard utility as the ultimate appeal on all ethical questions' (Mill 1859, Chapter 1, Section 11). I will take Mill at his word here, and see whether he is right to think that liberty and utility can be combined. Since Mill thinks we have *moral right* to liberty, I will focus on the more general question of whether moral rights and utility can be combined.

Utilitarians do not have any problems acknowledging the existence of *legal* or *conventional* rights, the rights that are enshrined in laws and conventions. What is at issue is the existence of *moral* rights. Unlike Bentham, who thought the very notion of moral rights was 'nonsense upon stilts', Mill defended its coherence. He also thought his version of utilitarianism was perfectly compatible with the existence of moral rights. To see whether he succeeds in this, let us first see what Mill says about the notion of a moral right.

Mill thinks that, by definition, a right (no matter whether it is legal, conventional or moral) corresponds to a perfect obligation. For example, I have a right, against you, to walk on the pavement just in case you have a perfect obligation to me, not to prevent me from walking on the pavement. Imperfect obligations, such as obligations of generosity or beneficence, are those that do not 'give birth to any right'. Mill then identifies justice with perfect obligations: 'Justice implies something which it is not only right to do, and wrong not to do, but which some individual person can claim from us as his moral right' (Mill 1871, Chapter 5, Section 15). Mill also thinks that it is part of the meaning of moral rights that they are associated with sanctions, in the sense that, if I fail to provide what you have a moral right to, then I ought to be punished in some way – either by law, the opinion of other people or my own conscience. Mill sums this all up by saying that 'To have a (moral) right, then, is, I conceive, to have something which society ought to defend me in the possession of' (Mill 1871, Chapter 5, Section 25).

So far, this is only an elucidation of the concept of moral right and what it takes for it to exist. Mill's utilitarianism comes in when he says that the only reason why society ought to defend rights and sanction rights-violations is general utility. One way to understand this is to put yourself in the position of a utilitarian legislator. As a *legislator*, you need to design a system of legal and conventional rights, which, by definition, will correspond to a system of legal and conventional perfect obligations with associated sanctions. As a *utilitarian*, you will be guided only by general utility and go for the system of rights that has the best consequences, that is, the one that will maximize overall happiness in the long run. A *moral* right can, therefore, be seen as a legal or conventional right that is part of the system of rights that has the best consequences. This will hold for all moral rights, including the right to liberty.

So far, Mill seems to have done a pretty good job at showing how a utilitarian can consistently embrace moral rights. The problem occurs when we consider a particular case in which we know that the only way to maximize overall happiness is to violate someone's moral right. Suppose you are a judge who knows that the only way to prevent a riot, which will harm many people, is to execute an innocent person, whom the potential rioters think is guilty of killing one of their gang-members. If Mill wants to stay true to *act*-utilitarianism, he seems to be forced to say that the judge should not respect the moral right of the innocent person in this particular case. Of course, this is not to deny that the person has a moral right not to be executed, for it is still true that this right is part of the best possible legal system; it is just to say that in this particular case, it should not be respected because we know that violating the right has better consequences. But one could argue that this admission shows that Mill does not take rights seriously enough. Shouldn't rights trump general utility in cases like this?

Conclusion

It is clear that Mill's utilitarianism is far from the simple-minded version of utilitarianism you find in contemporary introductions to ethics. Mill departs from simplistic hedonism by assessing pleasures not just by their intensity and duration but also by their quality. He also seems to be much more focused on the *things* we take pleasure in than the pleasure we take in things. When it comes to assessing actions, it is clear that he would not tell agents always consciously to apply the act-utilitarian principle. He would tell us to rely on rules of thumb that will select actions that typically maximize overall happiness. This does not mean that Mill is a rule-utilitarian, but that asking what would happen if everyone did the same, or followed the same rule, could help us determine the tendency of the individual act to promote overall happiness.

Unlike previous utilitarians, such as Bentham, Mill embraced moral rights. Moral rights, like the right to liberty, are legal and conventional rights that are part of the best system of such rights. The best system is simply the one that would have the best consequences in terms of overall happiness. This means that moral rights cannot be grounded in considerations that are independent of overall happiness. Whether this is to give too little weight to moral rights is a controversial question. What is beyond doubt, however, is that by stretching the utilitarian doctrine to its limits, Mill showed us both its potential and limitations.

I would like to thank Roger Crisp for very helpful comments on an earlier draft of this chapter.

References

Mill, J. S. (1852), 'Whewell on moral philosophy', in *The Collected Works of John Stuart Mill*, (1961–91), ed. J. Robson, Toronto: University of Toronto Press.

—(1859), 'On Liberty', in *The Collected Works of John Stuart Mill*, (1961–91), ed. J. Robson, Toronto: University of Toronto Press.

—(1868), 'Letter to Henry Jones', in *The Collected Works of John Stuart Mill*, (1961–91), ed. J. Robson, Toronto: University of Toronto Press.

—(1871), 'Utilitarianism', in *The Collected Works of John Stuart Mill*, (1961–91), ed. J. Robson, Toronto. See also, *Utilitarianism*, ed. R. Crisp (1998), Oxford: Oxford University Press.

—(1872), 'Letter to John Venn', in *The Collected Works of John Stuart Mill*, (1961–91), ed. J. Robson, Toronto: University of Toronto Press.

—(1873), 'Autobiography', in *The Collected Works of John Stuart Mill*, (1961–91), ed. J. Robson, Toronto: University of Toronto Press.

Recommended reading

Crisp, R. (1997), *Mill on Utilitarianism* (Routledge Philosophy Guidebooks). London and New York: Routledge.

Lyons, D. (1994), *Rights, Welfare, and Mill's Moral Theory*. Oxford: Oxford University Press.

Skorupski, J. (1989), *John Stuart Mill*. London and New York: Routledge.

—(ed.) (1998), *The Cambridge Companion to Mill*. Cambridge: Cambridge University Press.

West, H. R. (2004), *An Introduction to Mill's Utilitarian Ethics*. Cambridge: Cambridge University Press.

10

Nietzsche

Ken Gemes and Christoph Schuringa

Introduction

Nietzsche never presented a worked-out normative ethical theory and appeared to regard any attempt to do so as woefully misguided. He poured scorn on the main contenders for such a theory in his day, and in ours – Kantian ethics and utilitarianism. Moreover, he repeatedly referred to himself as an 'immoralist' and gave one of his books the title *Beyond Good and Evil*, thus seeming only to confirm the impression that he was more interested in demolishing, and even abolishing morality altogether than in making any constructive contribution to the subject. While the topic of morality appears as a central and almost obsessive interest in his works – especially in the sequence of books from *Daybreak: Thoughts on the Prejudices of Morality* (1881) to *On the Genealogy of Morality* (1887) – it generally does so as the target of relentless criticism. Many have concluded, not surprisingly, that Nietzsche, rather than being interested in replacing an existing conception of morality with a better one of his own, was in the business of advising us to abandon morality altogether – to live, in some sense, without morality.

If that was indeed what he was recommending, what could holding such a position amount to? One might think that an injunction to live without morality tells us to live in such a way as to deliberately subvert the felt claims of morality. But such a claim would seem itself ultimately to constitute a distinctive ethical position, albeit perhaps an unsavoury one, rather than a desertion of the notion that there is a set of values by which one should live. (In the same way, an egoistic ethics that recommends suppressing all impulses to altruism in favour of pure self-interest, whatever else may be said against it, cannot be criticized on the grounds of failing to present any values.) 'Immoralism' seems, however, to be something different; Nietzsche's objections to morality certainly seem to go much deeper than a mere call to subvert the status quo.

It is tempting to suppose that Nietzsche's apparent wholesale rejection of morality amounts, instead, to a distinctive *meta*-ethical viewpoint. On this interpretation, it is not so much that we are urged to abandon some notion of morality, but that we simply *couldn't be* moral even if we tried, because the claims of morality are illusory in some way. Nietzsche might thus, for example, be thought of as an early moral error theorist who concluded that the claims of morality should be abandoned because they aspired to correspond to a realm of moral facts that does not exist (cf. *D* 3). His rejection of moral facts is strongly evidenced in such claims as 'There are no moral phenomena at all, but only a moral interpretation of phenomena' (*BGE* 108). But Nietzsche, as we shall see, does not simply regard morality as illusory; he often characterizes it as inimical to what he calls healthy or life-affirming values. In the end, though, it remains difficult to establish whether Nietzsche's rhetoric against moral facts is a final considered meta-ethical position or a strategic move to loosen the grip of a morality he believes to be detrimental to his preferred values.

In his attacks on morality, it appears that Nietzsche, rather than presenting an overarching meta-ethical critique of morality, opposes one or more types of morality, but not others. According to one commentator (Leiter 2002), Nietzsche criticizes 'morality in the pejorative sense' (MPS) while reserving other non-pejorative senses for the word 'morality'. But while Nietzsche does leave scope for morality in an affirmative sense, this type of morality takes on a radically different character from those moralities he condemns. Such a morality lacks certain features Nietzsche takes to be essential to morality in the forms in which it has existed, and thus he urges us, as he sometimes says, to be 'supra-moral' rather than just moral in a different way.[1] While Nietzsche does have some positive injunctions to deliver, he explicitly does *not* claim to offer a new morality or to be a moral teacher of any kind.[2]

Nietzsche's approach, then, resists inclusion in any standard schema either of possible moral theories or of meta-ethical positions. This is unsurprising once we recognize that he in fact takes up a novel stance in relation to morality. Part of its novelty consists in suggesting that we should, in assessing our morality, take note of the particular historical and cultural context in which it has arisen and persists, and of the particular psychological states that are reflected in that morality. This clearly sets Nietzsche apart from most others who write about morality; more often than not Nietzsche writes about morality as if it were a symptom of deeper-lying psychological states, with the uncovering of these states being his real focus of interest. Nietzsche's role, here as elsewhere, is above all that of a diagnostician of the ills of contemporary culture. He is not interested in universalistic claims about what it is right to do at all times and places, but in uncovering the extent to which our practices and values are time-bound and formed by cultural processes of which we are unaware. Once we realize the way in which we have come to acquire our values, we will be in a better position to transcend them. This is because carrying out the critique of our (particular, contingent) morality will show us how it is the product of a process Nietzsche calls 'revaluation'. This very historical knowledge will, as a matter of psychological fact, loosen the hold those received values have on us. It also points the way for how we might, in turn, overcome these values. The particular revaluation of values which took place through the overturning of pagan morality by Christianity serves as an exemplar for a new 'revaluation' that will take us to a 'supra-moral' standpoint. We will not thereby *return* to pre-Christian values or simply negate Christian values: we will have transformed them into a set of values that will allow us to flourish in new ways – ways that had been blocked off by features of our morality thus far.[3]

Immoralism and the scope problem

Nietzsche frequently uses the term 'immoralist' to describe himself, and in his autobiographical work *Ecce Homo*, he several times calls himself the 'first immoralist' (*EH* UM 2; *EH* HH 6; *EH* Destiny 2).[4] While clearly designed to be provocative, it is not immediately clear what Nietzsche intends to convey with this self-description. An immoralist is, obviously enough, some sort of opponent of existing morality. But is immoralism targeted at just some particular morality or a range of moralities, or does it intend to undercut the viability or desirability of any morality whatsoever?

Brian Leiter has identified this problem as the 'scope problem' of Nietzsche's critique of morality (Leiter 2002, 74). According to Leiter, we should reject two ways of construing Nietzsche's critique that seem plausible at first sight. The first of these regards Nietzsche as simply a critic of *all* morality, attacking all possible candidates at one fell swoop. The second takes Nietzsche as a critic of only some one particular kind of morality (say Judaeo-Christian morality as it has developed in Europe).

Now, Nietzsche at many junctures refers to 'moralities' in the plural and emphasizes that there can be, and have been, many different sorts of moral systems. He thus leaves open the possibility of criticizing some of these moral systems while sparing others from the critique. And, indeed, he speaks of 'higher' moralities as if they represented viable options, in contrast to the 'lower' moralities he condemns, in such a way as to suggest that these higher moralities might earn his approval, while the lower ones do not. For example, in *Beyond Good and Evil* he writes: 'our moral philosophers . . . never laid eyes on the real problems of morality; for these emerge only when we compare *many* moralities' (*BGE* 186). And further: '*Morality* [Moral] *in Europe today is herd animal morality* – in other words, as we understand it, merely *one* type of human morality beside which, before which, and after which many other types, above all *higher* moralities, are, or ought to be, possible' (*BGE* 202). Nietzsche thus seems to suggest that he is willing to discriminate between moralities to be endorsed and those to be rejected, rather than issuing an all-out attack on any form of morality whatsoever.

At the same time that Nietzsche appears to demarcate those moralities he is willing to endorse from those he condemns, there is much that suggests that his critique is not simply a matter of expressing a preference for one kind of moral system over another. He often speaks as if he strikes the very idea of a morality right at its core. Thus, he writes in the Preface to *On the Genealogy of Morality*: 'an immense new vista opens up . . ., the belief in morality, in all morality totters' (*GM* Preface 6). Similarly, Nietzsche said of *Daybreak* that 'with this book my campaign against morality begins' (*EH D* 1). *Prima facie* this is not a campaign against some particular morality, in the interests of some other, but a campaign against morality as such. It would appear that Nietzsche can be seen as confining his criticism to, say, just Christian morality here only by reading the texts considerably against the grain.

We are helped to see what Nietzsche's campaign is directed against if we recognize the distinction he draws between morality 'in the narrower sense' – which he thinks has been dominant in some form for the last 10,000 years – and a future kind of morality which he proposes 'should be designated negatively, to begin with, as *extra-moral*' (*BGE* 32). This morality in the narrower sense corresponds closely to that of Christianity, that is, the tradition that has overwhelmingly shaped European culture. (It is important to note here that Nietzsche essentially regards Jewish and Christian morality as being continuous and forming one unified phenomenon.)[5] This is for Nietzsche the most salient target of a critique of morality since Judaeo-Christian morality is the system of moral constraints under which, thanks to a series of contingent historical developments, we do in fact operate. There might be other such moralities, but these fall largely outside Nietzsche's real interests since, as a cultural critic, he is primarily interested in those conditions that are available for study in the here and now.[6] In principle, of course, Nietzsche's critique could be extended to all morality systems that are structured in relevantly similar ways. Thus, the target of Nietzsche's critique would be a certain *form* of moral system with a number of structural features. This way of construing Nietzsche's target would conform to Leiter's notion of MPS, which constitutes not some particular moral system but the set of all possible instantiations of a particular structure: 'Nietzsche believes that all normative systems which perform something like the role we associate with "morality" share certain structural characteristics' (Leiter 2002, 78). On Leiter's picture, MPS contains both a descriptive and a normative component.[7] The descriptive component requires that agents (i) have free will; (ii) are sufficiently transparent to themselves that they can distinguish the individual motives of their actions and (iii) are similar in the relevant respects, so that morality has universal application. The normative component involves injunctions that entail that one's primary duty is to help the worst off, and hence, claims Leiter, an MPS harms the 'highest men' while favouring the 'lowest' men.

However, it is not clear that Nietzsche always opposes the conception of free will that Leiter associates with MPS; in some cases, indeed, he appears to regard something like it as required for human flourishing (see Gemes 2009). Indeed, as Leiter himself observes, utilitarianism is a form of MPS that typically does not embrace the claim of free will. Nor, for that matter, need it embrace any position about the transparency of motives. Arguably, there is something un-Nietzschean in the supposition that Nietzsche is interested in extending his critique to any possible morality system that possesses some specified set of structural features. We should expect Nietzsche to be little interested in such an exercise, since he regards it as well-nigh impossible for us to know what the effects of such systems will be abstracted from any specific cultural context. We would be attempting to construct a hypothetical moral system in isolation from the very historical and cultural context that gives it genuine specificity. Nietzsche teaches us that a morality can arise only within a set of highly complex cultural and historical conditions.[8] Thus it is always possible that within some individual cultural context the very belief in free will, transparency and perhaps even universality could be conducive to the flourishing of the 'higher types' that Leiter claims Nietzsche so values. Finally, the idea that what Nietzsche valued above all else was the flourishing of great individuals is itself questionable. It can be argued that Nietzsche's early project of cultural renewal still provided his most important axiological end even in the later works. On this reading he valued great individuals because he believed that they constituted the best hope for cultural renewal.

The Christian morality system

For Nietzsche, the morality associated with Christianity is of particular significance, since it has, he claims, pervaded European culture and has continued to shape the human beings who belong to that culture, often in ways they cannot themselves see. It has been, to borrow a phrase from Bernard Williams, the dominant 'morality system' under which we have lived.[9] As elsewhere in his work, Nietzsche's interest is above all in the cultural conditions in which he found himself and the ways in which these foster, or thwart, individual and cultural flourishing.

It is difficult to overestimate the role that Christianity, as a belief system and as a cultural phenomenon, played in Nietzsche's life and philosophical trajectory. Much of his philosophical project can be thought of as a protracted settling of scores with his Christian background and environment, and with his profound sense of Christianity's decay and collapse, which he regarded as having reached completion within his lifetime and which he summed up in the memorable phrase 'God is dead'.[10] Nietzsche, like many prominent German intellectuals of the nineteenth century, came from a family of clergymen; his father and both of his grandfathers were pastors. Born in the small village of Röcken in Saxony in 1844 in a house that adjoined the churchyard, Nietzsche would literally grow up in the shadow of the church. His father having died when he was five years old, the expectations of his family were that the young Nietzsche would train for the priesthood himself. In keeping with these expectations, Nietzsche duly enrolled as a theology student at the University of Bonn. While a student at Bonn, however, he experienced a decisive crisis of faith which prompted him to take the highly confrontational step of refusing communion in front of his family on Easter Sunday 1865. He then switched the subject of his studies to philology, at the same time moving to the University of Leipzig. From this time on, Nietzsche would reflect deeply on the nature of the Christian religion, the reasons for its hold on Western civilization and the decline that it was experiencing in the nineteenth century.

Nietzsche was writing at a time when both the Christian faith and established morality appeared to be subject to a grave threat, particularly from the ideas of Darwin. Darwin's *The Descent of Man*, published in 1871, controversially extrapolated the implications of his theory of natural selection to the human species. Darwin's work had suggested to many the possibility that human beings could be thought of as entirely natural creatures, that is, as continuous with other species of life, without any need for a divine explanation. Even the achievements of intelligence – and of morality – could now be explained as simply more highly evolved versions of the capacities and behaviour of other animals. In his early work on morality, Nietzsche himself was clearly influenced by a current of thought influenced by Darwin, and was keenly aware of the wide-ranging implications of Darwinism for nineteenth-century conceptions of morality. Nietzsche was quick to see that these implications, if fully accepted, had to be deeply shocking to those who clung to theological ideas. Indeed, Nietzsche accused those who did not accept the full implications of the new sciences of being guilty of some form of self-deception. He pointedly summed up their predicament:

> Formerly one sought the feeling of the grandeur of man by pointing to his divine *origin*: this has now become a forbidden way, for at its portal stands the ape, together with other gruesome beasts, grinning knowingly as if to say: no further in this direction! (*D* 49)

At the same time, he saw that the degree of this shock factor depended entirely on one's pre-existing conceptions about what ought to be the basis of morality. For Nietzsche, our link to the apes need not be regarded as a cause of despair; for him, it functioned instead as merely a reminder of our animal past.

Although in earlier works such as *Human, All Too Human* Nietzsche himself followed the Darwinian approach to morality closely, he would later come to distance himself both from Darwin generally and from the Darwinian approach to morality in particular.[11] He would now become more interested in tracing the ways in which values had been culturally transformed through a process he called 'revaluation'. Rather than building hypotheses invoking mechanisms of natural selection, he was increasingly interested in tracing the cultural evolution of morality, for instance through the texts of the Old Testament.[12] Nietzsche's development of this approach would allow him to deliver a much more trenchant critique of Christianity as a morality, since it would show the ways in which it continues to have a hold on us at the same time as pointing out the ways in which it had originally established that hold. The ways in which it did so, according to Nietzsche, are highly specific and complex, and ought to unsettle us in ways that a mere blanket appeal to the rootedness of our morality in animal evolution will not.

The first revaluation: The slave revolt

Nietzsche regarded the Christian morality system as the outcome of a process of 'revaluation' that transformed an existing system that he labels '*pre-moral*' (*BGE* 32). While Nietzsche most frequently reserves the term 'revaluation' for his own announced project of transforming our present Christian morality into something else, he also refers to the emergence of Christian morality itself as a 'revaluation'. He describes Christianity as 'promis[ing] a revaluation of all the values of antiquity' (*BGE* 46) and speaks of the 'radical revaluation of their enemies' values' by the Jewish priestly caste and of the 'revaluation of all values' by 'Israel' (*GM* I 7, 8). The pre-moral system from which the Judaeo-Christian morality system arises shares certain of the features of this morality 'in the narrower sense' – but these exist in a form that undergoes considerable change through the process of 'moralization'.

Nietzsche lays out the form he supposed such pre-moral systems to take in detail from the period of *Human, All Too Human* on. Here, he begins to describe such a system, giving it the label *Sittlichkeit der Sitte*, usually translated 'morality of custom' or 'morality of mores'.[13] It should be emphasized, however, that the German phrase does not contain any cognate of *moralisch* or *Moral*: the customs referred to have, importantly, not yet been 'moralized'. Rather than a system in which human actions are assessed in terms of motivation, the morality of custom is simply a societal system of rules designed to hold the community together and protect it from external threats. It demands from its subjects absolute obedience and conformity to existing practices, and its reach extends to practices such as hygienic and dietary practices that would now normally be considered as outside the realm of morality. What mattered under the morality of custom was absolute obedience, regardless of the individual's motivation for obeying. Indeed, the individual was entirely unimportant, and individuals were to be discouraged from acting on their own initiative. Signs of individuality and eccentricity presented a danger to the system that threatened to destabilize it and put its well-established customs in question. What was required above all was continuity and uniformity: 'change was accounted immoral [*das Unsittliche*] and pregnant with disaster' (*D* 18).

This account of the morality of custom is elaborated and expanded in the Second Treatise of *On the Genealogy of Morality* (1887). Here, Nietzsche describes in detail the process of moralization that takes us from a pre-moral set-up dominated by custom to a fully moral system. To take an example of this transition, in the pre-moral set-up, the members of the community stood to one another in reciprocal relationships that, if disturbed by a transgression by one member of the community against another, generated certain expectations of recompense on the part of the offended party. The equilibrium between individuals could be restored by the settling of the debt that had thus been created by means of an appropriate repayment. To be guilty here was simply to be in a state of debt. This Nietzsche sees as an antecedent of the moralized conception of guilt, drawing on the etymological connection between the terms for 'debts' (*Schulden*) and 'guilt' (*Schuld*) in German. This process of moralization of the concept of debt into that of (moralized) guilt involves the elaboration of a complex psychological machinery that gives rise to the emergence of bad (or guilty) conscience. Nietzsche argues that this concept of bad conscience has been exacerbated into a disfiguring pathology by the Christian conception of our infinite debt to, and guilt before God.

The Third Treatise of *GM* further fills in some of the details of how the transition from morality of custom to full-blown morality is effected. Here, Nietzsche fleshes out the story already offered in *GM* I by elaborating the role of priests as instruments of the revaluation. As Nietzsche had hinted in *HH* and *D*, since conformity was the principal requirement exacted by the morality of custom, something extraordinary had to happen for any proposed change to be accepted. For the individual proposing the change to be taken seriously, he had to claim an extraordinary status for himself. Effectively, the person with this power is the priest, who claimed to be possessed by divine inspiration. The priest is particularly important in the role he plays on behalf of the weak, slavish mass Nietzsche refers to as the 'herd'. This herd, which constitutes the vast majority, is subjugated by a minority of powerful nobles. According to the account in *GM* I, the nobles operate with a value system according to which they – the strong, flourishing types – are 'good', and the weak slaves are 'bad'. These terms, significantly, lack any moral connotations – the bad are bad simply in virtue of being weak, ugly and in other ways little worthy of the nobles' consideration, rather than being the object of the nobles' moral reproof. The good (the nobles) do not at all consider it their mission to convert the bad (the slaves). Indeed, the very existence of the slaves is a precondition for the existence of noble society. The weak, or the 'bad' as the nobles call them, live in a state of *ressentiment* – a festering, pent-up hatred of their masters, on whom they do not, due to their inferior strength, have the means of exacting revenge. They thus look for a way to bring about an 'imaginary revenge', and this they manage to do with the aid of the priests. This imaginary revenge consists in branding themselves 'good' and the nobles not 'bad' but 'evil'.[14] It now becomes the mission of the good to convert the evil, allegedly for their own good. The very qualities on which the nobles had prided themselves – pride, strength, carefreeness and aggression – are now branded as sins for which there must be some punishment in another world. This moral valuation allows the weak to get their revenge on the strong, by suggesting that the values of the weak – compassion and related moral emotions – though previously associated by the strong with feebleness and servitude, are the true values, while the values of the strong are to be met with the most terrible punishments in the imagined afterlife.

This story is important for Nietzsche in showing, first, that Christian morality is not the unique standard by which to measure human action but a contingent development arising from earlier value systems. Second, it shows that the origins of Christian morality involve strategies of revenge and cruelty which appear incompatible with the self-understanding of the Christian religion. The first of these results may seem to have a limited impact, affecting only those who uphold Christian morality as an unassailable system with a unique sanction (i.e. the word of God). The second, however, more obviously has a wider application. It would seem that almost any extant moral system describes itself as upholding the values of kindness and compassion. For any such moral system, it would be, at the very least, embarrassing if it turns out to have arisen in a haphazard, piecemeal and contingent fashion from a diffuse set of practices which have nothing to do with those values.

It would be a mistake to suppose that the critical force which Nietzsche takes these points to have led him simply to reject 'moralized' morality outright. It is almost never Nietzsche's position, where he criticizes a phenomenon or an idea, that the object of his critique should be straightforwardly rejected by everyone in all circumstances. Rather, Nietzsche criticizes a thing's suitability *for* some type of person or some use. Christianity he regards as having many laudable aspects, even if he thinks it is now predominantly harmful to the kind of human beings he would like to see flourish. As a cultural phenomenon, the Judaeo-Christian tradition has given us much that we should embrace; Nietzsche is certainly not advising us to try and somehow turn the clock back to a pre-Christian era. Indeed, Christianity has made man into an 'interesting animal' (*GM* I 6), with greater psychological complexity and a greater capacity to produce great works of the spirit, especially artworks, than would have been possible otherwise. Furthermore, it is Christianity that has endowed us with the will to truth that Nietzsche values so highly – and which becomes, in his hands, the instrument of Christianity's own demise (see Williams 2002, 12–16). The point, then, is not to reject the Christian heritage outright but to overcome it through the means it has itself provided (see Jaspers 1961).

Genealogy and critique

Before we consider how Nietzsche thinks 'moralized' values can be overcome, it is worth paying some attention to the details of his critique and how it is meant to function. How can telling us a story about how our morality has come to be have the function of motivating us to take up a critical stance towards it? It would seem that merely pointing to the disreputable origins of our practices does not serve to discredit them instantly; to think along these lines seems to be to fall victim to the 'genetic fallacy' (the error of inferring the present value of a thing from the value of its origins). That a thinker of Nietzsche's acuity should commit such an error would seem highly surprising; indeed, he seems to warn against it himself in several places.[15]

We can see how Nietzsche avoids this error by examining what he himself takes genealogy to be. There is a tendency in current discussion to speak of 'genealogy' as if it were something like a technique or method invented by Nietzsche, or even a distinctive argument form with a special logical force of its own.[16] Nietzsche never gives any indication, however, that he thought of genealogy as a novel way of doing philosophy that could, by itself, deliver a special kind of critical force. Indeed, he does not use 'genealogy' as a term of art. (Uses of the term 'genealogy' and its cognates in GM are relatively sparse, and he does not use it in this context in any other published works or his unpublished notebooks.)[17] Rather, he tends to speak of giving a 'history' of our 'moral valuations', our 'moral sensations' or similar phrases (see N 1883 8[15], 16[33]; N 1884 26[130], 26[164]). There is no indication, then, that a genealogy is for Nietzsche anything distinct from the telling of a historical narrative. There is a separate question as to whether Nietzsche's claim to deliver a 'real history' in GM should be taken at face value, in the sense of whether the stories have to be literally true, or can be partly or entirely fictional, but this does not affect their structure as narratives (for opposing views on their aspiration to be genuinely historical, see, e.g., May 1999 and Geuss 1999).

A genealogy, then, is simply a developmental story. The telling of such a story does not implicate the teller in the genetic fallacy if it is told with a specific intent: if it is told to discredit, and displace an existing story of a similar nature, then it has the potential to perform a vital critical function. It may show the original story to be questionable – because its claims to be the only right and true story have been undermined by the narrator's ability to tell another, radically different story. This appears to be precisely the case with Nietzsche's genealogy of morality. Moralists have tended to tell a story about the origination of values (whether the origin is taken to be a divine source, or, say, a moral law that we can sense within us) which is incompatible with the truth of the new story. Of course, the new story has no particular critical function for the upholder of a moral system who is not inclined to tell the original story in the first place. But for Nietzsche it is enough that his audience, in general, *did* in fact rely on such original stories. To shock them out of their faith in such stories was for him a major aim. As for those who proposed to uphold something like Christian morality without making claims to a divine origin, the question to be directed at them was presumably what could possibly justify such a freely dangling belief system. Indeed, Nietzsche had harsh words for those who professed to continue to uphold Christian values even while accepting the insights of Darwinism and other modern developments that put the theological underpinning of those values in serious question.[18] They were hypocrites, well-meaning perhaps, but behind the times: the news of the death of God had somehow not fully reached them.

We have seen that a genealogy constitutes an important part of the process of weaning us off our morality. It is a first stage in drawing us away from this morality and will need to be followed by a critical reappraisal. It is not itself critique; what genealogy provides us with is a preparation for the desired critique, in the form of the 'knowledge of the conditions and circumstances out of which they [our values] have grown' (Schacht 1994, 429). This knowledge was, ultimately, to be put in the service of what Nietzsche took to be his most important project: that of our own revaluation of all our values. It is to this project that we now turn.

The second revaluation:
The philosophy of the future

Having diagnosed what he saw as the decayed and irremediable state of contemporary morality, Nietzsche considered the time to be ripe for an extremely daring and ambitious project which he called for repeatedly: a new 'revaluation of all values'. In the period (roughly his last two active years before he succumbed to insanity in January 1889) in which he was formulating plans to write a systematic *magnum opus* bringing together all his ideas – a work which never materialized – his preferred working title for this systematic work was *Attempt at a Revaluation of All Values*. (Another title with which Nietzsche persistently toyed was *The Will to Power*; the work which was eventually posthumously published under that name, under the editorship of Nietzsche's sister, is a collection of fragments from Nietzsche's notebooks that crudely imposes a spurious order on them, and has no claim to be considered a book by Nietzsche.) If Nietzsche never published a systematic revaluation of all values, calls for such a project had nonetheless been appearing in his work long before this, beginning with *Beyond Good and Evil* in 1886. While he eventually billed *The Antichrist* as a 'revaluation of all values', this text cannot be considered as the execution of this project. Here, Nietzsche confines himself to a critique of Judaeo-Christian values, rather than elaborating what is to supplant them.

What could such a revaluation amount to? In *BGE*, Nietzsche had told us that the 'new philosophers' who are to take the place of traditional metaphysicians will 'put . . . an end to that gruesome dominion of nonsense and accident that has so far been called "history"', in part through a 'revaluation of values under whose new pressure and hammer a conscience would be steeled, a heart turned to bronze, in order to endure the weight of such responsibility' (*BGE* 203). These 'philosophers of the future', who will be 'free, *very* free spirits' (*BGE* 44), are called on to effect the 'overcoming of morality, in a certain sense even the self-overcoming of morality' (*BGE* 32). Their task is ultimately to '*create values*' (*BGE* 211).

In light of Nietzsche's insistence that philosophers should create values, it is surprising that he has often been portrayed as a nihilist. Sure enough, Nietzsche emphasizes the destruction of hitherto existing values that is summed up in his characterization of the contemporary predicament as marked by the 'death of God' (see *GS* 343). Nietzsche takes the death of God to spell an era in which there will be no ultimate values – that is, no values that can give ultimate meaning to existence – and predicts that this absence of ultimate values will mark the history of Europe for the next 200 years. This lack of ultimate values is the condition that Nietzsche diagnoses as nihilism, an attitude in which he is far from willing to acquiesce, and instead regards with horror. For Nietzsche, the loss of belief prompted by the death of God is much more troubling and far-reaching than most secularists would accept. Modern humanists, utilitarians, socialists and communists typically continue to espouse a morality of compassion which, by Nietzsche's lights, is simply Judaeo-Christian morality shorn of the usual religious metaphysics (God, heaven, hell, etc.) Nietzsche's prediction is that without that metaphysical underpinning these values will eventually cease to have a hold on us.

For Nietzsche, the truly pressing and disconcerting prospect is not the absence of value but the misdirection of man's will in such a way that he believes in nothingness, rather than not believe in anything at all. Man 'would much rather will *nothingness* than *not* will'. This is because

> Man, the bravest animal and the one most accustomed to suffering, does *not* negate suffering in itself: he *wants* it, he even seeks it out, provided one shows him a *meaning* for it, a *to-this-end* of suffering. The meaninglessness of suffering, not the suffering itself, was the curse that thus far lay stretched out over humanity. (*GM* III 28)

Nietzsche is very far from endorsing those who would forego the search for meaning. In fact he derides them as the 'last men', devoid of any great vision: '"What is love? What is creation? What is longing? What is a star?" – thus asks the last man, and he blinks' (*Z* I Prologue 5). Nihilism, then, is not to be succumbed to but to be overcome by those of sufficient strength to create their own values without relying on some external sanction. In *The Gay Science*, after first presenting the idea of the death of God as a thunderous and earth-shattering event, Nietzsche later returns to that theme in a much more lighthearted, even joyous vein, telling us that 'we philosophers and "free sprits" feel, when we hear the news that "the old god is dead", as if a new dawn shone on us; our heart overflows with gratitude, amazement, premonitions, expectation' (*GS* 343). Nietzsche's message appears to be that with the old god dead we, or at least the free spirits among us, are free to create our own, individual values.

In Nietzsche's frequent calls on the 'new' philosophers to be 'legislators', and to create their own values, it is not clear what the criteria are by which they should legislate. Nietzsche is clearly not simply an advocate of the capricious exertion of power, or even of the promotion of one particular kind of human being, for he thinks that different moralities are suitable in different contexts. In particular, 'moralities must be forced to bow first of all before the *order of rank*' (*BGE* 221); it is appropriate for herd morality to 'rule in the herd', but not among creative geniuses. Furthermore, Nietzsche was severely critical of the view that there is one correct moral standard:

My demand upon the philosopher is known, that he take his stand *beyond* good and evil and leave the illusion of moral judgment *beneath* himself. This demand follows from an insight which I was the first to formulate: that *there are altogether no moral facts*. . . . Morality is merely an interpretation of certain phenomena – more precisely, a misinterpretation. (*TI* 'Improvers' 1)

Arguably, it would seem that it is creativity itself that is given a higher value than anything else by Nietzsche. Nietzsche's spokesman Zarathustra, in the fictional work *Thus Spoke Zarathustra*, proclaims creation to be 'the great redemption from suffering, and life's growing light' (*Z* II 2). This prioritization of creativity helps to make better sense both of Nietzsche's reluctance to accept the existence of moral facts, fixed once and for all, and his call for philosophers to be creators of value. Such creation is the philosopher's ultimate task, and it is only in order to clear the ground for this that he must often be destructive. Thus, sometimes the philosopher is 'at his most useful when *there is much to destroy*, in times of the chaotic or of degeneration' (N 1873 28[2]). While Nietzsche liked to describe himself as 'dynamite' (*EH* Destiny 1), he destroyed in order to create space for the new, not merely to obliterate the old.

It can be argued, however, that Nietzsche himself does espouse several distinct positive values beyond the value of self-creation. The early Nietzsche of *The Birth of Tragedy* clearly subscribed to the project of the renewal of a high culture. Here, he appears close to Romantic thinkers such as his one-time hero, the poet Friedrich Hölderlin, who claimed that, while the Greeks had a genuine high culture, we moderns have a mere sham or philistine culture. The early Nietzsche's effusive enthusiasm for the music of Richard Wagner was based on the idea that Wagner could be the harbinger of a renewal of high culture (see *BT* 16).[19] Arguably, as Nietzsche realized how deep the roots of philistine culture went, he gave up on the idea of a shared high culture and moved to the position that culture is to be preserved and developed by a privileged elite. Part of his objection to the morality of compassion is that with its democratic levelling effect it hinders the development of such an elite. Apart from portraying himself as a romantic apostle of high culture, he presents himself as an advocate of other values, such as the greater psychological health of both the culture and the individual, or alternatively as an apostle of the value of life-affirmation.[20] A key question that remains over, however, is how these values can be grounded, given Nietzsche's scepticism about the existence of moral 'facts' and his privileging of rank-ordering and perspective.

While there remains a debate about what, if any, Nietzsche's ultimate values are, it is arguable that some of his values in fact came to fruition through the inspiration he provided to subsequent generations. One might argue that Nietzsche's most significant legacy is to be found, not in some wholesale destruction of morality, or in any specific philosophical doctrine, but in the myriad creative artists and thinkers who found inspiration in his work. Poets like Rainer Maria Rilke, W. B. Yeats and Stefan George, novelists like Thomas Mann, Hermann Hesse and D. H. Lawrence, and playwrights like Eugene O'Neill and George Bernard Shaw were crucially inspired by Nietzsche to find their own unique voices. Like these artists, philosophers like Martin Heidegger and Michel Foucault, who produced their own distinctive transformations of Nietzsche's thought, might be seen as practising just the kind of self-creation that Nietzsche called for. Such individuals arguably realize Nietzsche's project in a more distinctively Nietzschean vein than those who merely attempt to discern what Nietzsche's views on morality might have been.

Notes

1 Cf. *GS* 107: 'We should be *able* also to stand *above* morality'.

2 See, for example, *GS* 292: 'I do not wish to promote any morality'. See the contrast between becoming a new kind of moral lawgiver – something which Nietzsche advocates – and being a *moralist*, brought out at *GS* 335: 'Let us therefore *limit* ourselves to the purification of our opinions and valuations and to the *creation of our own new tables of what is good*, and let us stop brooding about the

"moral value of our actions"! Yes, my friends, regarding all the moral chatter of some about others it is time to feel nauseous. Sitting in moral judgment should offend our taste'.

3 Note what Nietzsche writes in the Preface added in 1886 to *Daybreak*: 'in this book faith in morality is withdrawn – but why? *Out of morality!*' 'In us there is accomplished – supposing you want a formula – the *self-sublimation of morality* [die Selbstaufhebung der Moral]' (*D* Preface 4).

4 See also *EH* Destiny 4 and the references to himself as an 'immoralist' in the period 1885–88, at *BGE* 32, 226; *D* Preface 4; *GS* 346, 381; *TI* Maxims 36, Morality 3, 6, Errors 7, Skirmishes 32.

5 This view has a number of complications. Nietzsche sees modern Christianity as essentially the creation of Saul of Tarsus (St Paul), not of Jesus of Nazareth. He sees Paul's version of Christianity as being remarkably continuous with the Jewish priestly culture of the Second Temple period. (See *AC*.)

6 Nietzsche often mentions Buddhism unfavourably, typically in places where he criticizes it, along with Christianity, as being a religion built on the all-encompassing value of compassion. This probably represents the influence of Schopenhauer, one of his main philosophical sources. Schopenhauer, an advocate of compassion and withdrawal from this world, often cited Eastern religions, including Buddhism.

7 Leiter regards only the normative component as essential but emphasizes that Nietzsche's full critique encompasses both.

8 Cf. Nietzsche's complaints about the hypothetical nature of the methods of the 'English genealogists' in *GM* Preface 7 and *GM* I 2: they think they are entitled to suppose what the basic ingredients of any moral system are, when they are in fact retrojecting highly specific and contingently developed features of their own worldview into the distant past.

9 See Williams 1985.

10 See, in particular, the famous passage at *GS* 125. The pronouncement 'God is dead' appears explicitly for the first time at *GS* 108, but see also *HH* II/2 84 for an important prefiguration, and a later elaboration in *Z* IV 6–7.

11 It is generally agreed that Nietzsche did not himself read Darwin. He appears to have gained most of his knowledge of Darwinism through Paul Rée, a philosopher he befriended and with whom he had a fruitful period of intellectual exchange at the time of the composition of *HH*.

12 This is the approach Nietzsche took in *The Antichrist*. See, especially, *AC* 27ff.

13 The phrase itself first appears at *D* 9, but the concept is evidently already in play in *HH* (see *HH* I 96, 99; *HH* II/1 89).

14 This account of the history of the value-oppositions 'good-bad' and 'good-evil' is a recurrent theme reaching back as far as *HH*. See *HH* I 45 and also *BGE* 260 for earlier accounts of this revaluation of terms. The revenge is *imaginary* presumably only in the sense that no material harm is inflicted on the strong – only a supposed spiritual harm.

15 A passage frequently cited in this context is *GS* 345, although it is doubtful that Nietzsche is referring to this specific fallacy there. See, nevertheless, the *Nachlaß* notes N 1883 16[33], N 1885 34[55] and N 1885–86 2[189]. Alternatively one might argue that Nietzsche was less interested in providing rigorous logical arguments against received morality than actually subverting its influence, and believed that the mere display of Christianity's unsavoury roots would effect such a subversion.

16 The notion that Nietzsche invented a method called 'genealogy' that was then later picked up by other authors such as Foucault has been criticized by Raymond Geuss (Geuss 1999, 1).

17 For the few mentions of 'genealogy' in *GM*, see *GM* Preface 4, 7; *GM* I 2, 4; *GM* II 4, 12.

18 See, in particular, Nietzsche's critique, in the first of his *Untimely Meditations*, of David Friedrich Strauss, a theologian who continued to uphold a form of Christianity despite claiming to endorse Darwinism.

19 Indeed, the later Nietzsche came to register embarrassment at this early naive enthusiasm (cf. *BT*, 'Attempt at a Self-Criticism'). However, to the end Nietzsche maintained that the case of Wagner was the most instructive one of our age.

20 See Reginster 2006 for an interpretation of Nietzsche's philosophy that gives a central role to a positive project of promoting the affirmation of life.

References

We use the following standard conventions for abbreviating the titles of Nietzsche's books: *AC* = *The Antichrist*; *BGE* = *Beyond Good and Evil*; *BT* = *The Birth of Tragedy*; *D* = *Daybreak*; *EH* = *Ecce Homo*; *GM* = *On the Genealogy of Morality*; *GS* = *The Gay Science*; *HH* = *Human, All Too Human*; *TI* = *Twilight of the Idols*; *Z* = *Thus Spoke Zarathustra*. The numbers following these abbreviations refer to sections, not pages. Translations cited are those of Walter Kaufmann, except for *D* and *HH* (translated by R. J. Hollingdale) and *GM* (translated by Maudemarie Clark and Alan Swensen). Unpublished notes are cited as N, followed by date and fragment number (any translations are our own).

Gemes, K. (2009), 'Nietzsche on free will, autonomy, and the sovereign individual', in K. Gemes and S. May (eds), *Nietzsche on Freedom and Autonomy*. Oxford: Oxford University Press, pp. 33–49.

Geuss, R. (1999), 'Nietzsche and genealogy', in his *Morality, Culture, and History*. Cambridge: Cambridge University Press, pp. 1–28.

Jaspers, K. (1961), *Nietzsche and Christianity*. South Bend: Regnery.

Leiter, B. (2002), *Nietzsche on Morality*. London: Routledge.

May, S. (1999), *Nietzsche's Ethics and His War on 'Morality'*. Oxford: Clarendon Press.

Nietzsche, F. (1973) [1886], *Beyond Good and Evil*, trans. W. Kaufmann. New York: Vintage.

—(1997) [1881], *Daybreak*, trans. R. J. Hollingdale. Cambridge: Cambridge University Press.

—(1998) [1887], *On the Genealogy of Morality*, trans. M. Clark and A. J. Swensen. Indianapolis: Hackett.

Reginster, B. (2006), *The Affirmation of Life: Nietzsche on Overcoming Nihilism*. Cambridge MA: Harvard University Press.

Schacht, R. (1994), 'Of morals and *Menschen*', in R. Schacht (ed.), *Nietzsche, Genealogy, Morality*. Berkeley: University of California Press, pp. 427–48.

Williams, B. (1985), *Ethics and the Limits of Philosophy*. London: Fontana.

—(2002), *Truth and Truthfulness: An Essay in Genealogy*. Princeton: Princeton University Press.

Recommended reading

General works on Nietzsche:

Clark, M. (1990), *Nietzsche on Truth and Philosophy*. Cambridge: Cambridge University Press.

Kaufmann, W. (1974), *Nietzsche: Philosopher, Psychologist, Antichrist*. Princeton: Princeton University Press (4th ed.)

Nehamas, A. (1985), *Nietzsche: Life as Literature*. Cambridge MA: Harvard University Press.

On Nietzsche and ethics:

Acampora, C. (ed.) (2006), *Nietzsche's On the Genealogy of Morals: Critical Essays*. Lanham MD: Rowman & Littlefield.

Clark, M. (1994), 'Nietzsche's immoralism and the concept of morality',
    in R. Schacht (ed.), *Nietzsche, Genealogy, Morality*. Berkeley:
    University of California Press, pp. 15–34.
Foot, P. (1994), 'Nietzsche's immoralism', in R. Schacht (ed.), *Nietzsche,
    Genealogy, Morality*. Berkeley: University of California Press,
    pp. 3–14.
—(2002), 'Nietzsche: the revaluation of values', in her *Virtues and Vices*.
    Oxford: Oxford University Press, pp. 81–95.
Gemes, K. and May, S. (eds) (2009), *Nietzsche on Freedom and
    Autonomy*. Oxford: Oxford University Press.
Hunt, L. H. (1991), *Nietzsche and the Origin of Virtue*. London/New York:
    Routledge.
Janaway, C. (2007), *Beyond Selflessness: Reading Nietzsche's
    Genealogy*. Oxford: Oxford University Press.
Leiter, B. (2002), *Nietzsche on Morality*. London: Routledge.
Leiter, B. and Sinhababu, N. (eds) (2007), *Nietzsche and Morality*.
    Oxford: Oxford University Press.
Schacht, R. (ed.) (1994), *Nietzsche, Genealogy, Morality*. Berkeley:
    University of California Press.
—(2001), *Nietzsche's Postmoralism*. Cambridge: Cambridge University
    Press.

11

MacIntyre

David Solomon

By the time Alasdair MacIntyre entered Moral Philosophy,[1] the state of discussion within classical meta-ethics was well defined. Three broadly different views were on offer: (1) the intuitionism of Moore, Prichard and Ross, which held that ethical judgements are fitted to express truths about how we should behave, but that these truths cannot be expressed in naturalistic terms; (2) the naturalism that held that moral concepts can be defined (or analysed, as philosophers increasingly said) into natural properties and that moral judgements are, therefore, suited to express truths about the natural world and (3) various versions of non-cognitivism, which rejected the cognitivism of both the intuitionists and the naturalists, by maintaining that the function of moral judgements is not to express truths at all, but rather merely to express attitudes or emotional responses towards possible actions and possible objects of pursuit.

Non-cognitivism, especially its most prominent form, emotivism, appeared to both intuitionists and naturalists to be quite radical and to give up altogether on the traditional ambitions of moral philosophy to achieve knowledge – or at least well-justified belief – about how we should behave and what objects are genuinely good or genuinely worthy of pursuit. If the task of moral language is only to express our contingently formed attitudes or emotions, it is impossible, so it seemed to many, to speak of truth in ethics or to regard moral disagreements as having rationally compelling resolutions. When

MacIntyre first comes on the scene in ethics, then, these three views dominate the ethical landscape, and all three have powerful arguments for their positions and well worked-out responses to the arguments of their opponents. Philosophers are beginning to talk about a stalemate in ethics.

MacIntyre's career in ethics is best understood as involving two great projects. The first is to respond to this stalemate in classical meta-ethics. He does this not by taking any one of the three options on offer at mid-century, but rather by raising fundamental questions about the adequacy of classical meta-ethics in its approach to the meaning of moral concepts. Although his response to the mistakes of classical meta-ethics develops and deepens over the three decades leading up to the publication of *After Virtue* in 1981, he consistently accuses classical meta-ethicists of treating moral concepts as if they are timeless and unchangeable, and of using semantic techniques for investigating them that are insufficiently sensitive to the historical and social determinants of meaning.

His second major project is to participate in the revival of traditional normative theory. The importance of G. E. Moore lies not simply in what he initiated – classical meta-ethics – but also in what he helped to bring to an end (at least for a time): traditional normative theory. As we have seen in earlier chapters of this book, ethics in the nineteenth century was dominated by the articulation and defence of comprehensive normative theories, theories anchored in reason and purporting to justify concrete and determinate action. The two most prominent normative ethical theories in the nineteenth century were Kantian rationalism and Benthamite utilitarianism. By the end of the nineteenth century, however, especially in the Anglophone world, both these normative theories had encountered severe headwinds. Henry Sidgwick, the most sophisticated and systematic of the utilitarians, had carried the utilitarian project much further than the point where Bentham and Mill had left it. Unfortunately for utilitarianism, Sidgwick had pushed the theory to the point, as he feared, of incoherence. He believed that he had irrefutable arguments that demonstrated that utilitarianism could be rationally compelling only if it could be shown that, ultimately, the demands on any agent that he maximize his own utility were consistent with the demands on him that he maximize universal utility. In other words, for utilitarianism to be rationally compelling, the demands of personal fulfilment must be perfectly compatible with the demands of universal benevolence. Unfortunately, he could find no arguments to demonstrate that these two demands necessarily converge. As a result, Sidgwick died a broken man, with his hopes for a compelling defence of utilitarianism dashed.[2]

At the same time, the ambitions of the Kantian alternative to utilitarianism had also encountered severe criticism – not least from the powerful arguments put forward by Nietzsche, but also from the various naturalistic projects of those like Spencer who were unfriendly to the special metaphysical requirements of Kantian theory. While there were some who would continue to defend and further articulate both the Kantian and utilitarian theoretical options, academic philosophers, especially in the English-speaking universities, increasingly withdrew from the very project of normative ethical theory. It is one of the most remarkable features of the first half of the twentieth century that while the world underwent some of the culturally most stressful events in human history – two world wars, a worldwide depression, a vast transformation of the basic conditions of human life by new technologies and the rise of two brutal and repressive totalitarianisms on a scale never encountered before – academic moral philosophers in the English-speaking world for the most part had no comment. The retreat from normative theory in favour of tidier – and morally neutral – investigations of classical meta-ethics was almost total.

As the second half of the twentieth century unfolded, it was impossible for this ethical quietism to be sustained. The revival of normative theory was surely inevitable, and, hurried on no doubt by the cultural turmoil of the 1960s, it arrived in a rush with the publication in 1971 of John Rawls' magisterial *A Theory of Justice*.[3] Though primarily focused on political philosophy, this book showed the way for a more general revival of a broadly Kantian approach to ethics. Rawls and his very talented and productive students[4] have continued this revival, which has made Kantian ethical theory increasingly the dominant ethical approach among academic philosophers. Rawls' revival of the Kantian ethical project was followed quite quickly by several revamped and updated versions of utilitarian theory, first seen in Derek Parfit's powerful book, *Reasons and Persons*. Like Rawls, Parfit too has become the centre of a school of talented and creative moral philosophers tending the revival of normative theory, but in Parfit's case, of course, his and their collective goal is a form of utilitarianism that can withstand the criticisms which brought Sidgwick low.

It appeared for a time in the late 1970s that the race for dominance in normative theory within academic ethics would be only two-way. There were certainly many moral philosophers who then thought – and many who still think – that a revived Kantianism and a revived utilitarianism were the only credible options. There had been, however, a number of philosophers lurking in the neighbourhood who had argued (in a modest way) for a third alternative – a revived Aristotelianism, which placed the classical notion of virtue at the heart of normative theory. Three remarkable British women, Phillipa Foot, Elizabeth Anscombe and Iris Murdoch, all friends and all Oxford graduates, played an especially powerful role in keeping this Aristotelian option part of the discussion.[5] Although they disagreed among themselves on a number of matters, they were at one in rejecting the quietism of classical meta-ethics and also at one in rejecting both Kantian and utilitarian approaches to ethics. Elizabeth Anscombe's 1958 article, 'Modern Moral Philosophy', regarded by many as the most important article in twentieth-century ethics, was an especially powerful statement and defence of this Aristotelian alternative. In the 1970s what the Aristotelian option lacked was a powerful and comprehensive defence, taking into consideration the state of play within academic ethics after the collapse of classical meta-ethics. When *After Virtue* appeared in 1981, it seemed to many to fill this void.

After Virtue provided not only a sophisticated and un-nostalgic defence of a broadly Aristotelian approach to ethics but also incorporated in this defence a devastating critique (as it seemed to many) of the Kantian and utilitarian alternatives. It argued that, far from being the only alternatives in normative theory, Kantianism and utilitarianism were actually quite similar in their theoretical claims, being simple variants of a single approach to ethics which MacIntyre dubbed the 'Enlightenment Project', a project that he argued not only failed but 'had to fail'.[6] He also included within this revived Aristotelianism his response to the problems within classical meta-ethics that he had been working on for thirty years. *After Virtue* is not only one of the most significant and influential books in twentieth-century moral philosophy, but also the best introduction to Alasdair MacIntyre's larger intellectual project. The two most memorable parts of *After Virtue* are its opening and closing paragraphs. The beginning asks us to contemplate a hypothetical situation in which a catastrophe has overtaken the natural sciences, and we are left with only fragments of natural scientific work and theory built up over centuries. This hypothetical situation is explored as an introduction to MacIntyre's claim that in morality, there has been an *actual* catastrophe with the result that contemporary moral life is lived out among *actual* fragments of a once coherent morality. The last pages of the book evoke an image of contemporary culture as one in which we have for 'some time been governed by barbarians', and our only hope lies in the emergence of a 'new, doubtless quite different, St Benedict'. Both the catastrophe image that opens the book and the apocalyptic image that ends it have captured the imagination of many readers of *After Virtue*.[7] Many others find both these images hyperbolic, melodramatic and insufficiently argued for. There is no doubt, however, that MacIntyre takes them seriously. The bulk of *After Virtue* provides the conceptual and historical resources that MacIntyre argues make these two images credible.

In his description of the hypothetical situation with which he begins the book, MacIntyre envisions a catastrophe that results in textbooks being destroyed, research centres and libraries disappearing, but various fragments of the sciences being left behind. This catastrophe narrative is, of course, a familiar one to fans of science fiction novels.[8] MacIntyre is not particularly interested, however, in exploring what this picture might help us to understand about science; he introduces this hypothetical situation rather as a vehicle for suggesting that this is the *actual* situation in which we find ourselves in contemporary morality. His suggestion is that an actual catastrophic event has struck the institution of morality, with the result that its coherent structure has been shattered. We live in a social world in which we make use of what is left of 'traditional' morality in an effort to think coherently about our lives. The fragments in question, then, are concepts like 'rights', 'duties', 'the good for man' and 'utility'.

Macintyre's thesis, of course, encounters immediate difficulties. First, if such a catastrophic event occurred, why is it that most people are unaware of it? In the science fiction scenarios documenting the destruction of the natural sciences, the event is usually taken to be something like a nuclear catastrophe, a devastating earthquake or meteor storm or perhaps a crippling epidemic. These events, while shattering the coherence of science, will be remembered by those who survive them and live among the fragments left behind. There seems to be no such memory of a catastrophic event in the case of morality. Most people, when reading the opening pages of *After Virtue*, come across this hypothesis for the first time.

This is a serious objection to MacIntyre's thesis and one that has continued to be raised by many of his critics. MacIntyre has, however, a ready response to it. His claim is that the very catastrophe that brought about the fragmentation of morality also transformed the practice of history, in such a way that the historical sciences are unable to discern this event. It is one of the effects of the catastrophe that it blinds us (at least partially) to its occurrence.[9] This is one of the first clues that the catastrophe MacIntyre has in mind is quite different from a nuclear holocaust or a devastating 'natural disaster'. The catastrophe turns out in fact to be a series of events, many of them events in philosophical argument, which occur in early modernity and that transform the way human beings think of themselves and their relation to nature, to God and to one another. In the first half of *After Virtue*, MacIntyre strives to make good his claim about this catastrophe, employing an account of the history of ethics in the modern period to help specify exactly what the catastrophe was. He also works backwards from an account of our present moral and cultural situation, which he argues demonstrates that we live in a world of moral fragments that could have been brought about only by some such catastrophe.

MacIntyre's account of the 'fragmentation thesis' rests on his exploration of contemporary moral disagreement. He argues that moral disagreement is not only ubiquitous in modern culture, but also has an intractable and interminable character, which signals that morality is now 'merely a collection of fragments'. In the second chapter of *After Virtue*, he considers in some detail three contemporary debates in which moral disagreement is particularly deep – debates about the justification of war, about the moral assessment of abortion and about the demands of economic justice.[10] In each of these three areas, MacIntyre explores arguments defending incompatible positions. The arguments are schematic, but worked out in sufficient detail for anyone to recognize them as representing positions common in contemporary discussion.

MacIntyre claims that these arguments share three features which are commonly found in well-worked-out areas of contemporary moral disagreement. All of the arguments are valid[11] – or at least could be made valid by the addition of trivial premises. The arguments draw on considerations that are incommensurable with those in competing arguments. And finally, the arguments rest on premises drawn from particular figures or positions that are rooted in particular historical situations. Although MacIntyre explores moral disagreements in detail only in these three areas, his clear intent is to suggest that all moral arguments in contemporary culture share these features. He thinks that the formulations of moral arguments by philosophers, especially in various areas of applied ethics, vindicate his claim. He has remarked on a number of occasions that what philosophers typically do when they reflect carefully on real moral problems is to take problems difficult to resolve – such as, for example, those related to war, abortion or economic justice – and by careful analysis demonstrate that these are 'actually impossible to resolve'.[12]

MacIntyre's primary reason for focusing on the phenomenon of moral disagreement is that he believes this feature of contemporary moral discussion is the key to establishing the fragmentation of morality. While all of the well-worked-out moral arguments in contemporary disputes can be 'made valid' by careful formulation of their premises, we are still left with disagreement over the truth of these. The incommensurability of the concepts employed in these premises further suggests that there will be no 'common measure' for resolving such disagreement.[13] And with no 'common measure', there would appear no rational method for resolving these disputes. MacIntyre combines this line of thought with the third feature of contemporary moral disagreement – the fact that competing moral arguments have disparate, but fairly concrete historical origins – to conclude that these arguments are intractable, because they draw on mere fragments of earlier moral traditions now no longer extant as coherent and complete moral systems. This line of argument comprises MacIntyre's way of arguing from the present state of moral disagreement – and the state of the moral culture that enables such disagreement – to the fragmentation thesis.

Once again, however, many deeply dispute MacIntyre's account of moral disagreement. Some argue that he is simply wrong in asserting that none of the arguments can establish their superiority in contemporary moral debate. There are countless Kantian and utilitarian moral theorists – not to mention natural law theorists of various stripes and Hobbesian game theorists – who think that they have arguments that will win the day, if people would simply carefully consider them. MacIntyre's response to this objection, however, is quite straightforward. He can merely point to *the large number of different – and conflicting – normative theories that make this claim*, and by doing so call attention to the fact that they simply reproduce moral disagreement at the level of normative theory. All of these schools of normative ethical theory are engaged in disagreement that replicates the three features of first-order moral disagreement. MacIntyre asks these theorists the question: if moral philosophy has the resources to resolve moral disagreement, why are there so many different schools of moral philosophy, all at one another's throats?[14]

A more serious objection to MacIntyre's treatment of moral disagreement comes from those who object to his claim that the intractability and interminability of moral argument is distinctive of modernity. These objectors claim that it is of the very nature of morality – or practical discussion generally – that there will be no rational route to the solution of moral disagreement. We should not expect the same kind of rational resolution of difficulties in ethics that we find in, for example, the sciences. These critics agree with MacIntyre that moral disagreement in modern culture is intractable and interminable, but they disagree with his claim that this is peculiar to modern culture. On their view, it has always been so, since it is of the nature of moral disputes to lack rational means of resolution.

This objection resurrects the emotivist position so carefully formulated in the discussions within classical meta-ethics. The deeper view lying behind this objection holds that moral judgements are themselves just the expression of the preferences, desires and attitudes of the individuals who express those judgements. Since there is, in the words of one of the most influential classical meta-ethicists, R. M. Hare, 'no logical limit to one's desires', there can be no logical limit to the ethical views one holds as an expression of those desires.

MacIntyre takes this emotivist objection very seriously, and his response to it is nuanced, taking us to the heart of his complicated interpretation of the main features of contemporary culture and moral discourse. It is clear that if emotivism is true – and if moral disagreement is, by its very nature, intractable – then MacIntyre's attempt to use this feature of moral judgement in contemporary culture as the key to understanding particular features of modernity will fail. Intractability of moral argument cannot establish anything peculiar to modern life, if it is universally true of moral discussion wherever it occurs.

MacIntyre's direct response to the emotivist is that he is correct about the contemporary *use* of moral judgements but mistaken about their *meaning*. One should recall that when emotivism was first put forward as a meta-ethical position, it was put forward as a semantic account of moral language – it purported to tell us what we *mean* when we use moral language. As an account of meaning, MacIntyre argues, relying on familiar arguments used by other philosophers such as Foot, Anscombe and Geach, emotivism is simply false. The most important argument to show this appeals to the fact that if moral terms like 'good' and 'right' merely express positive attitudes towards some object, they could not at the same time be used to commend that object. To put it most simply, moral terms are normative and purport to give reasons as to why some object is to be approved. If, however, they are merely expressions of approval (or disapproval in the case of words like 'bad' or 'wrong'), they cannot be used to give reasons for that very approval (or disapproval).

While MacIntyre argues that emotivism is false as an account of the *meaning* of moral judgements, he nevertheless thinks that there is something right about the view, something that explains why it has been such a widely held view among moral philosophers, social scientists and even ordinary people. His suggestion is that while emotivism certainly fails as an account of meaning, it succeeds as an account of the peculiar use of moral language in modernity. In making this argument, MacIntyre is asserting that for us moderns, the use and meaning of moral language come apart.[15] He believes that traditional naturalists were correct in their account of the meaning of moral language, but emotivists were right about its use. MacIntyre believes, in other words, that in contemporary culture we use language – whose meaning is suited for expressing cognitive claims about ethics – in such a way that we merely express our attitudes and desires in using this language.

MacIntyre's defence of this split between meaning and use takes us to the heart of his concrete critique of modern culture. MacIntyre suggests that the emotive use of moral language is evidenced by the prominence of certain modes of behaviour in contemporary culture, modes of behaviour that he relates to what he calls the 'characters' of modern culture – the manager, the therapist and the aesthete. Characters in a particular culture are, for MacIntyre, social roles that have a special prominence in that culture insofar as they express central features of its social structure. MacIntyre draws on the work of a number of social critics of contemporary culture to argue that managerial, therapeutic and aesthetic modes of behaviour are especially prominent in contemporary culture. Vis-à-vis his account of the use of moral language, the significance of these three characters is that they all embody a broadly emotivist attitude towards practical choices. While all three use reason in pursuing their goals, their use of reason is largely confined to determining concrete means to achieving certain ends that are specified in some sense externally to their own reasoning. The manager represents certain skills in maximizing efficiency in the pursuit of given ends, but he neither claims nor possesses any special skills in discerning ultimate ends to be pursued. Similarly, the therapist (at least on one popular conception of his or her task) has the goal of assisting others to adjust to the various situations in which they find themselves. We do not turn to therapists for assistance in determining which ultimate ends to pursue. Finally, the aesthete, too, determined to avoid boredom by pursuing pleasure in whatever form it arises, is hardly qualified to discern proper ends for human life.

The prominence of the managerial, therapeutic and aesthetic modes of rationality in contemporary life suggests to MacIntyre that contemporary culture is an emotivist culture – a culture in which we all use moral language as if emotivism were true. We confine our rational discernment to the realm of means to certain ends, while the determination of which ends are worthwhile is left strictly up to our attitudes and desires. As he puts it, 'In our own time emotivism is a theory embodied in characters who all share the emotivist view of the distinction between rational and non-rational discourse, but who represent the embodiment of that distinction in very different social contexts' (30).

The emotivist character of contemporary culture also shows itself in the concept of the self widely accepted by many prominent contemporary theorists. MacIntyre says of this self:

> The specifically modern self, the self that I have called emotivist, finds no limits set to that on which it may pass judgement for such limits could only derive from rational criteria for evaluation and, as we have seen, the emotivist self lacks any such criteria. Everything may be criticized from whatever standpoint the self has adopted, including the self's choice of standpoint to adopt. It is in this capacity of the self to evade any necessary identification with any particular contingent state of affairs that some modern philosophers, both analytical and existentialist, have seen the essence of moral agency. (34)

It can seem plausible to take this concept of the self as the essence of moral agency only if our culture is indeed emotivist.

MacIntyre's treatment of moral disagreement in the opening chapters of *After Virtue*, and especially his claim that the culture we now occupy is 'an emotivist culture', prepares us for the complicated conceptual and historical argument that makes up the remainder of *After Virtue*. The overall argument of the book following this treatment of the nature of contemporary moral disagreement moves through the following main stages.

MacIntyre first addresses the question of how we came to live in an emotivist culture, in which the meaning and use of moral language so dramatically come apart, with the consequence that our moral disagreements are interminable. He suggests that the answer to this lies in a series of episodes in the history of modern philosophy that replace a classical conception of ethics – a conception that he identifies with the Aristotelian view – with a modern conception dominated by what he terms the 'Enlightenment Project'. The philosophical episodes in question are those in early modernity associated with both the Scientific Revolution and the Reformation, which replace a classical teleological conception of the universe with a modern conception in which final causes are eschewed, and there is no longer room for the distinction (central to classical ethics) between human nature as we encounter it and human nature as perfected. MacIntyre claims that in classical ethics the familiar moral rules (which we largely share with the classical world) were justified by showing that following them provided the bridge between human nature as we find it and human nature as it would be if perfected. With the collapse of a teleological conception of the universe and, with it, a rich notion of perfected human nature, the justification of standard moral rules had to be rethought. MacIntyre suggests that the modern alternative – the Enlightenment Project – was an attempt to justify these moral rules (i.e. morality) by appealing to features of human nature as we find it. The two main features of human nature as we find it that attracted the attention of philosophers were the structures of human reason and the structures of human desire. Kantian-style modern theories strove to justify the received moral rules on the basis of reason, while Humean-style theories chose the structure of human desires (and other affective states) as the basis for their justificatory theories.

The main goal of MacIntyre's account of the history of modern ethics is to demonstrate that all of the Enlightenment theories that eschew teleology altogether not only fail but *must* fail. They must fail because their method is discrepant with the natural history of those moral rules that make human social life possible. These moral rules were formed in order to transform human nature into what it should be. Moral rules are fundamentally corrective. If the justification of these rules is based simply on facts about human nature (while rejecting the view that there is any way human nature *should* be), it cannot possibly justify corrective rules – at least it cannot justify corrective rules the aim of which is fundamentally to transform human beings into what they should be, as moral rules were conceived to be on the classical conception.

It is also part of MacIntyre's account of the history of modern ethics that this failure of the Enlightenment Project was already clearly perceived in the nineteenth century by figures as otherwise different as Kierkegaard and Nietzsche. This recognition of the failure of Enlightenment ambitions for ethical theory explains the many positions in twentieth-century ethics (e.g. certain forms of existentialism, pragmatism and morally neutral classical meta-ethics) that completely give up on justificatory theories in moral philosophy. Intuitionists like Moore and Prichard recognized the failure of the Enlightenment Project but wanted to hold onto the cognitive content of traditional moral rules without any 'real justification' – hence their appeal to 'intuition'. Emotivists in meta-ethics wanted to make the failure of justification in ethics merely a semantic feature of ethical language, with no connection to historical developments in ethics.

MacIntyre concludes the first half of *After Virtue* with a hinge chapter, entitled 'Aristotle or Nietzsche?', in which he outlines his own view of where the failure of the Enlightenment Project leaves us. He suggests that, in the wake of this failure, moral philosophers are left with only two real options: (1) to accept not only Nietzsche's negative critique of modern moral philosophy (with which MacIntyre largely agrees) but also his positive view that 'belief in the tenets of morality needs to be explained in terms of a set of rationalizations which conceal the fundamentally non-rational phenomena of the will' or (2) to attempt to vindicate the classical tradition in ethics, best expressed in the Aristotelian tradition, which was rejected in those dramatic early modern philosophical episodes when the complete rejection of this tradition ushered in the philosophical ambitions of the Enlightenment. In the second half of *After Virtue*, MacIntyre begins the task of showing what would need to be done to carry out this second task.

In attempting to vindicate an Aristotelian view of ethics, MacIntyre is clear that he is not bound to all of the details of Aristotle's own account. He treats Aristotelianism rather as a tradition in which the texts of Aristotle – especially the *Nicomachean Ethics* and *Politics* – play a peculiarly formative role. He particularly puts distance between himself and what he calls Aristotle's 'metaphysical biology', namely, Aristotle's comprehensive teleological view of nature. It is somewhat surprising that MacIntyre is so critical of Aristotle's teleology, since he had earlier argued that it was the rejection of Aristotle's views on this matter which sounded the death-knell for classical ethics and ushered in the new ethics of the Enlightenment Project. It becomes clear, however, that while MacIntyre is (in this book at least) rejecting Aristotle's comprehensive account of final causality and its role in nature, he believes he has other ways of bringing teleology into his vindication of classical ethics.

Much of the second half of *After Virtue* is taken up with a rich historical account of the history of the virtues, with the aim of demonstrating that developments in the conception of the role of the virtues, as well as of their concrete content, is central to the history of the classical conception of ethics. While this history makes clear that there is enormous diversity in the accounts philosophers (as well as literary sources) have given of the virtues, MacIntyre believes it is possible to give an account that captures what lies at the heart of this historical development and that can justifiably be called Aristotelian.

MacIntyre's general strategy for developing a broadly Aristotelian account of the virtues is to locate the virtues in a socially constituted context, now that the metaphysically constituted context of the traditional Aristotelian conception is no longer available.[16] The social context is constituted by three levels of social organization – that of human practices, the narrative unity of human life and the traditions in which our lives are embedded. Although we cannot examine each of these notions in detail, it is important to notice that each situates the choices of human beings in a framework much richer than that in which the emotivist self of late modernity operates.

MacIntyre's proposal to define the virtues by locating them within these layered contexts is the key to his defence of the broadly Aristotelian alternative to Nietzschean self-assertion. Although each of these notions is discussed in great detail by MacIntyre, we can comment here only on their main features and their significance for his overall project. Practices are defined by MacIntyre in one of the most well-known – not to say notorious – sentences in *After Virtue*:

> By a practice I am going to mean any coherent and complex form of socially established cooperative human activity through which goods internal to that form of activity are realized in the course of trying to achieve those standards of excellence which are appropriate to, and partially definitive of, that form of activity, with the result that human powers to achieve excellence, and human conceptions of the ends and goods involved, are systematically extended. (187)

Examples of practices given by MacIntyre are farming, physics, politics and other similarly complicated spheres of human activity which meet the standards of this definition. Of first importance is MacIntyre's claim that practices make possible the achievement of goods internal to them. In contrast to what he calls external goods – for example, money, status and prestige – internal goods are not objects of competition but can be recognized and realized only by those who fully participate in practices. Virtues are required for full participation in practices, in order (1) to define our relation to others within practices, (2) to define our relation to past participants and (3) to allow us to resist the corruption of practices by institutions. At this first level, then, virtues are to be understood as those dispositions to act which allow us to participate fully in practices and to achieve the goods internal to them.

The notion of a practice, however, is not sufficient fully to define a virtue. We may need to criticize a particular practice, or to understand how participation in it might contribute to the overall good of a human life. MacIntyre is particularly insistent that a good human life involves not just participation in a series of arbitrarily chosen practices. These difficulties move the discussion to the second level of the social underpinning of the virtues. MacIntyre argues that contemporary culture, as well as contemporary philosophy, encourages us to think of human lives as a mere series of episodes connected by the thinnest sort of physical and psychological continuity. He suggests that we should regard the unity of a human life as, instead, the narrative unity of a quest. In developing this notion, MacIntyre draws on the mediaeval notion of a quest, in which the object of the quest is not determined by a fully specified or well-defined end but is itself a quest for the good life for man. But what is the good life? MacIntyre defines it as 'the life spent in seeking for the good life for man, and the virtues necessary for the seeking are those which will enable us to understand what more and what else the good life for man is' (219).

Practices and the narrative unity of a life, however, even taken together, are not sufficient to provide a full setting for the virtues. Both practices and the forms of narrative quest that give unity to our lives have histories, and the historical background for these features of the social setting for human lives is organized into traditions.

MacIntyre defines a tradition as 'an historically extended, socially embodied argument, and an argument precisely in part about the goods which constitute that tradition' (222), and he argues that virtues are necessary 'to sustain traditions and to govern our relation to them'.

MacIntyre's account of the virtues, then, which he claims captures the heart of the Aristotelian tradition while eschewing Aristotle's resort to metaphysical biology, is constituted by this layered involvement of the virtues in the contents of practices, narrative unity and tradition. He sums up this account in the following way:

> The virtues find their point and purpose not only in sustaining those relationships necessary if the variety of goods internal to practices are to be achieved and not only in sustaining the form of an individual life in which that individual may seek out his or her good as the good of his or her whole life, but also in sustaining those traditions which provide both practices and individual lives with their necessary historical context. (223)

This account of the layered social world of practice, narrative unity and tradition is not intended, however, merely to provide a frame for the virtues. It is also intended to provide an alternative sociology to that of the emotivist culture MacIntyre had depicted in the first half of the book. In an important sense, MacIntyre opposes his social world of practice, narrative unity and tradition to the social world of the manager, the therapist and the aesthete. But if he has now given content to the stark choice that stands at the heart of *After Virtue* – Aristotle or Nietzsche? – what are the crucial arguments for determining which option to pick? How do we determine the superior view? And how can either view rationally vindicate itself?[17] There are, of course, throughout MacIntyre's work a number of arguments brought for and against particular positions implicated either in the Nietzschean or in the Aristotelian position, but he admits at the end of *After Virtue* that he lacks the resources in this book for fully defending his favoured Aristotelian position. He argues that if philosophical disputes are to be settled, 'it is necessary to stand back from the disputes and ask in a systematic way what the appropriate rational procedures are for settling this particular kind of dispute. It is my own view that the time has come once more when it is imperative to perform this task for moral philosophy; but I do not pretend to have embarked upon it in this present book. My negative and positive evaluations of particular arguments do indeed presuppose a *systematic*, although here unstated, account of rationality' (260).

MacIntyre turns in his later work to give a more comprehensive account of rationality which more fully expresses his Aristotelian alternative to Nietzsche and goes a considerable distance towards vindicating it – although there are many philosophers still unconvinced. *After Virtue* is in fact the first of a tetralogy of works, including MacIntyre's Carlyle Lectures, *Whose Justice? Which Rationality?*, his Gifford Lectures, *Three Rival Versions of Moral Enquiry* and his Carus Lectures, *Dependent Rational Animals*, which together constitute the fullest expression of his views in ethics. Any appraisal of the overall adequacy of his views must take into account all of these works, especially since they sometimes demonstrate significant changes of mind on significant matters.

MacIntyre is sometimes given credit on the basis of this body of work for pioneering a kind of 'virtue ethics', which can stand as an alternative to the deontological and consequentialist views that have so dominated normative ethics in the last few decades. While there is something right about this, since MacIntyre is certainly seeking to place the notion of virtue back at the centre of moral philosophy, he is not simply proposing an alternative to these other theories, with the claim that he can do what they are trying to do, only better. His critique of modern ethics is much more radical than that.[18] He proposes, as we suggested at the beginning of this chapter, to transform the relation of moral philosophy to its history, to social structure, to moral formation and to community life.

Some sense of the radical nature of this critique can be discerned in the famous last paragraph of *After Virtue*, to which I referred earlier. In that paragraph, MacIntyre says:

> It is always dangerous to draw too precise parallels between one historical period and another; and among the most misleading of such parallels are those which have been drawn between our own age in Europe and North America and the epoch in which the Roman Empire declined into the Dark Ages. Nonetheless

certain parallels there are. A crucial turning point in that earlier history occurred when men and women of good will turned aside from the task of shoring up the Roman imperium and ceased to identify the continuation of civility and moral community with the maintenance of that imperium. What they set themselves to achieve instead – often not recognizing fully what they were doing – was the construction of new forms of community within which the moral life could be sustained so that both morality and civility might survive the coming ages of barbarism and darkness. If my account of our moral condition is correct, we ought also to conclude that for some time now we too have reached that turning point. What matters at this stage is the construction of local forms of community within which civility and the intellectual and moral life can be sustained through the new dark ages which are already upon us. And if the tradition of the virtues was able to survive the horrors of the last dark ages, we are not entirely without grounds for hope. This time, however, the barbarians are not waiting beyond the frontiers, they have already been governing us for quite some time. And it is our lack of consciousness of this that constitutes part of our predicament. We are waiting not for a Godot, but for another – doubtless very different – St Benedict. (263)

Given MacIntyre's widely noticed entry into the Roman Catholic Church shortly after the publication of *After Virtue*, some have suggested that the reference in this passage to the world waiting for 'another – doubtless very different – St Benedict' might be a suggestion on MacIntyre's part that the world needs more religion – or that we should all be joining monasteries.[19] Surely not. MacIntyre's comparison of our Age with that period when high classical culture was slipping into the 'dark ages' is surely to be taken seriously. The darkness of our Age is for him expressed in the tragedy of the stunted lives available in emotivist culture. What Saint Benedict did in the late classical period was to create a new social form – the monastic community – which protected and preserved the classical tradition of the virtues behind the stone walls of monastic buildings, and the discipline and orderly practices of the monastic way of life. MacIntyre's suggestion is surely that the hope today of those committed to the life of the virtues as understood in the classical tradition will require something as radical as the invention – or discovery – of new forms of social life in which those virtues can be nurtured, even in the midst of the darkness of contemporary culture. What are needed are not philosophical theories but new forms of community. In the context of contemporary conceptions of normative ethical theory, this is surely a radical suggestion.

Notes

1 MacIntyre's Master's thesis, completed in 1951, is his first lengthy engagement with the issues in twentieth-century ethics. His point of departure in this work is the impasse in meta-ethics involving intuitionism, naturalism and emotivism. He argues that each of these views is right about some things and wrong about others, but that no one of them is adequate to the complexity of the modern ethical sensibility. Although this thesis has never been published and is not officially available in any archive, it has been widely circulated in typescript and is widely admired. It both signals the arrival of a brilliant new voice on the scene of academic ethics, and foreshadows much of MacIntyre's later work.

2 Since Sidgwick's failure, the hope of every utilitarian is to overcome this problem. As I am writing this chapter, I have on my desk the formidable new two-volume defence of utilitarianism by the most respected utilitarian of our day, Derek Parfit. The main burden of this defence is that Sidgwick's problem can finally be overcome. We shall see whether Parfit's critics agree.

3 There had, of course, been earlier gestures in the direction of reviving classical normative theory by utilitarians and Kantians, but there is no doubt that the appearance of *A Theory of Justice* signalled the return of moral philosophy to cultural relevance. Many moral philosophers were almost giddy with the prospect of a new-found cultural relevance after the long wandering in the cultural wilderness that was classical meta-ethics. One particularly enthusiastic expression of that giddiness is the young Peter Singer's 1974 piece in the *New York Times' Magazine*, entitled 'Philosophers Are Back on the Job'.

4 Among these students are such distinguished moral philosophers as Thomas Nagel, Christine Korsgaard, Barbara Herman, Onora O'Neill and Paul Weithman.

5 Foot's most important contribution was seen in two influential articles, 'Moral Arguments' and 'Moral Beliefs' (Chapters VII and VIII, respectively, of Foot 1978), while Murdoch's influence was exerted

through her book of essays, *The Sovereignty of Good*. Anscombe's 1958 article, 'Modern Moral Philosophy', was the most influential of all.

6 MacIntyre was not alone in arguing that the differences between Kantian and utilitarian normative theories did not run deep. Bernard Williams argued for a similar view in a number of places but with a quite different intent.

7 The concluding paragraphs of *After Virtue* are especially dramatic. It is some measure of their rhetorical power that they constitute the only instance (to my knowledge) of the words of a twentieth-century analytic philosopher being set to music by a serious composer. James McMillan, the distinguished Scottish composer, did just that.

8 Although a number of science fiction works explore this theme, MacIntyre clearly has the remarkable 1950s apocalyptic novel, Walter Miller's *A Canticle for Leibowitz*, especially in mind. This underground classic combines an account of the destruction of the natural sciences with one of the fragmentation of morality. Set in a monastery in the western part of the United States, this bleak novel follows the attempt of a relatively isolated group of Catholic monks to maintain a coherent life in the midst of both scientific and moral fragmentation.

9 It can't blind us completely, of course, since MacIntyre will provide evidence of an indirect sort that the catastrophe occurred.

10 One might notice that he takes these three areas from quite different areas of moral dispute – the justification of war involves disagreements about how nations should treat one another, the moral assessment of abortion is perhaps best seen as a matter of individual decision and the demands of economic justice involve social issues within a particular political entity.

11 MacIntyre is using validity in the semi-technical sense typically used by philosophers. In this sense, an argument is valid just in case it is such that if its premises are assumed true, then its conclusion must be true. By assessing the validity of an argument in this sense, we make no commitment to the truth of its premises nor, obviously, to the truth of its conclusion. Assessment of validity is merely the assessment of the logical relation between premises and conclusions – and is thereby not directly related to an assessment of truth.

12 I do not know of any instance where MacIntyre says this in print, but he has frequently expressed it in conversation. This goes a long way towards explaining, of course, MacIntyre's great disdain for applied ethics, at least the kind of applied ethics in which philosophers promise to bring their expertise to bear to resolve deep moral disagreements. MacIntyre's view is that, by using their genuine skills of clarification, analysis and careful formulation of arguments, philosophers actually make moral disagreement more stark and the prospect of genuine convergence of opinion more distant.

13 Incommensurability is one of the most difficult concepts in contemporary philosophy. Perhaps the most careful work on this concept has been done within the philosophy of science, especially by major figures like Kuhn, Feyerabend and Lakatos, who were concerned primarily with the rationality of theory-change or -development within the history of science. MacIntyre was a significant contributor to these discussions in the philosophy of science (especially in the philosophy of the social sciences). For more on MacIntyre's relation to Kuhn and Lakatos, see Angier 2011.

14 One of the most poignant – and I think ill-conceived – responses to MacIntyre on this point is the claim (made in slightly different forms by Derek Parfit and Thomas Nagel) that moral philosophy cannot resolve these disagreements because it is still in a 'primitive' state – much as pre-modern science was – and needs to be given more time to find its Newton (or perhaps its Descartes). Others, such as the late Alan Gewirth and the late Bernie Gert, seem to have believed that moral philosophy's Newton is already among us.

15 This is certainly one of the most difficult notions in MacIntyre to grasp. He elaborates on it in a number of places in *After Virtue*, saying at one point that 'the meaning and use of moral expressions were, or at the very least had become, radically discrepant with each other. Meaning and use would be at odds in such a way that meaning would tend to conceal use. We could not safely infer what someone who uttered a moral judgement was doing merely by listening to what he said. Moreover the agent himself might well be among those for whom use was concealed by meaning. He might well, precisely because he was self-conscious about the meaning of the words that he used, be assured that he was appealing to independent impersonal criteria, when all that he was in fact doing was expressing his feelings to others in a manipulative way' (14).

16 The following three pages follow closely an earlier discussion of mine found in 'MacIntyre and Contemporary Moral Philosophy', Chapter 5 of Murphy 2003.

17 Even to pose this question is, of course, to take sides in the debate, since the clash between Aristotle and Nietzsche is, in part, a clash about whether rational vindication is possible or even coherent.

18 I develop this point at length in my piece, 'Virtue Ethics: Radical or Routine?', Chapter 3 of DePaul and Zagzebski 2003.

19 There was also notice taken when Cardinal Joseph Ratzinger, the distinguished Catholic theologian and student of MacIntyre's work, took the name 'Benedict' when he was named Pope in 2005. There was much chatter at the time that this was a conscious nod to MacIntyre's reference to St Benedict in this passage. However that may be, it is surely significant that both MacIntyre and Ratzinger had Benedict in the front of their minds when thinking about fundamental issues facing contemporary culture.

References

Works by MacIntyre:

After Virtue: A Study in Moral Theory, London: Duckworth 1981.
Dependent Rational Animals: Why Human Beings Need the Virtues. London: Duckworth 1999.
Three Rival Versions of Moral Enquiry: Encyclopaedia, Genealogy, and Tradition. London: Duckworth 1990.
Whose Justice? Which Rationality? London: Duckworth 1988.

Other works:

Anscombe, G. E. M. (1958), 'Modern Moral Philosophy'. *Philosophy* 33, 124: 1–19.
DePaul, M. and Zagzebski, L. (eds) (2003), *Intellectual Virtue: Perspectives from Ethics and Epistemology.* Oxford: Oxford University Press.
Foot, P. (1978), *Virtues and Vices and Other Essays in Moral Philosophy.* Berkeley and Los Angeles: University of California Press.
Miller, W. (1959), *A Canticle for Leibowitz.* New York: Lippincott, Williams & Wilkins.
Murdoch, I. (1970), *The Sovereignty of Good.* London: Routledge and Kegan Paul.
Murphy, M. C. (ed.) (2003), *Alasdair MacIntyre.* Cambridge: Cambridge University Press.
Parfit, D. (1984), *Reasons and Persons.* Oxford: Oxford University Press.
—(2011), *On What Matters* (2 vols). Oxford: Oxford University Press.
Rawls, J. (1971), *A Theory of Justice.* Cambridge, MA: Harvard University Press.
Sidgwick, H. (1981), *The Methods of Ethics.* Indianapolis: Hackett.
Singer, P. (July 7th 1974), *Philosophers Are Back on the Job.* New York Times' Magazine.

Recommended reading

Angier, T. (2011), 'Alasdair MacIntyre's Analysis of Tradition'. *European Journal of Philosophy* (published online 28.12.11; forthcoming in hard copy).

Blackledge, P. and Knight, K. (eds) (2011), *Virtue and Politics: Alasdair MacIntyre's Revolutionary Aristotelianism*. Notre Dame: University of Notre Dame Press.

D'Andrea, T. D. (2006), *Tradition, Rationality and Virtue: The Thought of Alasdair MacIntyre*. London: Ashgate Publishing.

Horton, J. and Mendus, S. (eds) (1994), *After MacIntyre: Critical Perspectives on the Work of Alasdair MacIntyre*. London: Polity Press.

Lutz, C. S. (2009), *Tradition in the Ethics of Alasdair MacIntyre: Relativism, Thomism, and Philosophy*. Lanham, MD: Lexington Books.

—(2012), *Reading Alasdair MacIntyre's After Virtue*. London: Continuum Press.

McMylor, P. (1993), *Alasdair MacIntyre: Critic of Modernity*. London: Routledge.

Murphy, M. C. (ed.) (2003), *Alasdair MacIntyre*. Cambridge: Cambridge University Press.

Index